Venice
Shortlist

timeout.com / venice

28

59

Contents

68

Punta della Dogana and the Giudecca Canal

ABOUT THE GUIDE

The *Time Out Venice Shortlist* is one of a series of pocket guides to cities around the globe. Drawing on the expertise of local authors, it distils their knowledge into a handy, easy-to-use format that ensures you get the most from your trip, whether you're a first-time or a return visitor.

Time Out Venice Shortlist is divided into four sections:

Welcome to Venice introduces the city and provides inspiration for your visit.

Venice Day by Day helps you plan your trip with an events calendar and customised itineraries.

Venice by Area is the main visitor section of the guide. It includes detailed listings and reviews for the very best sights and museums; restaurants 🔟; cafés, bars & gelaterie 🔟; shops 🔟, and entertainment venues 🔟, all organised by area with a corresponding street map. To help navigation, each area of Venice has been assigned its own colour.

Venice Essentials provides practical visitor information, including accommodation options and details of public transport.

Shortlists & highlights

We have selected a Shortlist of stand-out venues in each area, which are marked with a heart ❤ in the text. The very best of these appear in the Highlights feature (*see p10*) and receive extended coverage in the guide.

Maps

There's an overview map on *p8* and individual street maps for each area of the city. Venues featured in the guide have been given a grid reference so that you can find them easily on the maps and on the ground.

Prices

All our **restaurant listings** are marked with a euro symbol category from budget to blowout (€-€€€€), indicating the price you should expect to pay for one main dish (*secondo*): € = under €10; €€ = €10-€25; €€€ = €25-€40; €€€€ = over €40.

A similar system is used in our **Accommodation** chapter based on the hotel's standard prices for one night in a double room: Budget = up to €150; Moderate = €150-€250; Expensive €250-€500; Luxury = €500+.

Introduction

Venice owes its very existence to its unique relationship with water. Built on marshy land, surrounded by a lagoon, today's city is a network of over 100 islands connected by more than 400 bridges. For centuries, its brilliance shone out over the eastern Mediterranean as the Most Serene Republic dominated trade and shipping, the resultant wealth enabling an outpouring of artistic creativity that continues to dazzle to this day. And now, with its future threatened by rising water levels and floods of tourists, Venice offers us a bravura lesson in survival against the odds.

There are several ways of experiencing Venice: take a boat down the Grand Canal to admire the architecture and ambition of the *palazzi*, or head further out to explore the lagoon and its islands; witness the greatness of Titian and Tintoretto in innumerable churches and *scuole*, or assess the achievements of their successors in the city's contemporary art galleries. Come for the masks and mayhem of Carnevale or the glitz and glam of the Film Festival. Most importantly, give yourself time to get lost: let your curiosity tempt you away from the main thoroughfares into the intricate labyrinth of alleyways, where you will find a hidden Venice of quiet squares and neighbourhood bars; or take a stroll very early in the morning, when even the tourist honeypots are mostly deserted and Venice is once again a city of water and dreams.

Welcome to Venice

Canale Sacche

Canale delle Fondamenta

Fond. San Girolamo

Fond. Batelo

Campo di Sant'Alvise

Fond. de la Sensa

Fond. degli Ormesini

Fond. de Misericordia

Fondamente Nove

Campo del Ghetto Nuovo

Rio Terà San Leonardo

CANNAREGIO

Campo dei Gesuiti

Calle de la Racheta

Rio Terà Barba Frutariol

Calle Rielo

Campo San Geremia

Campo San Felice

Strada Nova

Campo Santi Apostoli

Riva de Biasio

Campo Nazario Sauro

**SAN POLO &
SANTA CROCE**

♥ Mercato di Rialto

Riva del Vin

Campo Sant'Aponal

Campo San Polo

♥ **Grand Canal**

Calle dei Fabbri

SAN MARCO

Piazza San Marco

Ponte della Libertà

Fond. Sant'Andrea

Piazzale Roma

♥ **Scuola Grande
di San Rocco** ♥ **I Frari**

Campo dei Frari

Rio Terà dei Pensieri

C. Corte Contarini

Fond. Cereri

Campo Santa Margherita

Campo Sant'Anzolo

Campo Santo Stefano

La Fenice ♥

C. Larga XXII Marzo

Fond. Briati

C. Longa de San Barnaba

Campo San Barnaba

Campo San Maurizio

DORSODURO

Fond. Barbarigo

Fond. de Ognisanti

Fond. Zattere al Ponte Longo

♥ **Gallerie
dell'Accademia** ♥ **Peggy
Guggenhaim
Collection** ♥ **Punta della
Dogana** ♥

Fond. Zattere allo Santo Spirito

Canale della Giudecca

C. Larga dei Lavraneri

Fond. San Biagio

Fond. Santa Eufemia

Fond. del Ponte Piccolo

Fondamenta San Giacomo

Fondamenta Croce

Campiello Priuli

Fond. Convertite

Campo San Cosmo

Campo del SS. Redentore

LA GIUDECCA

ISLANDS OF THE LAGOON

Aeroporto Marco Polo

♥ TORCELLO

BURANO

Laguna di Venezia

SAN MICHELE

MURANO

Museo del Vetro

SANT' ERASMO

TRE PORTI

VENEZIA

Porto di Tre Porti

LIDO

♥ Venice Film Festival

Golfo di Venezia

Porto di Lido

Laguna di Venezia

Calle Stella

Fondamente Nove

♥ Santi Giovanni e Paolo

Campo San Lorenzo

CASTELLO

Campo delle Gate

Darsena Grande

Campo San Severo

Campo San Zaccaria

Campo Bandiera e Moro

Campo de l'Arsenal

♥ Biennale

Campo Ruga

ISOLA DI SAN PIETRO

Basilica di San Marco ♥

Riva degli Schiavoni

Palazzo Ducale ♥

Bacino San Marco

Via Giuseppe Garibaldi

Riva dei Sette Martiri

Campo San Giuseppe

Riva dei Partigiani

♥ San Giorgio Maggiore

SAN GIORGIO MAGGIORE

Fond. San Giovanni

Canale Ortanello

ISLANDS OF THE LAGOON

0   500 m
0   500 yds

© Copyright Time Out Group 2017

9

Highlights

Every corner and stone in Venice oozes beauty and history. But given its labyrinthine nature, it's easy to get overwhelmed, or miss a spot. Here's a selection of quintessential sites and experiences, from art-filled churches to history-filled palaces, and remote islands to world-class events.

01

Grand Canal *p24*

Some say that Venice is best seen from the water, and nothing beats the Grand Canal in that regard. Take a boat ride down this winding watery route, lined with magnificent *palazzi*, for a crash course in the history of architecture, from Gothic to contemporary.

Basilica di San Marco *p68*

A heart-stopping sight lording it over piazza San Marco, the basilica of St Mark is equally magical inside where acres – literally – of glistening golden mosaic follow the sinuous curves of its domes. From the upstairs museum, where the four bronze horses are displayed, to the gem-encrusted Pala d'Oro, it's all wondrous.

03

I Frari *p130*

A remarkable repository of fine art, this huge hangar-like church is dominated by Titian's glorious *Assumption of the Virgin*, swirling heavenwards wrapped in her scarlet gown and blue cape. Also here is a *Madonna and Child with saints* by Giovanni Bellini, arguably one of his greatest works, and Titian's magnificent *Madonna di Ca' Pesaro*.

04

Mercato di Rialto *p122*

Venetians stock up each morning (Mon-Sat) at the north-west foot of the Rialto Bridge, where stalls are piled high with fruit and vegetables, and – in the Pescaria – slimy, slithering creatures of the deep, many of which you'll be hard-pressed to identify. With its Grand Canal frontage, this must surely count as one of the world's most atmospheric shopping venues.

05

La Fenice *p85*

Venice's opera house is a gem – and one with a long season of top-rate operas and concerts. If you can't catch a performance, there are guided tours of the building, offering a chance to see the gilded, stuccoed extravaganza of the auditorium and the state-of-the-art backstage areas.

06

Gallerie dell'Accademia *p144*

One of the world's great galleries, the Accademia expanded into neighbouring premises in 2015, giving curators a chance to pull some forgotten treasures out of storage, and arrange familiar masterpieces in a more effective way. From the stiff icon-like first stirrings of Venetian art to the greats of the Renaissance, they're all here, in all their glory.

07

Gondolas *p150*

Eight varieties of tree, 280 pieces of wood, one expensive ride – but gliding beneath Venice's bridges, along its quiet canals, with just the splash of the single oar as it propels you through the labyrinth in this oh-so-Venetian craft is certainly a unique experience.

08

Palazzo Ducale (Doge's Palace) *p74*

This iconic building was where Venice wielded its power and displayed its might, in public rooms designed to instil shock and awe, and with artworks to drive the Serene Republic's self-important message home. Meeting halls, private apartments, torture rooms and prison cells – they're all here in the fulcrum of power.

09

Torcello *p161*

'Mother and daughter, you behold them both in their widowhood: Torcello and Venice', wrote John Ruskin. A powerful player well before Venice proper, the island of Torcello today is picturesquely forlorn and almost uninhabited. Only a cathedral with remarkable mosaics, a little museum and a pretty round church remain as testimonies to its more important former self.

10

Punta della Dogana *p147*

The stunning makeover by Japanese archi-star Tadao Ando of the Serene Republic's bonded customs warehouse at the southern end of the Grand Canal, facing across the water to St Mark's square, is worth a visit simply for the spaces. But there's also a chance to see a selection from French tycoon Francois Pinault's contemporary art collection too.

11

Traditional bacari *p31*

The *ombra*, a small, cheap glass of wine is one of the best examples of the tourist/local contrast in Venice. To experience it in its most salt-of-the-earth form, head to a traditional *bacaro*, such as Da Lele (see *p132*). It opens at dawn but there's no coffee machine: just alcohol. Unadorned and always busy, it's the epitome of hard-working Venice – the flip side of the city's finery and pomp.

12

La Biennale *p101*

Officially the name of Venice's massive arts umbrella organisation, 'La Biennale' is used to refer to unmissable contemporary art (odd years) and architecture (even years) bonanzas that draw the world's finest practitioners, and its cognoscenti, for shows that last through the summer and fall months – offering a chance to get inside the otherwise-shut Arsenale and the Biennale gardens (*see p97*).

13

Rowing regattas *p59*

Voga alla Veneta is an essential part of Venetian life, with over 100 rowing events taking place each year. These range from the serious and ceremonial Regata Storica to the jolly Vogalonga, in which a multicoloured jumble of craft and rowers go on a madcap race around the city.

14

Santi Giovanni e Paolo *p93*

Once the final resting place for Venice's rulers, there are 25 doges buried in this huge church. But there are also artworks by Giovanni Bellini, Lorenzo Lotto and Paolo Veronese, as well as some very fine sculpture by the Lombardo family.

15

Scuola Grande di San Rocco *p129*

Tintoretto made the interior of this *scuola* his life's work: 50 dramatic paintings are spread across three rooms and along the walls of the staircase. Look out too for the intriguing wooden sculptures by Francesco Pianta.

16

Murano glass *p159*

Murano glass played a major role in the development of this trading city and remains one of the most popular and sought-after – yet misunderstood – Venetian products. Just beware cheap imitations from the Far East...

17

Carnevale *p56*

It may be a 1970s reincarnation of long-dead Venetian merry-making but it's no less exceptional for all that: for two weeks in the run-up to Lent, Venice shrugs off its winter lethargy and fills with masked-and-costumed revellers who flock for a programme of events that grows by the year.

18

San Giorgio Maggiore *p155*

Occupying a piece of prime real estate directly across the water from the Doge's Palace, this most elegant of churches was designed by the great Renaissance architect Palladio. There are artworks to admire by Tintoretto *et al*, but San Giorgio's biggest draw is its belltower, with spectacular views over Venice and far beyond.

19

Peggy Guggenheim Collection *p143*

Charmingly unfinished Grand Canal-side Palazzo Venier dei Leoni was the home of eccentric millionairess Peggy Guggenheim who brought her extraordinary collection of modern art (and artists) with her to the lagoon city in 1949. With garden, café and fascinating artworks, it's little wonder this is Venice's third-most-visited sight.

20

Venice Film Festival *p44*

Movie world A-listers, razzmatazz, hordes of paparazzi and furious bustle: you'd barely recognise Venice's sleepy seaside Lido island for those ten days in August-September when the Film Festival comes to town. The world's oldest – though no longer its most cutting edge – the Venice event (unlike many others) still offers the public a good chance to see the films on show.

Sightseeing

First encountered at a distance, mediated through the beautifying camera lens, many of the world's great cities are a let-down when you get there. But not Venice. Nobody can come here without some idea of what to expect. The surprise is that it's true. The streets really are made of water – everywhere. The *palazzi* really do have a fairy-tale quality. And it's not just a matter of a carefully preserved little tourist centre surrounded by the usual high-rise flats and car parks; the *whole* of Venice is the centre.

Then there are the highlights. The **Grand Canal** (*see p24*) is the city's iconic thoroughfare and a living lesson in architectural history; the **Basilica di San Marco** (*see p68*) is one of Christendom's greatest churches; the **Gallerie dell'Accademia** (*see p144*) contain an unparalleled selection of Renaissance art; and the **Rialto**

Art treasure houses
Gallerie dell'Accademia *p144*
I Frari *p130*
Scuola Grande di San Rocco *p129*
Punta della Dogana *p147*

Amazing architecture
Basilica di San Marco *p68*
Palazzo Ducale *p74*
San Giorgio Maggiore *p155*
Ca d'Oro *p107*

Best museums for children
Museo di Storia Naturale *p125*
Museo Storico Navale *p98*

Best viewpoints
Campanile di San Marco *p66*
Campanile di San Giorgio
Maggiore *p155*
Fondaco dei Tedeschi *p80*
Loggia dei Cavalli *p70*
Scala Contarini del Bòvolo *p82*

(*see p24*) is a powerful symbol of mercantile energy as well as a fine bridge. But Venice is much more than this, and the best way to get an impression of its full diversity is to leave the main routes.

Finding your way

With its double topography of streets and canals, Venice provides a challenge even to the most skilled map-readers. But when you lose your bearings, don't be alarmed: the *calli* will close in around you; you'll come to innumerable dead ends and find yourself returning inexplicably to the same (wrong) spot over and over again. But eventually you'll hit a busy thoroughfare or the Grand Canal and a vaporetto stop. Until that happens, enjoy the feel of village Venice – or, more appropriately, island Venice. The city is made up of over 100 islands, and every one has something – magnificent or quaint, historic or charming – to offer.

Venice is divided into six *sestieri*. They are worth getting to grips with, first and foremost because all addresses include the *sestiere* name. Cradled by the lower bend of the Grand Canal is the *sestiere* of **San Marco**, the heart of the city; east of here is **Castello**, one of the most lived-in areas; extending to the west and north is **Cannaregio**, whose western stretches are among the most peaceful parts of Venice. To the west of the Rialto

Bridge is **San Polo**, bristling with churches; west of that is **Santa Croce**, short on sights but not on atmosphere; while further south is **Dorsoduro**, one of the city's most elegant and artsy districts, with its wide Zattere promenade looking across to the long residential island of the **Giudecca** – the honorary seventh *sestiere*. Bear in mind that you may need more than an address to get to where you're going. Houses are counted by *sestiere* rather than by street, so don't be surprised if the number goes into the thousands. To complicate matters further, Venetians are not overly creative when it comes to street names, which are often linked to local trades or religious superstition (for instance, there's more than one 'baker street', *calle del Forno*, in each *sestiere*).

Visitor passes

The most comprehensive pass is the **Venezia Unica City Pass** (*see p184*), which combines admission to sights with public transport and other services. Note that the passes detailed below can be included as part of a Venezia Unica City Pass package.

Basilica di San Marco

Key Events

Venice in brief

5th century AD Barbarians force inhabitants of the north-east of the Italian peninsula to flee to the Venetian lagoon.

AD 552 Communities in the lagoon help the Byzantine Emperor Justinian I to take Rome.

From AD 697 Paoluccio Anafesto is elected *doge* (duke) of the confederacy of communities in the lagoon. The duchy becomes a centre of shipbuilding and trade.

AD 810 Angelo Partecipazio moves the lagoon's centre of power to the Rialto and inflicts a devastating defeat on the Frankish fleet. He becomes doge (811-827) of the newly named duchy of 'Venetia'.

AD 829 Venetian merchants steal the body of the Evangelist St Mark from Alexandria. Venice goes on to establish trading routes throughout the eastern Mediterranean.

From 1096 The crusades present Venice with its greatest opportunity yet for expanding trade routes and removing competition.

13 April 1204 Sacking of Constantinople. Venetian crusaders under Doge Enrico Dandolo loot the city's greatest treasures and go on to seize control of strategic Byzantine ports.

1297-1354 Access to the ruling council is restricted to a few aristocratic families. Civil unrest ensues, and the Council of Ten is given new draconian powers.

13th-15th centuries Venetian mercantile power is at its zenith. Vast fortunes are lavished on building and decorating the city's great *palazzi* and churches.

1348-49 More than half the city's population die in the Black Death.

1380-1454 Venice besieges the Genoese fleet, forcing an unconditional surrender. It then embarks on a campaign of aggressive mainland expansion.

1489 Vasco da Gama reaches Kolkata by sea, shattering Venice's monopoly on the riches of the East.

1497-1573 The Ottomans take control of most of Venice's territories.

16th century Despite a gradual loss of power and revenue, Venice experiences an explosion of art, architecture and music by the likes of Titian, Tintoretto, Veronese, Giorgione, Palladio, Sanmicheli and Scamozzi.

17th and 18th centuries Venice's financial situation worsens as the city becomes notorious for its decadence.

12 May 1797 The last doge, Lodovico Manin, is deposed by the French.

1805-1815 Napoleon closes churches and monasteries and 're-designs' parts of the city.

1815-1866 Venice under Austrian rule.

1866 Venice joins the newly united Kingdom of Italy.

1895 First Biennale art exhibition takes place.

1932 First Venice Film Festival takes place on the Lido.

1966 Devastating floods spoil artworks and damage buildings.

2003 Construction begins on the MOSE flood prevention scheme.

The museums around piazza San Marco (but not the paying parts of the basilica) can only be visited with one of the museum passes, which can be bought at the sights themselves (not all accept credit cards), by phone (041 4273 0892) or online (www.visitmuve.it). The **Musei di Piazza San Marco Pass** (€19, €12 reductions, under-5s free) is valid for three months, with one visit to each of the Doge's Palace (*p74*), Museo Correr (*p67*), Museo Nazionale Archeologico (*p71*) and Biblioteca Marciana (*p72*). The **Museum Pass** (€24, €18 reductions, under-5s free) is valid for six months, with one visit to each of the museums listed above plus Ca' Rezzonico (*p138*), Casa di Carlo Goldoni (*p123*), Ca' Pesaro (*p125*), Museo del Vetro (*p158*), Museo di Storia Naturale (*p125*) and Palazzo Mocenigo (*p125*).

Although Napoleon cleared away a good 40 or so parish churches in the city during his brief rule, there are still well over 100 left, containing inestimable artistic treasures. The **Chorus Pass** (www.chorusvenezia. org, €12, €8 students, €20 family, under-12s free) gives access to 18 of them, with the proceeds going towards upkeep and preservation costs. Individual entry to these churches costs €3.

Piazza San Marco

💙 Grand Canal

▶ *The best way to experience the Grand Canal is to catch vaporetto line 1 (slow and busy) or line 2 (faster) from the train station (Ferrovia) or from piazzale Roma towards San Marco. You can hop out at any of the vaporetto stops en route. To cross the canal when you're not near a bridge, use one of the traghetto services. For further details, see p174 Public transport.*

The Grand Canal is Venice's high street and provides a superb introduction to the city, telling you more about the way Venice works – and has always worked – than any historical tome.

From the 12th to the 18th century, every family of note had to have a *palazzo* along the three and a half kilometre (two-mile) sweep of the canal, and this was not just for social cachet. The *palazzi* are undeniably splendid, but they were first and foremost solid commercial enterprises, and their designs are as practical as they are eye-catching.

When a family decided to rebuild a *palazzo*, they usually maintained the same basic structure and foundations, resulting in Veneto-Byzantine or Gothic features being incorporated into Renaissance or Baroque buildings.

Each *palazzo* typically had a main water-entrance opening on to a large hall with storage space on either side; a *mezzanino* with offices; a *piano nobile* (main floor – sometimes two in grander buildings) consisting of a spacious reception hall lit by large central windows

and flanked on both sides by residential rooms; and a land entrance at the back. Over the centuries, architectural frills and trimmings were added, but the underlying form was stable – and, as always in Venice, it is form that follows function.

Many family names recur in descriptions of the most notable *palazzi*. Compound names indicate that the *palazzo* passed through various hands over time. Originally the term '*palazzo*' was reserved for the Doge's Palace; other *palazzi* were known as Casa ('house') or Ca' for short.

Grand Canal bridges

Dogged by controversy and over-spending, the newest and most westerly bridge over the Grand Canal opened in 2008 to link piazzale Roma with the train station. Officially named **Ponte della Costituzione**, it is still known to most Venetians as Ponte di Calatrava, after its Spanish designer, Santiago Calatrava. Its single, elegantly curving arch is constructed of steel, with a glass and Istrian stone pavement. Disabled access was added later in the form of a strange bubble that crosses the canal on the outside of the structure. Just beyond it, the **Ponte degli Scalzi** was built in stone by Eugenio Miozzi in 1934. As the vaporetto swings round the bend past the Rialto Mercato stop, the **Ponte di Rialto** comes into view. The current bridge was built in 1588-92 to a design by aptly named Antonio Da Ponte, after designs by Michelangelo, Vignola, Sansovino and Palladio had been rejected. Da Ponte's simple but effective project kept the utilitarian features of the previous wooden bridge, with its double row of shops (seen in Carpaccio's painting of *The Miracle of the True Cross* in the Accademia; *see p144*). Last but not least, the wooden **Ponte dell' Accademia**, links the Gallerie dell' Accademia with campo San Vidal. It was originally built in 1932 as a 'temporary' structure to replace an earlier iron bridge. However, by 1984, when the wooden bridge was deemed dangerously unstable, Venetians had grown so fond of it that they demanded it be rebuilt exactly as before.

Fondaco dei Turchi

Santa Maria della Salute and Dogana da Mar

❤ Best sights on the right bank

Fondaco dei Turchi
This 19th-century reconstruction of a Veneto-Byzantine building was leased to Turkish traders in the 17th century and now houses the Museo di Storia Naturale (*see p125*).

Ca' Pesaro *p125*
A splendid example of Venetian Baroque by Baldassare Longhena, now home to the city's modern art collection.

Fabbriche Nuove
The longest façade on the Grand Canal was designed by Sansovino and built in 1554-56 for Venice's financial judiciary.

Ca' Rezzonico *p138*
This Baroque masterpiece by Longhena, begun in 1667, was where Robert Browning died in 1889. It's now the museum of 18th-century Venice.

Palazzo Venier dei Leoni
Work on this single-storey building ground to a halt in 1749 and never resumed. It now provides a perfect setting for the Peggy Guggenheim Collection (*see p143*).

Santa Maria della Salute *p146*
Baldassare Longhena's audacious Baroque creation (1671) queens it over the end of the Grand Canal.

Dogana da Mar
The Customs House (1677), with its tower, gilded ball and weathervane figure of Fortune, is where the Grand Canal enters the Bacino di San Marco.

❤ Grand Canal *continued*

❤ Best sights on the left bank

Palazzo Vendramin Calergi
Venice's Casinò, with porphyry insets in the façade, is where Wagner died in 1883.

Ca' d'Oro *p107*
This is the most gorgeously ornate Gothic building on the canal.

Ca d'Oro

Fondaco dei Tedeschi *p80*
The grandiose residence-cum-warehouse for German traders from the 13th century onwards is now a luxury shopping mall.

From Rialto to Sant'Angelo
This stretch is rich in architectural highlights. Palazzo Manin Dolfin has a façade by Sansovino (late 1530s). Palazzo Farsetti and Palazzo Loredan are adjoining buildings that serve as the City Hall; they are rare surviving examples of typical 12th-century Veneto-Byzantine houses. Palazzo Grimani was designed by Michele Sanmicheli in assertive fashion, while Palazzo Corner Spinelli is one of the most beautiful early Renaissance buildings and now hosts the Rubelli textile archives (*see p39* Material Makers).

Ponte di Rialto

Palazzo Grassi *p81*
Now used by the French magnate François Pinault to showcase his art, the last of the great patrician *palazzi* was built in 1748-72 when the city was already in decline.

Ca' Giustinian
The offices of the Biennale (*see p101*) were once a hotel where Verdi, Ruskin and Proust stayed.

View from Fondaco dei Tedeschi

Gelato

Eating & Drinking

An average 70,000 visitors rush through Venice each day, and the majority of the city's restaurants operate with these diners in mind: clearly, there's little real incentive to shoot for culinary excellence when you can be certain that 95 per cent of your guests will drop in once and once only.

But a discerning, faithful clientele of residents keeps standards high in a selection of mainly well-hidden establishments. Seek these out, and you'll eat very well indeed. In most cases, it will cost you more than elsewhere in Italy – Venice simply isn't cheap – but you'll have the satisfaction of eating in the local tradition and rubbing shoulders with spirited Venetians rather than frazzled tourists.

❤ **Shortlist**

Best places for a drink
Skyline *p153*
Malvasia all'Adriatico Mar *p140*

Best fine dining spots
Estro Vino e Cucina *p139*
Venissa *p162*
Da Fiore *p127*
Gran Caffè Quadri *p73*

Best Venetian classics
Antiche Carampane *p123*
Anice Stellato *p115*
Cantinone *p149*
La Zucca *p128*

Best cicheti
Al Portego *p95*
Alla Vedova *p109*

Where to eat

Venice boasts the usual panoply of *ristoranti*, *trattorie*
and *osterie*, but it is the humble neighbourhood *bacaro*
(*see p31* Traditional bacari) that is the salvation of the
Venetian dining scene. These establishments serve cheap
wine and tapas-like snacks called *cicheti* from dawn to
dusk to a loyal local clientele. From creamed cod (*baccalà
mantecato*) to meatballs, to sardines stewed in onion
(*sarde in saor*), to tiny stuffed peppers, there is a huge
selection, to be eaten one at a time or piled on to a plate
to make what can add up to a pretty full meal. However,
except where you can perch on a bar stool or occupy any
front-of-house accommodation, this is actually on-the-
hoof food: the proper tables are for proper diners, opting
for the full pasta-plus-main meals that will appear from a
kitchen hidden away behind.

Cicheti are charged individually – anything between
€1.50 and €3 is normal, depending on what you choose.
So a well-filled plate can cost €10 or less. Most bar staff
have an uncanny gift for keeping track of who eats what,
and for totting up your bill at the end. Sitting down for a
proper meal in the same hostelry, however, may cost €30
or more (sometimes much more) a head. To complicate
arrangements still further, many clients will just be here
for a drink: they're generally the ones chatting, glass in
hand, in the *calle* outside.

At the higher end of Venice's dining scene, *trattorie* and *ristoranti* function much as in the rest of Italy, the difference being that their prices tend to be higher than elsewhere. Between the two comes the trap that many visitors fall into: the hostelry catering only to the tourist horde. You can eat exceptionally well in the lagoon city... as long as you avoid anything with a *menù turistico* in several languages and a determined enticer at the door. Pay for the best, or seek out some dark *bacaro*: anything else will not be authentically Venetian.

Etiquette

In more rustic eateries, menus are often recited out loud; waiters are used to doing off-the-cuff English translations, though these can be a little approximate. If you are unsure of the price of something you have ordered, always ask.

If there is a printed menu, note that fish is often quoted by weight – generally by the *etto* (100 grammes). Steer well clear of restaurants – mainly around San Marco – that employ sharply dressed waiters to stand outside and persuade passing tourists to come in for a meal: an immediate recipe for rip-off prices. Always ask for a written *conto* (bill) at the end of the meal, as it is, in theory, illegal to leave the restaurant without one.

In the know
Restaurant price codes

We use the following price codes for restaurant listings throughout the guide; they represent the average cost of one main dish (*secondo*).

€ = under €10

€€ = €10-25

€€€ = €25-40

€€€€ = over €40

Finally, bear in mind that there are two timescales for eating in Venice. The more upmarket restaurants follow standard Italian practice, serving lunch from around 1pm to 3pm and dinner from 7.30pm until at least 10pm. But *bacari* and neighbourhood *trattorie* tend to follow Venetian workers' rhythms, with lunch running from midday to 2pm and dinner from 6.30pm to 9pm, although newer, more contemporary venues may keep on cooking until 10pm or 10.30pm. As a rule, though, if you want to eat cheaply, eat early.

In the know
Venice's favourite fizz

It's difficult to avoid spritz in Venice: before lunch, early evening, after dinner – just about any time, in fact, you'll find crowds outside Venetian bars, glasses of amber-orange liquid in hand. But despite its jaunty hue and party-fun flavour, spritz comes in varying degrees of dangerous.

The origins of this ubiquitous drink are as obscure as its 'real' recipe. Perhaps invented by Venice's Austrian occupiers in the 19th century (they couldn't take the strength of local wines, one story goes, and so ordered it watered down), a classic version calls for one part prosecco, one part bitters and one part sparking seltz water, with a slice of orange and some ice to finish off the job. It's quite normal these days to find common or garden mineral water and white wine replacing seltz soda and prosecco, making it altogether a less tingling experience.

The real threat to navigation comes from your choice of bitter. When ordering, you can specify spritz all'Aperol (11% proof), with the very Venetian Select (14%) or with Campari (20+%). Whatever version you choose, a generous glass will cost somewhere between €2.50 and €3.50 in all but the most high-end bars.

What's on the plate?

If you want to eat well, eat local. Venice may be the most tourist-infested of Italian cities, but it has a long and glorious culinary tradition based on fresh seafood, game and vegetables, backed up by northern Italy's three main carbohydrate fixes: pasta, risotto and polenta.

Eating like the locals requires a certain spirit of open-minded experimentation. Not everybody has eaten *granseola* (spider-crab) before, or *garusoli* (sea snails) or *canoce* (mantis shrimps), but Venice is definitely the place to try these marine curios – as well as market garden rarities like *castraure*

💜 Traditional bacari

With their blackened beams and rickety wooden tables, *bacari* (emphasis on the first syllable) are local bars, often hidden down backstreets or in quiet campielli. These establishments – **Al Portego** (*see p95*), **Ca' d'Oro** (*see p107*), **Alla Ciurma** (*see p121*) and **Bottega ai Promessi Sposi** (*see p109*) are fine examples – serve alcohol and snacks (*cicheti; see p28*) to market traders, workers and students from early morning onwards, and cater for Venetians on a *giro di bacari* (pub crawl) at aperitivo time. They may have a dark room out the back with scant seating, but dominating the front of the premises is a high glass-fronted bar counter piled with *cicheti*. The drink of choice is the *ombra*, a small glass of house wine (*see p34*), which is usually priced at around €1, but you'll find beer and spirits, too. The most famous and most down-to-earth of Venice's bacari is **Da Lele** (*see p132*), situated near piazzale Roma in the back streets of Santa Croce. A drink here – don't ask for a coffee as it isn't served – will give you an unrivalled insight into local workaday Venice.

(baby artichokes) and *fiori di zucca* (courgette flowers). A writhing, glistening variety of seafood swims from the morning stalls of the Rialto and Chioggia markets into restaurant kitchens; it's not always cheap, but for dedicated pescivores, there are few better stamping grounds in the whole of Italy.

The once-strong creative tradition with meat – especially the more unmentionable parts – is kept alive in a couple of restaurants and one marvellous *trattoria*, **Dalla Marisa** (Cannaregio 652B, fondamenta San Giobbe, 041 720 211); it can also be found in bar-counter *cicheti* like *nervetti* (veal cartilage) and *cotechino* (spicy pig's intestine parcels filled with various cuts of pork).

There are still very few dedicated veggie restaurants in the city, but Venetian cuisine relies heavily on seasonal vegetables, so it is quite easy to eat a vegetarian meal. *Secondi* are often accompanied by a wide selection of grilled vegetables: aubergine, courgette, tomato or radicchio.

Where and what to drink

Italians are assiduous frequenters of their local café for morning cappuccino and of their favourite bar for evening *aperitivi* (in fact, one establishment may answer all their needs: the terms bar and café are generally interchangeable, and most venues are multi-purpose).

Unassuming places such as **Da Lele** (*see p132*) or **Alla Ciurma** (*see p121*) open their doors around 6am. But you'll search in vain for a coffee machine: market traders or workers arriving from the mainland drop by at sunrise for their first (alcoholic) drink of the day. It keeps – they'll tell you –the damp out of your bones. *Aperitivi*, on the other hand, are quite likely to be consumed in a *pasticceria* (cake shop), with some fruity, creamy pastry concoction as a chaser.

At *aperitivo* time, locals flock to *bacari* or *enoteche*, the best of which offer an enormous selection of top-quality wines by the glass, most from north-east Italy. As well as local prosecco, try white wines from the Collio and Colli Orientali appellations and gutsy Valpolicella classico and Amarone reds.

Venetian Menu

Choosing what to eat

Antipasti (starters)

The dozens of *cicheti* that are served from the counters of the city's traditional *bacari* (see p31) are essentially antipasti; the choice may include: *baccalà mantecato* – cod beaten into a cream with oil and milk, often served on grilled polenta; *bovoleti* – tiny snails cooked in olive oil, parsley and garlic; *carciofi* – artichokes, even better if they are *castraure* (baby artichokes); *canoce* (or *cicale di mare*) – mantis shrimps; *folpi/folpeti* – baby octopus; *garusoli* – sea snails; *moleche* – soft-shelled crabs, usually deep-fried; *museto* – a boiled pork brawn sausage, generally served on a slice of bread with mustard; *nervetti* – boiled veal cartilage; *polpette* – deep-fried meatballs; *polenta* – yellow or white cornmeal mush, served either runny or in firm sliceable slabs; *sarde in saor* – sardines marinated in onion, vinegar, pine nuts and raisins; *schie* – tiny grey shrimps, usually served on a bed of soft white polenta; *seppie in nero* – cuttlefish in its own ink; *spienza* – veal spleen, usually served on a skewer; *trippa e rissa* – tripe cooked in broth.

Primi (first courses)

Bigoli in salsa – fat spaghetti in an anchovy and onion sauce; *gnocchi con granseola* – potato gnocchi in spider-crab sauce; *pasta... e ceci* – pasta and chickpea soup; *... e fagioli* – pasta and borlotti bean soup; *spaghetti... alla busara* – in anchovy sauce; *... al nero di seppia* – in squid-ink sauce; *... con caparossoli/vongole veraci* – with clams; *risotto di zucca* – pumpkin risotto.

Secondi (main courses)

In addition to the antipasti mentioned above, you may find: *anguilla* – eel; *aragosta/astice* – spiny lobster/lobster; *branzino* – sea bass; *cape longhe* – razor clams; *cape sante* – scallops; *cernia* – grouper; *coda di rospo* – anglerfish; *cozze* – mussels; *granchio* – crab; *granseola* – spider crab; *orata* – gilt-headed bream; *rombo* – turbot; *pesce San Pietro* – John Dory; *pesce spada* – swordfish; *sogliola* – sole; *tonno* – tuna; *vongole/caparossoli* – clams.

Meat eaters are less well catered for in Venice; local specialities include: *fegato alla veneziana* – veal liver cooked in onions; *castradina* – a lamb and cabbage broth.

Dolci

The classic end to a meal here is a plate of *buranei* – sweet egg biscuits – served with a dessert wine such as Fragolino. Then it's quickly on to the more important matter of which grappa to order.

Granchio served at Riviera *p135*

33

In a city where everything seems to cost over the odds, a small glass of wine (*un'ombra*) costs anything from Da Lele's ridiculous 60c to around €1.50. And in all but the smartest bars, the ubiquitous spritz (*see p30* Venice's favourite fizz) comes in at €2.50. Or rather, it does when consumed standing. Sitting down incurs a surcharge: the privilege of occupying a table will push your bill up a little in smaller places but jaw-droppingly so in, say, piazza San Marco – especially in the evening, when palm court orchestras are playing. Cautionary tales of tourists paying €50 for a glass of mineral water may be apocryphal, but they give the general idea: don't expect much (if any) change from a €10 note.

In the know
Gelato

Gelato is an all-day stop-gap, indulged in by everyone during the hotter months. Quality varies greatly from place to place. A foolproof test of any shop is to eyeball the tub of banana ice-cream – if it's grey in colour, you know it's the real deal: bright yellow screams that the ice-cream's been made from a mix. Recent years have seen the spread – much to Venetians' indignation – of gastronomic chains using high-quality ingredients, which, though a reliable fallback, lack a certain local feel and individual character.

Shopping

Venice was once the crossroads between East and West, and merchants from all over Europe met those from the Levant here to trade throughout the city. Exotic spices and raw silks were among the goods imported from distant lands and sold by shrewd Venetian merchants, though humble salt was also a major player in Venetian trade. One of the most important events in Renaissance Venice was La Sensa fair (*see p57*), which lasted a fortnight and was particularly popular for purchasing wedding trousseaux.

Traders of different nations each had their *fondaco* (alternatively spelt *fontaco* or *fontego*), a warehouse-cum-lodging. So successful in their business – and so desirous of making an impression – were the German traders in Venice that their Fondaco dei Tedeschi (*see p80*) was bedecked with frescoes by Titian and Giorgione.

Best places to buy glass
Vittorio Costantini *p116*
Marina & Susanna Sent *p149*
Davide Penso *p158*
Seguso Viro *p160*

Best spots for fashion lovers
T Fondaco dei Tedeschi *p80*
Banco Lotto N10 *p102*
Mori & Bozzi *p110*
Bevilacqua *p79*

Best Venice-themed shops
Papier Maché *p96*
Signor Blum *p141*
Venetian Dreams *p83*

Best places to buy food
Drogheria Mascari *p121*
VizioVirtù *p96*
Mercato di Rialto *p122*

What to buy and where to buy it

The sumptuous brocades and damasks (*see p39*), Burano lace and Murano glassware (*see p159*) still produced and found in the city are all legacies of *La Serenissima*'s thriving commerce. Though the prices of such authentic Venetian-made goods can be prohibitive, a recent resurgence of local artisans – shoemakers, jewellers, carpenters, mask makers and blacksmiths – has led to slightly more competitive rates, and has helped to keep traditional techniques alive.

The **Mercerie** – the maze of crowded, narrow alleyways leading from piazza San Marco to the Rialto – and the streets known collectively as the **Frezzeria**, which wind between La Fenice and piazza San Marco, have been the main retail areas in this city for the past 600 years or so. The densest concentration of big-name fashion outlets can be found around the calle larga XXII Marzo, just west of the piazza, where the top names such as Prada, Fendi, Versace and Gucci have all stacked their boutiques.

Devotees of kitsch should not miss the stalls and shops near the train station, where plastic gondolas, illuminated gondolas, flashing gondolas, musical gondolas and even gondola cigarette lighters reign supreme.

For more tasteful souvenirs, Venice's glass, lace, fabrics and handmade paper are legendary – as are the much cheaper made-in-Taiwan substitutes that are passed off as the genuine article by unscrupulous traders. Sticking to the outlets listed in this guide will help you to avoid unpleasant surprises.

The steady demographic drop has led to the demise of 'everyday' shops: bread, fruit and veg, milk and meat are increasingly difficult to get hold of. And while new supermarkets have opened around the city and on the Giudecca, the flipside of this is the threat they pose to the livelihood of the few remaining greengrocers, bakers and butchers. This said, a string of daily and weekly food markets (*see p38*) takes place throughout the city and on neighbouring islands, meeting the locals' basic needs.

Opening hours and tax rebates

Most food shops are closed on Wednesday afternoons, while some non-food shops stay shut on Monday mornings. During high season (which in Venice includes Carnevale in February/March, Easter, the summer season from June to October and the four weeks leading up to Christmas) many shops abandon their lunchtime closing and stay open all day, even opening on Sundays.

Signor Blum *p141*

It pays to be sceptical about the hours posted on the doors of smaller shops: opening times are often dictated by volume of trade or personal whim. If you want to be sure of not finding the shutters drawn, call before you set out.

Incomprehensibly – given that summer is

Venice's busiest season – some shops close for holidays in August, but the majority of these are smaller ones that cater more to residents than tourists, such as *tabacchi*, photocopying centres or dry cleaners.

If you are not an EU citizen, remember to keep your official receipt (*scontrino*) as you are entitled to a rebate on IVA (sales tax) paid on purchases of personal goods costing more than €155, as long as they leave the country unused and are bought from a shop that provides this service. Make sure that there is a sign displayed in the window and also ask for the form that you'll need to show at customs upon departure. For more information about customs, see the Italian government website (www. agenziadogane.gov.it) for info in English.

For obvious reasons, which relate primarily to lack of space, Venice does not have modern shopping centres, with the exception of **T Fondaco dei Tedeschi** (at the luxury end of the market, *see p80*) and **Santa Lucia station**. If you are looking for a mall to fill all your needs, you'll have to journey to the mainland. The Centro Barche in Mestre offers everything from H&M to Feltrinelli International bookstore.

Markets

As befits a city that was once at the centre of a bustling trade in goods from around the world, Venice boasts a wide selection of daily and weekly markets, selling everything from tacky fridge magnets to pungent creatures of the lagoon. On market day, locals will come out of the woodwork, wheelie carts in hand, and gather to share news and stock their pantries. The historic **Rialto markets** (*see p122*) are by far the most visually stunning, but you need to go further afield to get a taste of day-to-day local life. Head to Sacca Fisola on Giudecca on a Friday morning, for example, and even a native Italian speaker will struggle to understand the

Material Makers

Sumptuous fabrics are a hallmark of the city

The fact that rich-hued brocades – from luscious silks to sad nylon rip-offs – adorn thousands of Venetian hotel rooms does not signal lack of imagination on the part of local interior designers. The choice, in fact, reflects a traditional craft that dates back to the 13th century, or perhaps earlier.

It was *La Serenissima*'s privileged trading position with the Orient and its close links with Byzantium that provided the initial impetus. Venetian merchants filled the holds of their ships with the raw materials – cotton and silk – on their return to Venice from the great trading centres of the eastern Mediterrean. It may have been weavers from Byzantium who first showed the Venetians how to make fabric. But craftsmen brought from Lucca, an earlier Italian centre of textile excellence, also played a part. By the 14th century, Venice's fabrics – from cheap low-grade cottons to the most luxurious of heavy silks – had become highly sought-after commodities around Europe and the Levant. If Venice had become an international byword for unimaginable richness, it was in large part due to its textiles.

Today, the lagoon city is more commonly associated with lace, but this is misleading: far more fabric is now produced in and around Venice than lace. Manufacturers of the very finest materials are household names with top designers everywhere.

Rubelli (Palazzo Corner Spinelli, San Marco 3877, campiello del Teatro, 041 241 7329, www. rubelli.com) has been weaving in the Veneto since 1835: its fabrics grace the La Fenice opera house (see *p85*) and all rooms of the Gritti Palace hotel (see *p168*). Its magnificent textile archive goes back far further than the company's own history, however, with examples of Venetian and many other fabrics dating from the 15th century onwards. It can be visited by appointment.

The **Bevilacqua** dynasty has operated in Venice for more than two centuries and some of its output is still produced on the original looms in its workshop in the Santa Croce district (Santa Croce 1320, campiello de la Comare, 041 721 566, www.luigi-bevilacqua. com). The shop at the same location sells fabric, household and apparel accessories and textile-related books, as well as holding the company's huge archive. There's more Bevilacqua fabrics, and homewares made with it, at the Bevilacqua shops near San Marco (see *p79*).

Spanish fashion designer-cum-polymath **Mario Fortuny** (see *p153*) opened his textile factory in a former convent on the Giudecca island in 1921, installing machinery specially designed by him that is still in use and remains a closely guarded secret. The factory's showroom can be visited, however: it positively glows with the colours emanating from the massive bolts of glorious fabrics that line the walls.

meticulously coiffed elderly locals as they argue with the greengrocer in thick Venetian dialect. At the other end of Giudecca, on Thursday mornings, the enterprising inmates of the women's prison sell organic vegetables from their 'Garden of Marvels', while boats piled high with fruit and veg make for unusual market stalls in via Garibaldi and fondamenta Gherardini.

The city's markets (see www.veneziaunica.it/en/content/markets for further details) have received a boost in recent years by the 'zero kilometre' movement, which calls for food miles to be kept to a minimum – a trend increasingly supported by restaurants serving only lagoon produce, and by eco-friendly cooperatives such as iSapori (www.isaporidisanterasmo.com), which delivers seasonal vegetables from the island of Sant'Erasmo (specialities include the distinctive purple artichoke) to various pick-up points across the city, and Valle Sacchetta e Sacchettina (www.pescherieonline.it), which exports fish all over Europe.

Tourist market

Entertainment

Venice was once famous for endless partying; these days, you'll be hard-pressed to find much of a scene. There's hardly a dancefloor in the city – but then again, that's not what Venice is about. If you're happy to settle for drinks, chat and the occasional bout of live music in one of the city's late-night bars, fine; if you're after serious clubbing, you'll have to go further afield. Classical and church music of varying standards is performed at concerts throughout the year, supplemented in summer by high-quality contemporary film, theatre, dance and music, as part of the Biennale. At the other end of the scale, numerous commercial organisations cater to a less rigorous public happy to crown their rose-tinted Venetian idyll with costumed renditions of Vivaldi's greatest hits.

Best live music spots
Venice Jazz club *p141*
Paradiso Perduto *p116*

Best classical music venues
San Vidal *p84*
Basilica dei Frari *p130*

Best for original language movies
Venice Film Festival *p44*

Best performing arts experience
La Biennale di Venezia, Danza-Musica-Teatro *p58*

Best theatres
La Fenice *p85*
Teatro Carlo Goldoni *p80*

Best free concerts
Fondazione Cini *p154*

Nightlife

A typical Venetian night out starts with a post-work and preprandial spritz (or three, *see p30* Venice's favourite fizz) in one of the bars around the Rialto market area, which might develop into a *giro de ombre* – a bar crawl Venetian-style. And for those still standing when the traditional bacari close, there's a network of late-opening bars: head for Cannaregio's 'party' **fondamenta della Misericordia**, or Dorsoduro's student headquarters of **campo Santa Margherita**. Many of the drinking establishments listed in this guide are open well into the evening. Try, for example, the **Skyline Bar** in Giudecca (*see p153*).

Stringent noise pollution regulations and lack of adequate venues have effectively pulled the plug on large music events. Rock 'n' roll royals who do dates in Venice are usually confined to the very formal setting of one of the local theatres. There's better news for jazz heads, with regular series of high-quality jazz and experimental music (www.caligola.it). And, thanks to the tenacity of a handful of bar owners, it's still possible to play and hear live music in various *locali* around town - mostly reggae, jazz or blues.

For serious club culture, make for the mainland. In winter, take a short bus or train ride to Mestre or Marghera; in summer, most of the dance action moves out to the seaside resort of Lido di Jesolo.

Film

If you pitch up in town during the world's longest-running film festival in late summer (*see p44*), you might mistake Venice for cinema heaven. But outside the once-a-year jamboree, the city lacks viable cinemas. The renaissance of the **Multisala Rossini** cinema (*see p83*) provided a little more choice for ardent cinemagoers, but many former picture palaces now house supermarkets.

One ray of hope is **Circuito Cinema**, a city hall-backed film promotion initiative that runs and programmes a group of local arthouse cinemas (see www.comune.venezia.it/cinema for details). In Italy, the dubber is king, so the selection of films in *versione originale* is limited.

Performing arts

Looking back to the days – in the 18th and 19th centuries – when Venice boasted no fewer than 18 hugely active theatres, you might think that contemporary Venice has become a backwater in the performing arts sector. But this town of fewer than 60,000 souls still boasts one of Europe's great opera houses, **La Fenice** (*see p85*), plus

Teatro Malibran

❤ Venice Film Festival

Palazzo del Cinema, lungomare Marconi 90, Lido (041 521 8711, www.labiennale.org). Vaporetto Lido. **Date** *11 days, starting late Aug/early Sept.*

Founded in 1932, the annual Venice Film Festival (Mostra Internazionale d'Arte Cinematografica) is the oldest film festival in the world and remains one of the most prestigious. For 11 days in late summer the glitterati of the film industry, plus their entourage of press and fans, take over the Lido (*see p154*). The main venue is the marble-and-glass Palazzo del Cinema, where official competition screenings take place. Other screens can be found in the Palazzo del Casinò, the striking red box of the Sala Giardino and the 1,700 seater Palabiennale marquee.

The best film of the festival is awarded the *Leone d'Oro* – won by *The Shape of Water* (Guillermo del Toro) in 2017 – with other prizes for best director, actor and actress. Many screenings are open to the public, with tickets from as little as €5 (in 2017) available online until two days before the event; multi-ticket subscriptions are also available. Note that competition films are likely to sell out quickly. Further details, including a full programme of screenings, are available on the official Biennale website.

George Clooney arriving at the 74th Venice Film Festival

Ensemble Hanatsu Miroir perform at 61st International Festival of Contemporary Music, Sale D'Armi

the summer **Biennale di Venezia, Danza-Musica-Teatro** (*see p58*), which brings high-quality international productions and artists to perform contemporary theatre, dance and music in the city. Stages here tend to be multi-purpose, with La Fenice, for instance, hosting opera, dance and other performances, and the **Teatro Malibran** (*see p110*) offering both classical music concerts and ballet.

The **Teatro Carlo Goldoni** (*see p80*), named after the city's enduringly popular 18th-century playwright, tends to serve up standard theatrical fare. You can find more cutting-edge work during the summer Biennale in theatre spaces created inside the Arsenale: the **Teatro alle Tese** and the **Teatro Piccolo Arsenale**.

When it comes to classical music, Venice has become a victim of its own musical tradition, with Vivaldi pouring out of its *scuole* and churches, usually performed by bewigged and costumed players with predictable programmes. But there are exceptions, such as the Venice Baroque Orchestra (www.venicebaroqueorchestra.it), Interpreti Veneziani (www.interpretiveneziani.com), and the orchestra of La Fenice, one of the best in the

LGBT Venice

Quietly cruising the city

Venice has everything and (next to) nothing for the gay traveller: enchanting, romantic, tolerant and indulgent...with hardly an LGBT-specific venue in sight. In the *centro storico* a quiet gay scene is tucked away in the private sphere: dinner parties or quiet drinks at the local *bacaro* define the way the city's gay community goes about its business. Buzzy Campo Santa Margherita is the focal point for young Venetians of all persuasions. Further north, in Santa Croce, La Zucca (*see p128*) is one of Venice's most gay-friendly restaurants. Behind the Procuratie Nuove, by the Giardinetti Reali, Il Muro is one of the city's oldest cruising institutions. Rarely frequented from October to May, it can still pull a crowd during summer.

The summer provides more scope for fun, when gay visitors in large numbers descend on Alberoni Beach on the Lido for nude sunbathing and cruising. If the weather's good, cruising starts as early as April.

country. Apart from La Fenice, Teatro Malibran, **San Vidal** (*see p84*) and **I Frari** (*see p130*) are among the best places to hear high-quality classical and church music in the city. Lovers of sacred music should aim to catch the sung Mass at St Mark's every Sunday at 9am or the Gregorian chant on the island of **San Giorgio**, also on Sunday at 11am.

Most dance events are limited to the summer Biennale or to classical ballet in the major theatres, although in the summer, tango aficionados can watch or even join performances in campo San Giacomo dell'Orio, on the steps of the station or in front of the Salute basilica (www.tangoaction.com).

In the know
Information and tickets

Day-to-day listings are carried by the two local papers, *Il Gazzettino* and *La Nuova Venezia*. For a fuller overview of concerts and festivals magazine *Venews* (www.venezianews.it) and www.veneziadavivere.com/events is indispensable. Tickets are usually available at the venue, but in some cases can be bought in advance at Venezia Unica outlets (*see p184*), or online via www.ticketone.it.

For high-profile or first-night productions at prestigious venues such as La Fenice, Teatro Carlo Goldoni or Teatro Malibran, the limited number of seats not taken by season-ticket holders will sell out days or even weeks in advance.

Smoking is strictly forbidden in indoor public spaces, except in designated rooms with extraction systems.

Venice
Day by Day

Acqua alta in piazza San Marco

Itineraries

Passing through and anxious to get the city's major sights under your belt? Much is possible in a single day, as long as you set off early and have laid the groundwork with some pre-booking. If you're here for longer, you'll be able to visit less-touristed areas. We also provide tailored itineraries for families and for those visitors on a tight budget, so that everyone can make the most of their time in *La Serenissima*.

ESSENTIAL WEEKEND

Venice in two days
Budget €265 per person
Getting around Vaporetti and lots of walking

DAY 1

Morning

St Mark's Basilica (*see p68*) doesn't open to tourists until 9.30 or 9.45am, so book your entry in advance for a €2 fee, but arrive earlier to stroll around the (relatively) uncrowded *piazza* and admire the architecture before entering. If you need refreshment, note that a coffee consumed at a café table in piazza San Marco may be the most expensive hot beverage of your life: drunk standing at the counter inside it costs a fraction of the price. Once inside the basilica, take time to climb up to the **Museo Marciano** in the loggia to see the famous bronze horses and enjoy the sweeping view of St Mark's square from the balcony.

A visit to the **Doge's Palace** (*see p74*) next door is essential to understand the mighty machinery of the Venetian state, and to get to grips with some seriously large-scale art.

From the San Zaccaria stop, take a vaporetto to the Palanca stop, admiring Palladio's splendid churches of **San Giorgio Maggiore** (*see p155*) and **Redentore** (*see p153*) en route.

▶ *Budgets include transport, meals and admission prices, but not accommodation and shopping.*

Afternoon

For lunch, grab a quick plate of excellent seafood at one of the canal-side tables at **Alla Palanca** (*see p153*). Then sail back to Zattere and head for the **Gallerie dell'Accademia** (*see p144*), Venice's foremost treasure trove for the grand masters of classical art. If, on the other hand, your preference is for something more up to date, head for the charming **Peggy Guggenheim Collection** (*see p143*), with its fine displays of modern art.

Take the route through campo San Barnaba to **campo Santa Margherita** and refresh yourself in one of the many café-bars in this happening square, before continuing on to the vast **Frari** church (*see p117*) for another art feast.

Evening

Backtrack just a little for your evening *aperitivo* to friendly **Estro Vino e Cucina** (*see p139*). Once you settle down here, you may opt to eat as well. But if you have the strength, take vaporetto 1 at San Tomà and steam along the Grand Canal, with the city bathed in sunset light, to the **ponte di Rialto**. Watching the evening draw in from the top of the bridge may be a cliché, but it's undeniably romantic. There are eateries for all budgets on both sides of the bridge.

DAY 2

Morning

Explore further afield today, starting off at the magnificent church of **Santi Giovanni e Paolo** (*see p93*), perhaps with a cappuccino stop at a pavement table at **Rosa Salva** (*see p80*) right next door.

A stroll along the lovely lagoon-side walkway will take you to the Fondamenta Nove vaporetto stop for the quick hop across to **Murano** (*see p157*). Ignore anyone trying to lure you into a glass showroom along the sniper's alley of shops. These peddle anything from stunning Murano creations to cheap tat imported from the other side of the globe. Head instead for the **Museo del Vetro** (*see p158*) for a fine introduction to Venice's long glass-making tradition. (Alternatively, you can leave the vaporetto at **San Michele** island (*see p157*) and languish among the famous graves of the city's picturesque cemetery.)

Afternoon

Back at Fondamenta Nove, weave your way to **Alla Frasca** (*see p115*) for lunch in a delightful campo. You'll need all your orienteering skills to get from here to the **Madonna dell'Orto** (*see p113*), where huge works by Tintoretto dominate the church. The artist is buried here too. Now wend your way south into the **Ghetto** (*see p110*) where the **Museo Ebraico** (*see p111*) charts the long history of Venice's Jewish community.

From the Guglie stop, take vaporetto 4.1 up the final reaches of the Grand Canal, under the **Ponte della Costituzione** (aka Ponte di Calatrava after its controversial Catalan designer), through what counts as Venice's industrial wasteland and on to Palanca, on the **Giudecca** island (*see p152*).

Evening

There are few finer places in the world to watch the sun set than at the **Skyline Bar** (*see p153*) on the roof of the Molino Stucky Hilton. From Palanca – or indeed from any of the stops along the Giudecca if you feel like a stroll – vaporetto 4.1 continues on to San Zaccaria. **CoVino** is a smart stop for a gourmet dinner, but be sure to book ahead.

Gallerie dell'Accademia

FAMILY DAY OUT

Travelling with tots or teens
Budget €250 for a family of four
Getting around Mainly walking, children under six travel free on public transport. Remember that *traghetti* (*see p175*) are a cheap and cheerful way to travel across the canals at a fraction of the price of a gondola.

Morning

A view over the city is a good place to begin a day's exploration. Give the over-subscribed campanile in St Mark's Square a miss, and take a vaporetto from the San Zaccaria stop to **San Giorgio**. The bird's-eye view from the tower is arguably better: you're one wide canal away from the main island, and so the whole sweep of the city is laid out before you, bisected by the backwards-S-shaped Grand Canal. On a clear day, you can see the faraway peaks – at times snow-covered – of the Dolomites.

Head back to San Zaccaria and turn left along the **Riva degli Schiavoni** promenade to the lagoon-facing façade of the **Doge's Palace** (*see p74*). (Note en route that the final bridge you cross gives a fine view to the Bridge of Sighs.) Stop at the third column from the palace's corner for the most famous Venetian game of all. Stand with your back touching the column and try to walk around it, all the way. Can you do it without slipping off the shoe-eroded edge of the marble pavement?

In **piazza San Marco**, on the north side of the basilica, crouch two little red marble lions, their backs worn smooth by generations of small bottoms: if you're longing for a photo of your child astride the symbol of St Mark – Venice's patron saint – this is the place.

DENONTIE SECRETE
CONTRO CHI OCCVLTERÀ
GRATIE ET OFFICII
Ó COLLVDERÀ PER
NASCONDER LA VERA

Doge's Palace

Afternoon

Grabbing a slab of pizza is often a good lunch option, though the big, noisy **Alla Basilica** diner right behind St Mark's Basilica also provides a (relatively) cheap lunch for starving children.

A ten-minute stroll north east of the piazza, the **Scuola di San Giorgio degli Schiavoni** (*see p99*) is a charming place to introduce children to the allure of Venetian painting. In the first years of the 16th century, artist Vittore Carpaccio was commissioned to decorate this social centre for Slav residents with stories from the lives of Dalmatian saints. Look out for St George rescuing the lovely princess of Trebizond from the fiery dragon; St Jerome looking

bewildered as his fellow monks scarper at the sight of a cuddly lion, and 12-year-old St Tryphon banishing a cheeky-looking basilisk-devil that had possessed the emperor's daughter. There are infinite engaging details in Carpaccio's dreamy world.

If it's all going well and you feel you can risk a little more art, check out the series of 18th-century scenes of Venetian life by Gabriel Bella at the nearby **Fondazione Querini Stampalia** (*see p91*). Between serious processions and doges going about their official duties are football matches, ice-skating parties on the frozen lagoon, bear- and bull-baiting fixtures and the unusual 'sport' of head-butting cats.

If, on the other hand, a change of tack is needed, head south-east for the **Museo Storico Navale** (*see p98*), containing models of Venetian ships from mighty galleons to the Doge's magnificent gilded *Bucintoro* barge. Its annexe, the **Padiglione delle Navi**, has full-size (real) gondolas, fishing boats, naval vessels and racing boats.

Padiglione delle Navi

Evening

You're far enough east now to collapse in some greenery, either in the *giardini* off via Garibaldi or – slightly further away – those in Sant'Elena. Both come with swings and slides and shady tree cover. If you make it to Sant'Elena, the **Vincent Bar** (Sant'Elena, Viale IV novembre 36, 041 520 4493) serves good café-style meals at outside tables from which you can watch your offspring play in the park. Nearer to via Garibaldi, **Dai Tosi** (*see p100*) offers good pizza and much else.

BUDGET BREAK

For the euro-conscious visitor
Budget €25 per person
Getting around Walking

Morning

For a very special take on **St Mark's Basilica** (*see p68*), enter by the piazza dei Leoncini door and attend the sung mass at 9am. You can't wander around – you're there for the service – but craning up at those acres of shimmering mosaic as the music drifts over you is unique. And it's free.

In calle degli Albanesi, just behind the basilica, grab a restorative cappuccino at **Da Bonifacio** (*see p95*) – in Italy, sitting down to consume your coffee costs more, but there's no danger of that here as there's nowhere to sit – before heading to the nearby church of **San Zaccaria** (*see p92*) with its Tintoretto, its Tiepolo and its marvellous *Madonna and Four Saints* by Giovanni Bellini – all for free.

Afternoon

As you wiggle your way north to campo Santi Giovanni e Paolo, pick up the ingredients for a picnic. You can eat it on the canal-side steps opposite the entrance to the massive church. To see the interior of **Santi Giovanni e Paolo** (*see p93*) you'll be charged €2.50 – a small

San Zaccaria

price for all those fine doges' tombs and great art. Next door at the **Scuola Grande di San Marco** (*see p94*), on the other hand, you can see the magnificent halls and the intriguing collection of historical medical-related artefacts – this medical science museum is located inside the city's hospital – for free.

Further west near the Rialto Bridge, the **Fondaco dei Tedeschi** (*see p80*) is a luxury shopping mall with little to entice the visitor on a tight budget. But if you can time your stopover here for just before sunset, climb to the rooftop viewing platform for an utterly magnificent and utterly *gratis* panorama over the city centre.

Evening

Shun the Fondaco's ground-floor bar if you want to save your *centesimi* and cross the Rialto bridge to **Al Mercà** (*see p121*). This hole-in-the-wall purveyor of snacks and drinks serves great spritzes at €2.50. One or two of these, consumed among the crowd of happy *aperitivo*-drinkers who fan out to occupy the campo, will set you up nicely for your evening meal. If you're not too late you might squeeze into **Alla Ciurma** (*see p121*) and eat a meal's-worth of delicious *cicheti* (bar snacks), but the place closes at 9pm: remember, to eat cheaply in Venice, be prepared to eat standing up and eat early.

Scuola Grande di San Marco

Diary

Venice has never shied away from merry-making: saints' days, military victories, even the arrival in town of a foreign diplomat – they were all good excuses for a party. The arrival of Napoleon's troops in 1797 ended this state of affairs. By that time, Venice's celebrations had become frantic and excessive, the tawdry death throes of a city in terminal decline. It wasn't until well into the 20th century that the city's traditional revelries began to be resuscitated – this time by officials with an eye firmly on tourist revenue. The most famous example is Carnevale, dusted off in 1979 and now a tourist draw so immense that new spaces for events are being opened up. The Regata Storica, too, is something of a historical pastiche, though in this case one that dates from 1899 when it was hoped it would lend the Biennale a little Venetian colour.

❤ Carnevale

www.carnevale.venezia.it.
Date *2 weeks before Shrove Tues.*

Venice's pre-Lenten Carnevale had existed since the Middle Ages, but it came into its own in the 18th century. As the Venetian Republic slipped into terminal decline, the city's pagan side began to emerge. Carnevale became an outlet for all that had been prohibited for centuries by the strong and sober arm of the doge. Elaborate structures would be set up in piazza San Marco as stages for acrobats, tumblers, wrestlers and other performers. Masks served not only as an escape from the drabness of everyday life but to conceal the wearer's identity – a useful ploy for nuns on the run or slumming patricians.

The Napoleonic invasion in 1797 brought an end to the fun and games, and Carnevale was not resuscitated until the late 1970s. When it was reintroduced, it was with money-earning in mind: the city authorities and hoteliers' association saw the potential, and today the heavily subsidised celebrations draw revellers to the city from all over the world.

But if Carnevale fills Venetian hotels and coffers, it also gives the locals a chance for fun and games. The party starts two weekends before *martedì grasso* (Shrove Tuesday). Visitors flock to piazza San Marco, where professional poseurs in ornate costumes occupy prime spots and wait for the world's press photographers to immortalise them. Since 2014, organisers have sought to relieve the pressure of numbers in St Mark's by moving some events into the Arsenale. Venetians, on the other hand, organise private masked and costumed celebrations, or gather in smaller squares. Consult the website for a full programme of events.

Spring

February is **Carnevale** month (*see p56*), so be prepared to wear a costume and embrace the mayhem in the streets. Venice is also a popular destination on Valentine's Day, so if you prefer to avoid the crowds, try the period after Carnevale and before Easter. You may get deals on hotels and airfares at this time, but pack an umbrella and warmish clothes, as the weather will be wet and nights can be cold. May is a gorgeous month to visit – you'll get sunshine and a clear atmosphere, which make strolling through the city pure bliss. However, if you want to avoid the worst of the crowds, don't visit over the first weekend in May.

Mar/Apr **Pasqua (Easter)**

At dusk on Maundy Thursday, the lights are turned off inside St Mark's basilica, and a fire is lit in the narthex (entrance porch) for the *benedizione del fuoco* (blessing of fire). Pasquetta (Easter Monday) is a public holiday, and museums and galleries may be closed.

Sun in mid Apr
Su e Zo per i Ponti

www.suezo.it
Literally 'Up and Down the Bridges'. Participants in this non-competitive, jolly race are given a map and a list of checkpoints (many of them bars) in the city of Venice to tick off. Proceeds go to charity.

25 Apr **Festa di San Marco**

Mass in the basilica, followed by a gondola regatta between the island of Sant'Elena and the punta della Dogana. Red rosebuds are given to wives and lovers.

1 May **Festa del Lavoro (Labour Day)**

Weekend after Ascension **Festa e Regata della Sensa**

Under the Republic, the doge boarded a glorious state barge and threw a gold ring overboard near the outlet to the Adriatic, to symbolise *lo sposalizio del mare* – marriage with the sea. Today, the mayor throws a wreath at San Nicolò on the Lido; a regatta follows.

Summer

June to August is when four elements combine to create arguably the worst time to visit: excessive humidity (and mosquitoes), intense heat, huge crowds and high prices. Some days may be hazy, while others will be punctuated by heavy showers. The tiny alleys (*calli*) can get clogged with people, making it difficult to circulate in the most popular areas of the city, notably around the Rialto Bridge and St Mark's square. Note too, that 15 August is **Ferragosto**, a national Italian holiday when Venetians tend to leave town, meaning that many authentic shops and eateries are closed. During the **Venice Biennale** (*see p101*) and the **Venice Film Festival** (*see p44*) prices inflate even more; queues for water taxis are long, and fares prohibitively expensive. But if glitz and glam are your thing, it's worth the hassle.

❤ May/Nov **Biennale d'Arte Contemporanea & Architecttura**

www.labiennale.org
See p101 La Biennale.

Festa del Redentore

June-Aug Biennale di Venezia, Danza-Musica-Teatro

www.labiennale.org

Venice's Biennale festival umbrella has expanded its dance, music and theatre department and enriched the city's cultural offering as a result. The international programme is staged in two spectacular venues inside the Arsenale – the **Teatro Tese** and the smaller **Teatro Piccolo Arsenale** – and in squares and venues around the city. There are also workshops and a host of side events.

Week around 29 June Festa di San Pietro

The most villagey of Venice's local festivals, this one, in Castello, has a week of concerts, food stands and bouncy castles.

❤ 3rd weekend in July Festa del Redentore

A pontoon bridge is built from San Marco to the Giudecca, to allow church and civic dignitaries to process to the Redentore church. On Saturday evening, illuminated boats full of picnickers gather off the punta della Dogana to watch a firework display.

Week around 25 July Festa di San Giacomo dell'Orio

Concerts, barbecues and a charity raffle in the eponymous campo.

15 Aug Ferragosto (Feast of the Assumption)

Venice closes down for this public holiday, and there's usually a free concert on the island of Torcello.

❤ Late Aug-early Sept Venice Film Festival

www.labiennale.org

See p44 Venice Film Festival.

❤ Late May/early Jun Vogalonga

www.vogalonga.com

See p59 Rowing regattas.

June-July Venezia Jazz Festival

www.venetojazz.com

This annual event draws serious jazz-heads for great music in fantastic venues around Venice and in the Veneto.

♥ Rowing regattas

The sight of a flotilla of boats being rowed full tilt across the lagoon or down the Grand Canal may well be the highlight of your stay as well as being evidence of the Venetian love of messing about in boats.

There are 120 'serious' fixtures on the lagoon during the rowing season from April to September, plus more to accompany every big Venetian feast day, including Carnevale (see p56), Festa della Sensa (see p57) and Il Redentore (see p58). The Regata delle Befane (see p60) is a light-hearted affair, but others are hard-fought battles between the city's famously excellent rowers displaying their own particular style of forward-facing rowing, known as *Voga alla Veneta*.

The most sumptuous of all the Venetian regattas, however, is the **Regata Storica** (www. regatastoricavenezia.it) on the first Sunday in September. This event begins with a procession of ornate boats down the Grand Canal, rowed by locals in 16th-century costume. The procession is followed by four races: one for young rowers, one for women, one for rowers of *caorline* – long canoe-like boats in which the prow and the stern are identical – and the Flast, the most eagerly awaited, featuring two-man sporting *gondolini*. The finish is at the sharp curve of the Grand Canal between Palazzo Barbi and Ca' Foscari: here, the judges sit in an ornate raft known as the *machina*, where the prize-giving takes place. Seating for spectators is on floating platforms near campo San Polo (tickets for non-residents €60; €30 reductions; book well in advance).

More riotously jolly is the **Vogalonga** (041 521 0544/www. vogalonga.com), which takes place on a Sunday in May or early June and is open to anyone with a boat and an oar. For this one chaotically colourful day, Venetians protest against motorboats by boarding any kind of rowing craft and following a 30-km (18-mile) route through the lagoon and along the city's two main canals. They are joined in this annual free-for-all on the water by a host of out-of-towners and foreigners. Boats set off from the Canale di Giudecca, off Punta della Dogana, at 9am.

Vogalonga

Autumn

Due to its mild temperatures, September is becoming a favourite month to be in Venice, and events such as the **Regata Storica** (see p59) draw thousands of curious onlookers to the shores of the canals. October can also be a good time to stroll through the city with fewer tourists, but you should expect changeable weather. By November, *acqua alta* (high-water flooding) is common and tends to frighten off visitors. However, the combination of thick fog and flooded streets creates an eerie and enchanting atmosphere that will appeal to many – just be sure to pack your wellies. And don't miss the celebration of **Festa della Madonna della Salute**.

❤ 1st Sun in Sept Regata Storica
www.regatastoricavenezia.it
See p59 Rowing regattas.

3rd Sun in Sept Sagra del Pesce
Fried fish and lots of white wine are consumed amid Burano's brightly painted houses.

1st weekend in Oct Sagra del Mosto
This festival on Sant'Erasmo is a great excuse for Venetians to get light-headed on the first pressing of wine.

Last Sun in Oct Venice Marathon
www.venicemarathon.it
The marathon starts in the town of Stra, near Padua, and ends on the riva dei Sette Martiri.

1 Nov Ognissanti (All Saints' Day)

11 Nov Festa di San Martino
Children armed with mamma's pots and spoons raise a ruckus around the city centre. Horse-and-rider-shaped San Martino cakes can be found in cake shops all over Venice.

21 Nov Festa della Madonna della Salute
The patriarch (archbishop) leads a procession across the Grand Canal on a pontoon bridge from campo Santa Maria del Giglio to the Salute church.

Winter

December is usually crowded, especially for the **Christmas holidays** (23 December to 6 January). At the beginning of the year, temperatures tend to drop, sometimes below freezing, so consider warming yourself up with a cup of hot chocolate, or some grappa.

Dec Le Giornate Wagneriane
arwvi@libero.it
Wagner is the star of a series of world-class concerts organised by the Associazione R Wagner; there are also conferences on the great man, and visits to the house he occupied while in Venice. Concerts are free, but get tickets in advance.

8 Dec L'Immacolata (Feast of the Immaculate Conception)

25 Dec Natale (Christmas Day)

26 Dec Santo Stefano (St Stephen's/Boxing Day)

31 Dec San Silvestro (New Year's Eve)
A massive outdoor party in St Mark's square has light shows, live music and DJ sets.

1 Jan New Year's Day
Hardy swimmers take a bracing dip in the waters off the Lido.

6 Jan La Befana (Epiphany)
A rowing race along the Grand Canal. Competitors, all aged over 50, are dressed up as an ugly witch, La Befana.

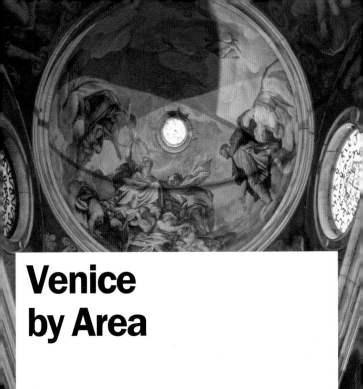

Venice
by Area

Scuola Grande di San Rocco

San Marco

Piazza San Marco, Napoleon said, is the 'drawing room of Europe'. It may not be homely, but it is a supremely civilised meeting place. At times, it appears that much of Europe's population is crammed into this great square and the pulsating shopping streets leading out of it.

Three main thoroughfares link the key points of this neighbourhood: one runs from piazza San Marco to the Rialto bridge; one from the Rialto to the Accademia bridge; and one from the Accademia back to piazza San Marco. For a respite from the crowds, wander off these routes; even in this tourist-packed *sestiere* you can find little havens of calm.

Iconic sights
The Basilica di San Marco (*p68*) is arguably one of the greatest churches in Christendom, and it's right next to the hub of Venetian power and magnificence, the Palazzo Ducale (*p74*).

Best shopping experience
Bevilacqua (*p79*) for Venetian textiles for a king. T Fondaco dei Tedeschi (*p80*) offers 21st-century consumerism in a 16th-century trading house. Venetian Dreams for authentic Venetian beads (*p83*)

Best view
Climb to the top of the Campanile (*p66*) to enjoy the splendour of piazza San Marco.

Best restaurant
Head to the Gran Caffè Quadri (*p73*) for the ultimate gourmet blow-out, or to Caffè Florian (*p79*) for a taste of history.

Best music
La Fenice (*p85*) serves up top-notch opera in an over-the-top setting. Or there's baroque at its best at San Vidal (*p84*).

Piazza San Marco & around

In magnificent piazza San Marco, Byzantine rubs shoulders with Gothic, late Renaissance and neoclassical. The Venetians have always kept the square clear of monuments; this is typical of Venice, where individual glory always plays second fiddle to the common weal. The north side of the square dates from the early 16th century. Its arches repeat a motif suggested by an earlier Byzantine structure. Here resided the procurators of St Mark's, who were in charge of maintaining the basilica – hence the name of this whole wing, the **Procuratie Vecchie**. At its eastern end is the **Torre dell'Orologio**. Construction of the **Procuratie Nuove**, opposite, went on for most of the first half of the 17th century, to designs by Vincenzo Scamozzi. Napoleon joined the two wings at the far end – not for the sake of symmetry, but in order to create the ballroom that was lacking in the Procuratie Nuove, which had become the imperial residence. So, in 1807,

down came Jacopo Sansovino's church of San Geminiano and up went the Ala Napoleonica, which now houses the **Museo Correr**. The **Campanile** and **Basilica di San Marco** close off the square to the east.

Between the basilica and the lagoon, the **piazzetta** is the real entrance to Venice, defined by two free-standing columns of granite. What appears to be a winged lion on top of the eastern column is in fact a chimera from Persia, Syria or maybe China; the wings and book are Venetian additions. St Theodore, who tops the other column, was Venice's first patron saint, before he was ousted by St Mark. The area directly in front of the **Palazzo Ducale** (Doge's Palace) was known as the *broglio*, and was the place where councillors conferred and connived (hence the term 'imbroglio'). Opposite the palace stands the **Biblioteca Marciana**, now the main city library. Most of the library's collections are housed in **La Zecca**, the former mint, designed by Sansovino in 1547.

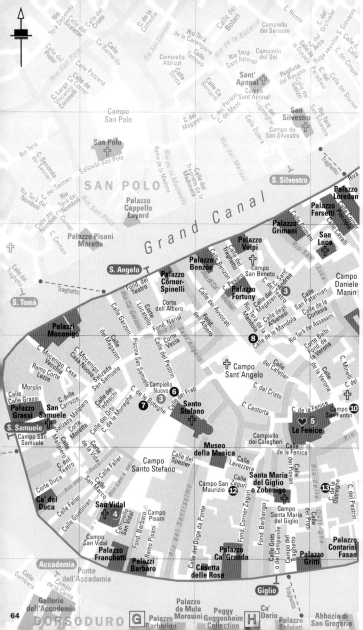

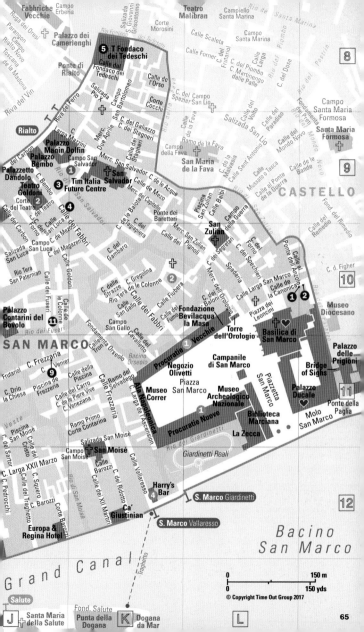

West of the piazzetta are the **Giardinetti Reali** (Royal Gardens), created by the French. The dainty neoclassical coffee house by Gustavo Selva is now a tourist information office. By the San Marco Vallaresso vaporetto stop is **Harry's Bar**, the city's most famous watering hole (*see p86*).

Heading east from the piazzetta, you will cross the **ponte della Paglia** (Bridge of Straw). If you can elbow your way to the side of the bridge, there is a photo-op view of the ponte dei Sospiri (Bridge of Sighs). From the Bridge of Straw, there is also a superb view of the Renaissance façade of the Palazzo Ducale.

Campanile

Sights & museums

❤ Campanile di San Marco
San Marco, piazza San Marco. Vaporetto San Marco Vallaresso or San Zaccaria. **Open** *Nov-Mar 9.30am-5.30pm daily. Apr 9am-5.30pm daily. May-Sept 8.30am-9pm daily.* **Admission** *€8. No cards.* **Map** *p64 L11.*

At almost 99m (325ft), the Campanile is the city's tallest building, originally built between 888 and 912. Its present appearance, with the stone spire and the gilded angel on top, dates from 1514. In July 1902 it collapsed, imploding in a neat pyramid of rubble; the only victim was the custodian's cat. It was rebuilt exactly 'as it was, where it was', as the town council of the day promised. The Campanile served both as a watchtower and a bell tower. It provided a site for public humiliations: people of 'scandalous behaviour' were hung in a cage from the top. More wholesome fun was provided by the *volo dell'anzolo* (flight of the angel), when an *arsenalotto* (shipwright) would slide down a rope strung between the

Campanile and the Palazzo Ducale at the end of Carnevale. The flight is still re-enacted today. Holy Roman Emperor Frederick III rode a horse to the top of the original in 1451; these days visitors take the lift. The view is superb, taking in the Lido, the whole lagoon and (on a clear day) the Dolomites in the distance. Sansovino's little Loggetta at the foot of the tower, which echoes the shape of a Roman triumphal arch, was also rebuilt using bits and pieces found in the rubble.

▶ *For an eye-to-eye view of the Campanile, climb up the Torre dell'Orologio, see p72.*

Museo Correr, Museo Archeologico & Biblioteca Marciana
San Marco 52, piazza San Marco/ sottoportego San Geminiano (041 240 5211, correr.visitmuve.it). Vaporetto San Marco Vallaresso. **Open** *10am-7pm daily.* **Admission** *€20, €13 reductions (with Palazzo Ducale. See p21 Visitior passes).* **Map** *p64 K11.*

These three adjoining museums are all entered by the same doorway, which is situated beneath the Ala Napoleonica at the western end of piazza San Marco.

Museo Correr

The Museo Correr is dedicated to the history of the Republic. Based on the private collection of Venetian nobleman Teodoro Correr (1750-1830), it has gems – including some very fine artworks – enough to elevate it well beyond mere curiosity. The museum is housed in the Ala Napoleonica, the wing that closes off the narrow western end of the piazza, and in a constantly expanding area of the Procuratie Nuove. Napoleon demolished the church of San Geminiano, which faced off across the piazza to the basilica, in order to make way for his exercise in neoclassical regularity, complete with that essential imperial accessory, a ballroom. It is through this ballroom that you enter the Museo Correr today. At the far end, in a secluded niche, stands an unlabelled statue (1811). This is the city's hated conqueror, Napoleon.

The route now leads through nine rooms that made up the suite occupied by Sissi, aka Empress Elizabeth of Austria, wife of Franz Joseph I. In fact the beautiful, tragedy-prone Sissi spent no more than a few months here, in 1861-62, but the stuccos and fittings – including beautiful textile reproductions by Rubelli (*see p39* Material Makers) – faithfully reflect the decor of the period.

Passing through the pretty oval 'everyday dining room', the spirit of these same years continues in Rooms 4 and 5, dedicated to the beautiful if icy sculpture of Antonio Canova, whose first Venetian commission – the statue of Daedalus and Icarus displayed here – brought him immediate acclaim. Some of the works on display are Canova's plaster models rather than his finished marble statues.

From Room 6, the historical collection – which occupies most of the first floor of the Procuratie Nuove building – documents Venetian history and social life in the 16th and 17th centuries through displays of globes, lutes, coins and

Museo Correr

💜 Basilica di San Marco

*San Marco, piazza San Marco (041 270 8311, www. basilicasanmarco.it). Vaporetto San Marco Vallaresso or San Zaccaria. **Open** Basilica, Chancel & Pala d'Oro, Treasury 9.30am-5pm Mon-Sat; 2-4.30pm Sun. Loggia & Museo Marciano 9.45am-4.45pm daily. **Admission** Basilica free. Chancel & Pala d'Oro €2. Treasury €3. Loggia & Museo Marciano €5. No cards. **Map** p64 L11.*

▶ *To skip the huge queues that form at the basilica entrance at busy times, you can book your visit (€2 fee) through www. venetoinside.com. Large bags or rucksacks must be deposited (free) in a building in calle San Basso, off the piazzetta dei Leoncini. The basilica is open for mass and private prayer from 7am to 11.45am, and 5pm to 7.30pm, with entrance from the piazzetta dei Leoncini door.*

Considered the living testimony of Venice's links with Byzantium, St Mark's Basilica is also an expression of the city's independence. In the Middle Ages any self-respecting city state had to have a truly important holy relic. So when two Venetian merchants swiped the body of St Mark from Alexandria in 828, concealed from prying Muslim eyes under a protective layer of pork, they were going for the very best – a gospel writer, and an entire body at that. Fortunately, there was a legend (or one was quickly cooked up) that the saint had once been caught in

the lagoon in a storm, and so it was fitting that this should be his final resting place. The basilica is encrusted with trophies brought back from Venice's greatest spoliatory exploit, the Sack of Constantinople in 1204, during the Fourth Crusade.

The present basilica is the third on the site. It was built mainly between 1063 and 1094, although the work of decoration continued until the 16th century. The church became Venice's cathedral only in 1807, ten years after the fall of the Republic; until then the bishop exerted his authority from San Pietro in Castello (*see p98*). Being next door to the Palazzo Ducale, Venice's most important church was associated with political as much as spiritual power. Worshipers were guests of the doge, not the pope.

Exterior

Viewing the basilica from the western end of the piazza is unforgettable. The façade consists of two orders of five arches, with clusters of columns in the lower order; the upper arches are topped by fantastic Gothic tracery. The only original mosaic (c1260) is over the northernmost door, *The Translation of the Body of St Mark to the Basilica*. The real treasures on show are the sculptures, particularly the group of three carved arches around the central portal.

In the narthex (covered porch), a small lozenge of porphyry by the central door is said to mark where Emperor Barbarossa paid homage to Pope Alexander III in 1177.

The south façade was the first side seen by visitors arriving by sea and is thus richly encrusted with trophies proclaiming *La Serenissima*'s might. At the corner by the Doge's Palace stand the Tetrarchs, a fourth-century porphyry. It comes from Constantinople and is usually accepted as representing Diocletian and his Imperial colleagues.

The north façade is also studded with loot. Note the 13th-century Moorish arches of the Porta dei Fiori, which enclose a Nativity scene.

Interior

A lifetime would hardly suffice to see everything contained in this cave of wonders. The basilica is Greek cross in form, surmounted by five great 11th-century domes. The surfaces are totally covered by more than four square kilometres (1.5 square miles) of mosaics, the result of 600 years of labour. The finest pieces, dating from the 12th and 13th centuries, are the work of Venetian craftsmen influenced by Byzantine art but developing their own style.

In the apse, beneath the *Christ Pantocrator* in what may be the oldest mosaics in the church, are four saint-protectors of Venice: Nicholas, Peter, Mark and Hermagoras. The central Dome of the Ascension dates from the early 13th century. The Pentecost dome (near the entrance) was probably the first to be decorated; it shows the *Descent of the Holy Spirit*.

In the right transept is the *Miraculous Rediscovery of the Body of St Mark*: this refers to an episode that occurred after the second basilica was destroyed by fire, when the body was lost. The Evangelist obligingly opened up the pillar where his sarcophagus had been hidden.

Pentecost dome

💜 Basilica di San Marco *continued*

Baptistry & Zen Chapel
The baptistry contains the Gothic tomb of Doge Andrea Dandolo and in the adjoining Zen Chapel is the bronze 16th-century tomb of Cardinal Zen. The baptistry and chapel are very rarely open.

Chancel & Pala d'Oro
The chancel is separated from the body of the church by the iconostasis – a red marble rood screen with statues of the Madonna, the apostles and St George. St Mark's sarcophagus is visible through the grate underneath the altar.

The indigestibly opulent Pala d'Oro (Gold Altarpiece) is a Byzantine work and, for a change, was acquired honestly. It was made in Constantinople in 976 and further enriched in later years with amethysts, emeralds, pearls, rubies, sapphires and topaz, topped off with a Gothic frame and resetting in 1345.

The left transept contains the chapel of the Madonna Nicopeia (the Victory Bringer), named after the tenth-century icon on the altar, another Fourth Crusade acquisition. The St Isidore Chapel beyond is reserved for private prayer and confessions, as is the adjacent Mascoli Chapel.

Loggia & Museo Marciano
Of all the pay-to-enter sections of the basilica, the Loggia dei Cavalli is the most worthwhile – and it's the only part of the church you can visit on a Sunday morning. Up a narrow stairway from the narthex are the bronze horses that vie with the lion of St Mark as the

city's symbol; here, too, is Paolo Veneziano's exquisite Pala Feriale, a painted panel that was used to cover the Pala d'Oro on weekdays. The Loggia also provides a marvellous view over the square. Since 1982, the original bronze horses are kept indoors. They were among the many treasures brought back from the Sack of Constantinople.

In 1797 it was Napoleon's turn to play looter; the horses didn't return to Venice from Paris until after his defeat at Waterloo.

Treasury
This contains a hoard of exquisite Byzantine gold and silver plunder. The highlights are a silver perfume censer in the form of a church and two 11th-century icons of the Archangel Michael.

The Tetrarchs

robes. Room 6 is devoted to the figure of the doge. Room 11 has a collection of Venetian coins, plus Tintoretto's fine *St Justine and the Treasurers*. Beyond are rooms dedicated to the Arsenale (*see p97*), a display of weaponry and some occasionally charming miniature bronzes.

Beyond Room 15 lies the nine-room Wunderkammer, charmingly laid out in a style inspired by the 18th-century passion for eclectic collecting. Curators went through the Museo Correr's store rooms, dusting off and restoring a few real gems, including a couple of early works by Vittore Carpaccio, and a remarkable portrait of dashing 16th-century mercenary Ferrante d'Avalos, formerly attributed to Leonardo da Vinci – an attribution once rubbished but now being reconsidered. Other rooms contain exquisite painted china produced for the Correr family, Renaissance bronzes and ivory carvings. In the final room of the Wunderkammer is the first-ever print of Jacopo de' Barbari's 1500 intricate bird's-eye view map of Venice, along with the original matrices in pear wood. This extraordinary woodcut is so finely detailed that every single church, *palazzo* and well-head in the city is clearly portrayed.

Stairs from the next room lead up to the Quadreria picture gallery – one of the best places to get a grip on the development of Venetian painting between the Byzantine stirrings of Paolo Veneziano and the full-blown Renaissance story-telling of Carpaccio. Rooms 25 to 29 are dedicated to Byzantine and Gothic painters; note Veneziano's fine *St John the Baptist* in Room 25 and the rare allegorical fresco fragments from a 14th-century private house in Room 27. Room 30 fast-forwards abruptly with the macabre, proto-Mannerist *Pietà* (c1460) of Cosmè Tura. The Renaissance gets into full swing in Room 34 with Antonello da Messina's *Pietà with Three Angels*, haunting despite the fact that the faces have nearly been erased by cack-handed restoration. The Bellinis get Room 36 to themselves. The gallery's most fascinating work, though, must be Vittore Carpaccio's *Two Venetian Noblewomen* – long known erroneously as *The Courtesans* – in Room 38. These two bored women are not angling for trade: they're waiting for their husbands to return from a hunt. This was confirmed when *A Hunt in the Valley* (in the Getty Museum in Los Angeles) was shown to be this painting's other half.

Back downstairs, the historical collection continues with rooms dedicated to the Bucintoro (state barge), festivities, trade guilds and fairground trials of strength. The atmosphere gets neoclassical again along the corridor to the exit, café and gift shop which is lined with reliefs by Canova.

Museo Archeologico

This collection of Greek and Roman art and artefacts is interesting not so much for the individual pieces as for the light they cast on the history of collecting. Assembled mainly by Cardinal Domenico Grimani and his nephew Giovanni, the collection is a discerning 16th-century humanist's attempt to surround himself with the classical ideal of beauty. Highlights are the original fifth-century BC Greek statues of goddesses in Room 4, the Grimani Altar in Room 6, and the intricate cameos and intaglios in Room 7. Room 9 contains a fine head of the Emperor Vespasian. Room 20 has a couple of Egyptian mummies.

Biblioteca Marciana/Libreria Sansoviniana

In 1468, the great humanist scholar Cardinal Bessarion of Trebizond left his collection of Greek and Latin manuscripts to the state. Venice didn't get round to constructing a proper home for them until 1537. Jacopo Sansovino, a Florentine architect who had settled in Venice after fleeing from the Sack of Rome in 1527, was appointed to create the library, a splendid building right opposite the Doge's Palace. With this building, Sansovino brought the ambitious new ideas of the Roman Renaissance to Venice. He also appealed to the Venetian love of surface decoration by endowing his creation with an abundance of statuary. His original plan included a barrel-vault ceiling. This collapsed shortly after construction, however, and the architect was immediately clapped into prison. His rowdy friends Titian and Aretino had to lobby hard to have him released.

The working part of Venice's main library is now housed inside La Zecca and contains approximately 750,000 volumes and around 13,500 manuscripts, most of them Greek.

The main room has a magnificent ceiling, with seven rows of allegorical medallion paintings, produced by a number of Venetian Mannerist artists as part of a competition. Veronese's *Music* (sixth row from the main entrance) was awarded the gold chain by Titian. Beyond this is the anteroom, in which a partial reconstruction has been made of Cardinal Grimani's collection of classical statues, as arranged by Scamozzi (1596). On the ceiling is *Wisdom*, a late work by Titian. Don't miss Fra Mauro's map of the world (1459), a fascinating testimony to the great precision of Venice's geographical knowledge, with surprisingly accurate depictions of China and India.

There are occasional free guided tours in English; call 041 240 5211 for information.

Torre dell'Orologio

San Marco 147, piazza San Marco (bookings 041 4273 0892, torreorologio.visitmuve.it/en/ home). Vaporetto San Marco Vallaresso or San Zaccaria. **Open** *Guided tours in English 10am, 11am Mon-Wed; 2pm, 3pm Thur-Sun.* **Admission** *€12; €7 reductions.* **Map** *p64 L10.*

Note that there is no lift and the stairs are steep and narrow. The clock tower can *only* be visited on a tour, which can be booked at the Museo Correr (*see p67*), online, or by calling the number given above.

The clock tower, designed by Maurizio Codussi, was built between 1496 and 1506; the wings were an addition, perhaps by Pietro Lombardo. Above the clock face is the Madonna. During Ascension week and at Epiphany, the Magi come out and bow to her every

Torre dell'Orologio

Gran Caffè Quadri

hour, in an angel-led procession. At other times of year the hours and minutes are indicated in Roman and Arabic numerals on either side of the Madonna; this feature dates from 1858 – one of the earliest examples of a digital clock. On the roof, statues of two burly Moors, made of gunmetal and cast in 1497, strike the hour. Another Moore (Roger) sent a villain flying through the clock face in the film *Moonraker*.

After lengthy restoration, the tower reopened in 2007. The tour reveals the workings of the clock, which dates from 1753 and was a remake of the original of 1499. Until 1998 the clock was wound manually by a *temperatore* who lived in the tower. Amid controversy the last incumbent was replaced by an electrical mechanism. The tour concludes on the roof of the tower with a fine view over piazza San Marco, the basilica and the palace.

Restaurants

❤ Gran Caffè Quadri €€€€
San Marco 120, piazza San Marco (041 522 2105, www.alajmo.it/grancaffe-quadri). Vaporetto San Marco Vallaresso or San Zaccaria. **Café** *9am-midnight daily.* **ABC Bistrot** *noon-3pm, 7-10.30pm daily.* **Restaurant** *12.30-2.30pm, 7.30-10.30pm Tue-Sun.* **Map** *p64 L11* ❶ *Modern Venetian*

Marcel Proust used to bring his *maman* to eat in this Venetian classic that has been operating since 1638, and you can still imagine the couple in the plush red upper dining room with its spectacular view across St Mark's square. But the food – the exquisite, sometimes surprising creations of star chef Massimiliano Alajmo – might surprise them (as might the bill). Since the advent of the Alajmos (brother Raffaele runs the house) in 2011, everything here is recherché, from the extraordinary coffee specially toasted for the café at piazza level, through the club sandwiches and deceptively simple pasta plates served (at slightly lower prices than the restaurant) in the ABC Bistrot, to the marvels cooked up (prawn and curried clam cappuccino, wild duck risotto with truffle and foie gras drops, seabass with olive, caper and chicory pesto) for what is arguably the city's finest eating experience, recognised with a Michelin star in 2017. There are taster menus at €170, €235 and €300. Originally called Il Rimedio, the Gran Caffè takes its name from Giorgio Quadri, who was among the first to bring Turkish-style coffee to Venice when he took the place over in the late 18th century. Stendhal, Wagner and Balzac were habitués. In the evening, a palm court orchestra competes out in the square with the one at Florian's (*see p79*) opposite, and romantics pay small fortunes to sip cocktails under the stars.

❤ Palazzo Ducale (Doge's Palace)

San Marco 1, piazzetta San Marco (041 271 5911, bookings 041 4273 0892, www.visitmuve. it). Vaporetto San Marco Vallaresso or San Zaccaria. **Open** 8.30am-7pm daily. Tours (book at least 2 days in advance) 9.55am, 10.45am, 11.35am daily. **Admission** €20, €13 reductions (with Museo Correr, Museo Archeologico, Biblioteca Marciana), see p21 Visitor passes. Audio guides €5. Tours €20, €14 reductions. **Map** p64 M11.

If the basilica was the Venetian Republic's spiritual nucleus, the Doge's Palace was its political and judicial hub. The present site was the seat of ducal power from the ninth century onwards, though most of what we see today dates from the mid 15th century.

The palace is the great Gothic building of the city, but is also curiously eastern in style, achieving an uncanny combination of lightness and strength. The ground floor was open to the public; the work of government went on above. The building gets heavier as it rises: the first level has an open arcade of simple Gothic arches, the second a closed loggia of ornate arcading. The top floor is a solid wall broken by a sequence of Gothic windows.

On the corner by the ponte di Paglia (Bridge of Straw) is an exquisite marble relief carving, the *Drunkenness of Noah*, from the early 15th century, while on the piazzetta corner is a statue of Adam and Eve from the late 14th century. The capitals of the pillars below date from the 14th to the 15th centuries, although many of them are 19th-century copies (some of the originals are on display inside the palace).

The Porta della Carta (Paper Gate – so called because this was where permits were checked), between the palace and the basilica, is a grand piece of florid Gothic architecture and sculpture (1438-42).

Behind the palace's fairy-tale exterior the complex machinery of empire whirred away with assembly-line efficiency. Anyone interested in the inner workings of the Venetian state should take the 90-minute Itinerari Segreti tour. This takes you into those parts of the palace that the official route does not touch, including the leads – the sweltering prison cells beneath the roof where Casanova staged his famous escape.

Following reorganisation, the main visit – for which an audio guide is recommended – now begins at the Porta del Frumento on the lagoon side of the palace. The Museo dell'Opera, has the best of the 14th-century capitals from the external loggia.

In the main courtyard stands the Arco dei Foscari, built by Antonio Bregno and Antonio Rizzo. Rizzo also sculpted the original figures of Adam and Eve, which earned him gushing accolades and led to his appointment as official architect in 1483, after a disastrous fire. Rizzo had time to oversee the building of the overblown Scala dei Giganti (where doges were crowned) and some of the interior before he was found to have embezzled 12,000 ducats; he promptly fled, and died soon afterwards.

The official route now leads up the ornate Scala d'Oro staircase by Jacopo Sansovino, with stuccoes by Vittoria outlined in 24-carat gold leaf.

First floor: Doge's apartments

The doge's private life was entirely at the service of *La Serenissima*; even his bedroom had to keep up the PR effort. These rooms are occasionally closed or used for temporary exhibitions; when open, the Sala delle Mappe merits scrutiny. Just to the right of the entrance is a detailed map of the New World with Bofton (Boston) and Isola Longa (Long Island) clearly marked.

Second floor: State rooms

This grandiose series of halls provided steady work for all the great 16th-century Venetian artists. Titian, Tintoretto, Veronese, Palma il Vecchio and Jacopo Bassano all left their mark.

The Sala delle Quattro Porte was where the Collegio – the inner cabinet of the Republic – met before the 1574 fire. After substantial renovation it became an ambassadorial waiting room. The Anticollegio, restored in part by Palladio, has a spectacular gilded stucco ceiling, four Tintorettos and Veronese's blowsy *Rape of Europa*.

Beyond here is the Sala del Collegio, where the inner cabinet convened. The propaganda paintings on the ceiling are by Veronese. But for real hubris, stroll into the Sala del Senato, where Tintoretto's ceiling

Sala del Collegio

❤ Palazzo Ducale *continued*

centrepiece shows *The Triumph of Venice*. Beyond again are the Sala del Consiglio dei Dieci and the Sala della Bussola, where the arcane body set up to act as a check on the doge considered matters of national security. In the former, note Veronese's ceiling panel, *Juno Offering Gifts to Venice*. The itinerary continues through an armoury.

First floor: State rooms

The Sala dei Censori leads down to a liagò (covered, L-shaped loggia), which gives on to the Sala della Quarantia Civil Vecchia (the civil court) and the Sala del Guariento. The latter's faded 14th-century fresco of *The Coronation of the Virgin* by Guariento looks strangely innocent amid all this worldly propaganda.

Next comes the Sala del Maggior Consiglio – the largest room in the palace. This was in effect the Republic's lower house. Before the fire of 1577 the hall had been decorated with paintings by Bellini, Titian, Carpaccio and Veronese. Their replacements are less exalted, with one or two exceptions. Tintoretto's *Paradise*, on the far wall, sketched out by the 70-year-old artist but completed after his death in 1594 by his son Domenico, is liable to induce vertigo. In the ceiling panels are works by Veronese and Palma il Giovane; note too the

Palazzo Ducale

Bridge of Sighs

frieze of ducal portraits made by Domenico Tintoretto and assistants.

On the left side of the hall, a balcony gives a fine view over the southern side of the lagoon. A door leads from the back of the hall into the Sala della Quarantia Civile and the large Sala dello Scrutinio, where the votes of the Maggior Consiglio were counted; the latter is flanked by vast paintings of victorious naval battles.

Criminal courts & prisons

Backtracking through the Sala del Maggior Consiglio, a small door on the left leads past the Scala dei Censori to the Sala della Quarantia Criminale – the criminal court.

The route now leads over the Bridge of Sighs to the Prigioni Nuove, where petty criminals were kept. Lifers were sent down to the waterlogged *pozzi* (wells) in the basement of the *palazzo* itself. When this new prison wing was built in 1589, it was acclaimed as a paragon of comfort.

Some of the cells have their number and capacity painted over the door; one has a trompe l'œil window, drawn in charcoal by an inmate. Back across the Bridge of Sighs, the tour ends on the lower floor in the Avogaria – the offices of the clerks of court.

▶ *For a primer on Venice's convoluted system of government, see p78 Machinery of State.*

Paradise (Tintoretto c1588)

Machinery of State

Navigating the corridors of power

The longevity of the Venetian republic was due, to a large extent, to a finely honed system of checks and balances that kept the powerful merchant aristocracy closely involved in the machinery of state without allowing any one person or dynasty to lord it over the others. Rules, numbers and duties changed. At the end of the 13th century, what had started out as something close to a democracy became an oligarchy, with only the members of the 200-odd powerful clans included in the Libro d'oro (Golden Book) eligible for office. Later, anyone with the necessary funds could buy into the machinery of state. The main ruling bodies were:

Collegio dei savi

College of Wise Men – a group of experts, elected by the Senato, who staffed special committees to oversee all aspects of internal, marine and war policy.

Consiglio dei dieci

Council of Ten – appointed by the Senato, the council's extensive network of spies brought any would-be subversives to a closed-door trial, in which defence lawyers were forbidden. In time, the increasingly powerful Consiglio dei dieci would have the Inquisition to assist it in its task.

Il doge

The Duke – elected for life in a complicated, cheat-proof system of multiple ballots, the sumptuously robed Duke of Venice was glorious to behold. He could not, however, indulge in business of his own, receive foreign ambassadors alone, leave Venice without permission, or accept personal gifts. If his city state tired of him, he could be deposed. With the doge's extended family

banned from high office for the term of his reign, many doges hailed from less politically adept clans. Most were very old by the time they donned the *biretta*, the distinctive horned hat – the average age of doges between 1400 and 1570 was 72. However, the doge was the only official privy to all state secrets and eligible to attend all meetings of state organs; he could, if he played his cards right, have a determining effect on Venetian policy.

Maggior consiglio

Great Council – the Republic's parliament – made up of all voting-age males from the clans that were included in the Libro d'oro – which elected (and provided the candidates for) most other state offices, including that of the doge.

Minor consiglio

Lesser Council – elected by and from the Maggior consiglio, this six-man team advised – or kept tabs on – the doge.

Pien collegio

Full College – made up of the Minor consiglio and the Collegio dei savi, this became Venice's real government, eventually supplanting the Senato.

Quarantie

The three supreme courts; the 40 members were chosen by the Senato.

Senato

Senate – known until the late 14th century as the Pregadi, the Senato was the upper house of the Venetian parliament; by the 16th century it had some 300 members.

Serenissima signoria

Most Serene Lordships – the Minor consiglio, the heads of the three Quarantie courts and the doge; this body was vested with ultimate executive power.

Cafés, bars & gelaterie

♥ Caffè Florian
*San Marco 56, piazza San Marco
(041 520 5641, www.caffeflorian.
com). Vaporetto San Marco
Vallaresso.* **Open** *9am-midnight
daily.* **Map** *p64 L11*
Florian sweeps you back to
18th-century Venice with its
mirrored, stuccoed and frescoed
interior. Founded in 1720 as Venezia
Trionfante, Florian's present
appearance dates from an 1859
remodelling. Rousseau, Goethe and
Byron hung out here – the last in
sympathy with those loyal Venetians
who boycotted the Quadri (*see p73*)
across the square, where Austrian
officers used to meet. These days,
having a drink at Florian is more
bank statement than political
statement, especially if you sit at one
of the outside tables, where not even
a humble *caffè* costs less than €10.

Shops & services

♥ Bevilacqua
*San Marco 337B, ponte della
Canonica (041 528 7581, www.
bevilacquatessuti.com). Vaporetto
San Zaccaria.* **Open** *10am-7pm
Mon-Sat; 10am-5pm Sun.* **Map** *p64
M10* ❶ *Fabric*
This diminutive shop offers
exquisite examples of hand- and
machine-woven silk brocades,
damasks and velvets. *See p39*
Material Makers. **Other location**
San Marco 2520, campo Santa
Maria del Giglio (041 241 0662).

Studium
*San Marco 337C, calle
Canonica (041 522 2382, www.
libreriastudium.eu). Vaporetto San
Zaccaria.* **Open** *9am-7.30pm Mon-
Sat; 9.30am-6pm Sun.* **Map** *p64
M10* ❷ *Books & music*
This shop stocks a wide selection
of works on Venice, as well as travel
books and novels in English. Its

true speciality is revealed as you
step into the back room, which is
filled with theology studies, icons
and prayer books.

Piazza San Marco to the Rialto

Piazza San Marco is linked to the
Rialto by the busiest, richest and
narrowest of shopping streets:
the **Mercerie**. The name is plural,
since it is divided into five parts:
the Merceria dell'Orologio; di San
Zulian (on which stands the church
of the same name); del Capitello; di
San Salvador and del 2 Aprile. The
church of **San Salvador** contains
two great Titians and some
splendid Veneto-Tuscan sculpture.

Mercerie means 'haberdashers',
but we know from John Evelyn's
1645 account of 'one of the most
delicious streets in the world'
that in among the textile emporia
were shops selling perfumes and
medicines too. Most of the big-
name fashion designers are to be
found here now. The ponte dei
Baretteri (Hatmakers' Bridge), in
the middle of the Mercerie, is a
record holder in Venice: six roads
lead directly off the bridge.

The Mercerie emerge near
campo San Bartolomeo, the square
at the foot of the Rialto, with the
statue of playwright Carlo Goldoni
looking amusedly down at the
milling crowds.

Caffè Florian

Cafés, bars & gelaterie

Rosa Salva

San Marco 950, calle Fiubera (041 521 0544, www.rosasalva. it). Vaporetto Rialto or San Marco Vallaresso. Open 8am-8pm Mon-Sat. No cards. Map p64 K10 ❷

This long-established family-owned café and *pasticciere* makes one of the smoothest *cappuccini* in town, and some very delicious cakes to go with it. If it's ice-cream you fancy, all the flavours are made on the premises. There's a good lunch spread, with interesting sandwiches and filled rolls, as well as pastas and simple salads. The candied fruit in intriguing jars and piles of sugared rose buds and violet leaves are delightful.

Shops & services

L'O.FT

San Marco 4773, calle dell'Ovo (041 522 5263, www.otticofabbricatore. com). Vaporetto Rialto. Open 9am-12.30pm, 3.30-7.30pm Mon-Sat; 11am-7pm Sun. Map p64 J9 ❸
Accessories

Also known as L'Ottico Fabbricatore, this ultra-modern shop specialises in designer eyewear – the kind you won't find anywhere else, with extraordinary frames in anything from buffalo horn to titanium. Pop in for a pair of sunglasses, or bring along your prescription and treat yourself to glasses the likes of which chain-store opticians can only dream of. The boutique also sells gossamer-like cashmere and sensual silk apparel, plus a selection of luxurious bags in materials ranging from calfskin to ostrich.

Rizzo Regali

San Marco 4739, calle dei Fabbri (041 522 5811). Vaporetto Rialto. Open 9am-8pm Mon-Sat. Map p64 K9 ❹ *Food & drink*

This old-fashioned shop sells traditional cakes, sweets and chocolates. For *pesce d'aprile* (April Fool's Day), you can buy bags of foil-wrapped chocolate goldfish. If you can't find the *torrone* (nougat) you're looking for here, then it doesn't exist.

❤ T Fondaco dei Tedeschi

San Marco, calle del Fontego dei Tedeschi (041 314 2000), Vaporetto Rialto. Open 10am-8pm daily. Map p64 K8 ❺ *Mall*

Venetians struggle to recognise this glitzy tax-free shopping mall as the gloomy if rather monumental building that served as their main post office until a few years ago. A radical makeover, courtesy of architects Rem Koolhaas and Jamie Fobert, has transformed what was the 16th-century headquarters of German traders into a sparkling (almost blindingly so) luxury haven for anyone with deep pockets and a taste for designer labels. The **AMO** café/restaurant (run by super-chef Massimiliano Alajmo) serves meals in the courtyard, but, for those not wishing to splash out, an *aperitivo* in the bar itself, beautifully decked out in onyx by Philippe Starck, is a worthy alternative. Make sure to head up to the roof terrace, which offers a stunning view of the Grand Canal.

Entertainment

If your heart is set on performers in wigs, head for the **Scuola Grande di San Teodoro** (❶ San Marco 4810, salizzada San Teodoro) to hear I Musici Veneziani (www. imusiciveneziani.com).

Teatro Carlo Goldoni

San Marco 4650B, calle Carbonera (041 240 2011, www. teatrostabileveneto.it). Vaporetto Rialto. Map p64 J9 ❷ *Theatre*

The Goldoni serves up Venetian classics by its namesake, supplemented by 20th-century and more contemporary Italian pieces.

From the Rialto to the Accademia bridge

The route from the Rialto to the Accademia passes through a series of ever-larger squares. From cosily cramped campo San Bartolomeo, the well-marked path leads to campo San Luca, then campo Manin with its 19th-century statue of Daniele Manin, leader of the 1848 uprising against the Austrians. An alley to the left of this campo will lead you to the **Scala del Bòvolo**, a striking Renaissance spiral staircase. Back on the main drag, the calle della Mandola leads to broad campo Sant'Angelo with its dramatic view of **Santo Stefano**'s leaning tower; off calle della Mandola to the right is the Gothic **Palazzo Fortuny**, once home to the Spanish fashion designer Mariano Fortuny, and occasionally open for exhibitions.

Just before the Accademia bridge, campo Santo Stefano is second in size only to piazza San Marco in the *sestiere*. The tables of several bars scarcely encroach on the space where kids play on their bikes or kick balls around the statue of Risorgimento ideologue Nicolò Tommaseo. (Poor Tommaseo is known locally as il cagalibri, 'the bookshitter', for reasons which become clear when the statue is viewed from the rear.) The 18th-century church of **San Vidal** lies at the Accademia bridge end of the square.

On the Grand Canal to the north-west of campo Santo Stefano is campo San Samuele, which holds a deconsecrated 11th-century church and the massive **Palazzo Grassi** exhibition centre. Leading there from the campo, **calle delle Botteghe** is a hotch-potch of fascinating shops. Nearby, in calle Malipiero, the 18th-century love machine Giacomo Casanova was born (though in which house exactly is not known). The neighbourhood is full of Casanova associations, including the site of the theatre where his mother performed (corte Teatro).

Sights & museums

Palazzo Grassi

San Marco 3231, campo San Samuele (041 240 1308, www. palazzograssi.it). Vaporetto San Samuele. **Open** *during exhibitions 10am-7pm Mon, Wed-Sun.* **Admission** *€15 (€18 Palazzo Grassi & Punta della Dogana; see p147); €10 (€15 both) reductions.* **Map** *p64 F11.*

This superbly – though boringly – regular 18th-century *palazzo* on the Grand Canal was bought in 2005 by French billionaire businessman François-Henri Pinault. Pinault brought in Japanese superstar-architect Tadao Ando for an expensive overhaul, which increased the exhibition space by 2,000sq m (21,000sq ft). Most of the *palazzo*'s shows centre on Pinault's own massive contemporary art collection. Next door at no.3260, the Teatrino Grassi – another Ando makeover – shows art videos and hosts events.

▶ *François-Henri Pinault's mega-gallery in the Punta della Dogana is even more impressive; see p147.*

Santo Stefano

San Marco, campo Santo Stefano (041 275 0462, www.chorusvenezia. org). Vaporetto Accademia or San Samuele. **Open** *10.30am-4.30pm Mon-Sat.* **Admission** *€3 (or Chorus; see p23).* **Map** *p64 G11.*

Santo Stefano is an Augustinian church, built in the 14th century and altered in the 15th. The façade has a magnificent portal in the florid Gothic style. The large interior, with its splendid ship's-keel roof, is a multicoloured treat,

Scala Contarini del Bòvolo

with different marbles used for the columns, capitals, altars and intarsia, and diamond-patterned walls. On the floor is a huge plaque to Doge Morosini (best known for blowing up the Parthenon) and a more modest one to composer Giovanni Gabrieli. On the interior façade to the left of the door is a Renaissance monument by Pietro Lombardo and his sons, decorated with skulls and festoons. In the sacristy are two tenebrous late works by Tintoretto, *The Washing of the Feet* and *The Agony in the Garden* (*The Last Supper* is by the great man's assistants), and three imaginative works by Gaspare Diziani (*Adoration of the Magi, Flight into Egypt, Massacre of the Innocents*).

Scala Contarini del Bòvolo & Sala del Tintoretto

Palazzo Contarini del Bòvolo, San Marco 4299, corte dei Risi (041 309 6605, www. scalacontarinidelbovolo. com). Vaporetto Rialto. **Open** *10am-1.30pm, 2-6pm daily. Last admission 30mins before closing.* **Admission** *€7.* **Map** *p64 J10.*

Follow the signs for the Scala del Bòvolo from campo Manin and you will emerge in a narrow courtyard entirely dominated by this elegant Renaissance spiral staircase, built sometime around 1499 by Giovanni Candi (spiral staircases are *scale a chiocciola*, snail staircases, in Italian; *bòvolo* is Venetian dialect for snail). It was beautifully restored in 1986 and again more recently, and offers a stunning view from the summit. Halfway up, a small doorway opens on to the Sala del Tintoretto, which houses a handful of artworks from Venetian private collections. The standout piece, which gives the room its name, is Tintoretto's study for his far more grandiose *Paradise* in the Palazzo Ducale.

Cafés, bars & gelaterie

Fiore
San Marco 3461, calle de le Botteghe. **Open** *9am-10.30pm Mon, Wed-Sun.* **Map** *p64 G11* ❸
At *aperitivo* and lunch time, locals flock to this friendly *osteria* just off campo Santo Stefano to wet their whistles and stave off hunger by choosing from a wide selection of *cicheti*. Perch at the bar or rest your drink precariously on the ledge outside and sample the local specialities spilling over the counter – meatballs, *folpéti* (octopus) and celery, battered fish, fresh vegetables.

Shops & services

Ebrû
San Marco 3471, campo Santo Stefano (041 523 8830, www. albertovallese-ebru.com). Vaporetto Accademia or Sant'Angelo. **Open** *10am-1.30pm, 2.30-7pm Mon-Wed; 10am-1pm, 2.30-7pm Thur-Sat; 11am-6pm Sun.* **Map** *p64 G11* ❻ *Accessories/ stationery*

Beautiful, marbled handcrafted paper, scarves and ties. These are Venetian originals, whose imitators can be found in other shops around town.

L'Isola – Carlo Moretti
San Marco 2970, calle delle Botteghe (041 5233 1973, www.lisola.com). Vaporetto Sant'Angelo or San Samuele. **Open** *10.30am-7.30pm daily.* **Map** *p64 G11* ❼ *Homewares*
This long-established family firm produces exquisitely coloured contemporary glasses, bowls, vases, light fixtures and much else. Each piece is hand-crafted, some are limited editions and many find their way into important glass collections. The showroom closes some Sundays in August and all Sundays from January to March.

❤ Venetian Dreams
San Marco 3805, calle della Mandola (041 523 0292, www. marisaconvento.it), Vaporetto Sant'Angelo. **Open** *10.30am-6pm Wed-Sun.* **Map** *p64 H11* ❽ *Beads*
A treasure trove glittering with jewellery, household items and other decorative pieces fashioned out of antique beads by owner Marisa Convento, who lovingly keeps alive the 19th-century craft of the *imperaresse* – women who sat on bridges and *fondamenta* painstakingly sorting and threading seed beads. Bead-threading classes and themed rambles can also be organised on request.

Entertainment

Multisala Rossini
San Marco 3997A, salizada de la Chiesa o del Teatro (041 241 7274). Vaporetto Rialto or Sant'Angelo. **No cards.** **Map** *p64 H10* ❸ *Cinema*
Besides a mix of big hits, smaller productions and retrospectives

(and occasional screenings in *linga originale*), the very centrally located Rossini has a bar run by the Marchini dynasty, a restaurant and even an in-house supermarket.

❤ San Vidal

*San Marco 2862B, campo San Vidal (041 277 0561, www. interpretiveneziani.com). Vaporetto Accademia. **Shows** 9pm daily (8.30pm in winter). Tickets €29; €24 reductions. **Map** p64 G12* ④ *Classical concerts*

For highly professional renditions of Vivaldi and other mainly baroque favourites, visit the church of San Vidal (*see p84*), where the no-frills Interpreti Veneziani play to a backdrop of Carpaccio's image of San Vitale on a white horse over the high altar. Tickets can be purchased on the door, or at the Museo della Musica.

The Accademia bridge to piazza San Marco

The route from campo Santo Stefano back to piazza San Marco zigzags at first, passing through small squares, including campo San Maurizio, with its 19th-century church now transformed into the **Museo della Musica** (041 241 1840, www. museodellamusica.com), and **campo Santa Maria del Giglio** (aka Santa Maria Zobenigo). It winds past banks, hotels and antique shops, to end in wide via XXII Marzo, with an intimidating view of the Baroque statuary of **San Moisè**. Off to the left is the opera house, **La Fenice**, and more streets of supersmart shops, in the Frezzeria district.

Press on and you will be ready for what is arguably the greatest view anywhere in the world: piazza San Marco from the west side.

Sights & museums

San Moisè

*San Marco, campo San Moisè (041 528 5840). Vaporetto San Marco Vallaresso. **Open** 9.30am-12.30pm, 3-6.30pm daily. **Map** p64 K12.*

The Baroque façade of San Moisè has been lambasted by just about everybody as one of Venice's truly ugly pieces of architecture. Inside, an extravagant Baroque sculpture occupies the high altar, representing not only Moses receiving the stone tablets but also Mount Sinai itself. Near the entrance is the grave of John Law, author of the disastrous Mississippi Bubble scheme that almost sank the French central bank in 1720.

Santa Maria del Giglio

*San Marco, campo Santa Maria Zobenigo (041 275 0462, www. chorusvenezia.org). Vaporetto Giglio. **Open** 10.30am-4.30pm Mon-Sat. **Admission** €3 (or Chorus; see p23). No cards. **Map** p64 H12.*

This church's façade totally lacks any Christian symbols (give or take a token angel or two). Built between 1678 and 1683, it's a huge exercise in defiant self-glorification by Admiral Antonio Barbaro, who was dismissed by Doge Francesco Morosini for incompetence in the War of Candia (Crete). On the plinths of the columns are relief plans of towns where he served; his own statue (in the centre) is flanked by representations of Honour, Virtue, Fame and Wisdom. The interior is more devotional. You may not have heard of the painter Antonio Zanchi (1631-1722), but this is his church. Particularly interesting is *Abraham Teaching the Egyptians Astrology* in the sacristy, while the Cappella Molin has *Ulysses Recognised by his Dog* (an odd subject for a church). The chapel also contains a *Madonna and Child*, which is proudly but erroneously attributed to Rubens. Behind the altar there

💜 La Fenice

San Marco 1983, campo San Fantin (box office 041 24 24, information 041 786 511, www.teatrolafenice. it). Vaporetto Giglio. **Box office** *10am-5pm daily. Tours 9.30am-6pm daily (rehearsals permitting). Tickets €15-€300. Tours €10; €7 reductions.* **Map** *p64 H11* ⑤

Venice's principal opera house – aptly named 'the phoenix' – has a long history of fiery destruction and rebirth. The 1792 theatre, designed by Giannantonio Selva, replaced the Teatro San Benedetto, which had burned down in 1774. Opera enjoyed huge popularity in Venice at the start of the 19th century and La Fenice was the focus of this enthusiasm, with famous composers, such as Donizetti, Bellini and Rossini, regularly providing the theatre with new works. Selva's building was itself destroyed by fire in 1836, but was rebuilt in the same style by the Meduna brothers. Besides Verdi's *Rigoletto* and

La Traviata, La Fenice hosted premières of Benjamin Britten's *The Turn of the Screw* and Igor Stravinsky's *The Rake's Progress*. In the 20th century, Luciano Berio and Venice's greatest modern composer, Luigi Nono, were commissioned to write for the opera house.

In 1996, another massive blaze broke out, courtesy of two electricians. After years of legal wrangling, the theatre was rebuilt and inaugurated in December 2003, reclaiming its position as one of the world's premier opera houses. La Fenice now offers opera, ballet and concert seasons, and its orchestra is one of the best in the country, but tickets don't come cheap. If you can't get a seat for a performance, explore the theatre on a tour (with audio guide; bookable at the box office). Hidden from view behind the ornate gilding and faux-Baroque plush are state-of-the-art technological innovations.

are two paintings of the Evangelists by Tintoretto, formerly organ doors.

Cafés, bars & gelaterie

Harry's Bar

San Marco 1323, calle Vallaresso (041 528 5777, www.cipriani.com). Vaporetto San Marco Vallaresso. **Open** *10.30am-11pm daily.* **Map** *p64 K12* ❹

This historic watering hole, founded by Giuseppe Cipriani in 1931, has changed little since the days when Ernest Hemingway came here to work on his next hangover… except for the prices and the numbers of tourists. But despite the crush, a Bellini at the bar is as much a part of the Venetian experience as a gondola ride. At mealtimes, diners enjoy Venetian-themed international comfort food at steep prices (€140-plus for three courses). Stick with a Bellini, and don't even think of coming in here wearing shorts or ordering a spritz.

Shops & services

Araba Fenice

San Marco 1822, Frezzeria (041 522 0664). Vaporetto Giglio or San Marco Vallaresso. **Open** *9.30am-7.30pm Mon-Sat.* **Map** *p64 J11* ❾ *Fashion/accessories*

A classic yet original line of women's clothing made exclusively for this boutique, plus jewellery in ebony and mother-of-pearl.

Bugno Art Gallery

San Marco 1996D, campo San Fantin (041 523 1305, www. bugnoartgallery.it). Vaporetto San Marco Vallaresso. **Open** *4-7.30pm Mon, Sun; 10.30am-7.30pm Tue-Sat.* **Map** *p64 J11* ❿ *Gallery*

Large windows overlooking the Fenice opera house reveal a space devoted to artists working in all types of media. Well-known local artists are also included in the gallery's

collection. So packed is the exhibition calendar that shows often spill over into a smaller exhibition space.

Daniela Ghezzo Segalin Venezia

San Marco 4365, calle dei Fuseri (041 522 2115, www.danielaghezzo. it). Vaporetto Rialto or San Marco Vallaresso. **Open** *10am-1pm, 3-7pm Mon-Fri; 10am-1pm Sat.* **Map** *p64 J10* ⓫ *Accessories*

The shoemaking tradition that was established by 'the Cobbler of Venice', Rolando Segalin, continues through his talented former apprentice Daniela Ghezzo. Check out the footwear in the window, including an extraordinary pair of gondola shoes. A pair of Ghezzo's creations will set you back anything between €650 and €1,800. Repairs are done as well.

Trois

San Marco 2666, campo San Maurizio (041 522 2905). Vaporetto Giglio. **Open** *4-7.30pm Mon; 10am-1pm, 4-7pm Tue-Sat.* **No cards.** **Map** *p64 H12* ⓬ *Fabric*

This is one of the best places in *La Serenissima* to buy original Fortuny fabrics – and at considerable savings on the prices you'd find in the UK and the US (though this still doesn't make them particularly cheap). Made-to-order beadwork, masks and accessories are also available.

Venetia Studium

San Marco 2425, calle delle Ostreghe (041 523 6953, www. venetiastudium.com). Vaporetto Giglio. **Open** *10am-7.30pm Mon-Sat; 11am-6pm Sun.* **Map** *p64 K8* ⓭ *Accessories/ homewares*

Venetia Studium is the sole authorised manufacturer of the distinctive Fortuny lamps. It also stocks splendid silk pillows, scarves, handbags and other accessories in a marvellous range of colours. They're certainly not cheap, but they do make perfect gifts.

Castello

Castello is not only Venice's largest sestiere, it's also the most remarkably varied, stretching from the bustle and splendour in the north-west around Santa Maria Formosa and Santi Giovanni e Paolo, to the homely, washing-festooned stretches around and beyond wide via Garibaldi. To this mix add the immense Arsenale complex – Venice's former shipbuilding centre and great military powerhouse – and the Giardini della Biennale, where the city's contemporary art and architecture shows take place through the summer. There's also a slew of remarkable churches, a football pitch whose days may be numbered and some seriously good restaurants. Castello really is a Venice unto itself.

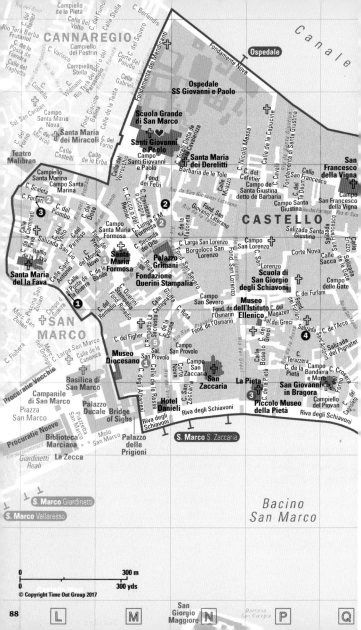

CANNAREGIO

Campiello de la Pietà
Calle del Volto
C. Berlendis
Rio Terà Barba Frutariol
Calle del Fumo
C. Stella
Canale
Rio Terà de la Posta de Fiandra
C. de Varisco
Campiello del Pestrin
Ospedale
Fondamente Nove
Calle del Traghetto
Campiello Stella
Rio Tera S. Sofia
Calle Gabriel
Corte de Paludo
Widmann
Fondamenta dei Mendicanti

Ospedale SS Giovanni e Paolo

Campo Santa Maria Nova
Santa Maria dei Miracoli
Calle Castelli
C. del Forno
C. de le Erbe
Scuola Grande di San Marco
Calle Detta de Cavaletizza

Teatro Malibran

Campiello Santa Marina
Campo Santa Marina
Santi Giovanni e Paolo
Campo Santi Giovanni e Paolo
Fond. dei Felzi
Santa Maria dei Derelitti

C. Scaleta
C. Fornieri
C. del Piombo
C. del Dose
Barbaria de le Tole
Calle del Cafetier
Calle de Capucine
C. Nicolò Massa
Campo de Santa Giustina detto de Barbaria
Fondamenta di Santa Giustina
C. Cavalli
C. del Deo
Calle San Francesco

San Francesco della Vigna

Campo San Francesco della Vigna
Rio di San Francesco

Santa Maria del la Fava
Ramo de la Fava
Calle Caminati
C. del Paradiso
C. del Nuovo
Campo Santa Maria Formosa
Campo Santa Maria Formosa
Santa Maria Formosa
C. Lunga S.M.
C. della Madoneta
C. de la Testa
Fond. San Giovanni Laterano
Rio de San Giovanni Laterano

CASTELLO

Salizada Santa Giustina
C. Erizzo
Calle Sacca
Salizada de le Gate
Campo delle Gate
C. dei Furlani
Rio de la Tana

Calle San Antonio
Calle del Mondo
C. Cocco
C. Trevisan
C. Cicogna
C. del Remedio
Campo Santa Maria Formosa
C. Seconda del Orbi
Borgoloco San Lorenzo
C. Larga San Lorenzo
Campo San Lorenzo
San Lorenzo
Corte Nova
Calle Salizada de Gate

Palazzo Grimani
Fondazione Querini Stampalia
Querini Stampalia
C. del Rimpeto
Campo San Severo
Fond. San Severo

Scuola di San Giorgio degli Schiavoni
C. dei Furlani
Calle San Antonin

SAN MARCO
Marzaria del Capitello
Piscina S. Zulian
C. del Figher
Fond. de l'Osmarin
Campo San Severo
Museo dell'Istituto Ellenico
Campo de la Pietà
C. del Magazen
Salizada dei Greci
C. de la Pietà
Salizada del Pignater
Terrazzera
C. de l'Arco

Santa Maria del la Fava
C. Fiubera
Marzaria del Capitello
C. Larga San Marco
Calle de la Canonica
Museo Diocesano
Sal. San Provolo
Calle de la Rasse
Campo San Provolo
Campo San Zaccaria
San Zaccaria
C. San Zaccaria
La Pietà
C. de la Pietà
San Giovanni in Bragora
Campo Bandiera e Moro
C. Crosera
Campiello del Piovan

Procuratie Vecchie
Basilica di San Marco
Campanile di San Marco
Piazza San Marco
Palazzo Ducale
Bridge of Sighs
Hotel Danieli
Piccolo Museo della Pietà
Riva degli Schiavoni

Procuratie Nuove
Biblioteca Marciana
La Zecca
Palazzo delle Prigioni
Molo San Marco
Riva degli Schiavoni

S. Marco S. Zaccaria

Giardinetti Reali

S. Marco Giardinetti
S. Marco Vallaresso

Bacino San Marco

0 ———— 300 m
0 ———— 300 yds
© Copyright Time Out Group 2017

L   M   N   P   Q

San Giorgio Maggiore

Darsena San Giorgio

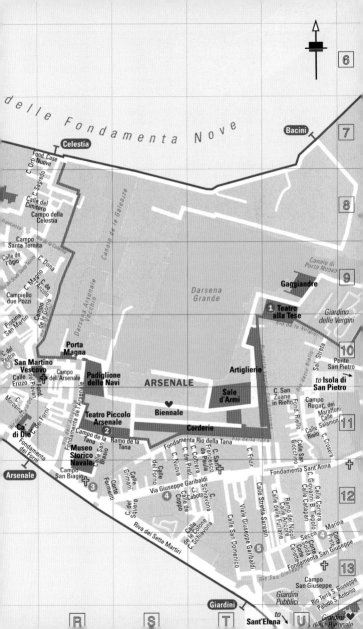

Best shops
If you're looking for hand-made masks with contemporary themes, Papier Mâché (*p96*) is for you. For quirkier stuff, Banco Lotto N.10 (*p102*) sells high fashion made behind bars. VizioVirtù has wonderful chocolate (*p96*).

Best art & architecture
Any chance to enter the fascinating complex of the Arsenale (*p97*) should be seized, especially during La Biennale (*p101*). The Scuola di San Giorgio degli Schiavoni (*p99*) has enchanting works by Carpaccio. Santi Giovanni e Paolo (*p93*) is full of monuments and masterpieces.

Best places to escape the crowds
San Francesco della Vigna is a little-visited campo, with an imposing church and two extraordinary cloisters (*p91*). Far from the centres of political power is San Pietro in Castello, Venice's former cathedral (*p98*).

Best restaurants
Feast on some of Venice's best *cicheti* at Al Portego (*p95*). Fish enthusiasts will like Alle Testiere (*p95*).

Best entertainment
Listen to Vivaldi music in the Vivaldi church, La Pietà (*p102*).

Northern & western Castello

The canal dividing the Doge's Palace from the prison marks the end of the sestiere of San Marco. This means that the **Museo Diocesano di Arte Sacra** (Castello 4312, ponte della Canonica, 041 522 9166, www.veneziaubt.org) and stately **San Zaccaria**, although closely associated with San Marco, actually belong to Castello. But the heart of northern and western Castello lies inland: **campo Santa Maria Formosa**, a large, bustling, irregular-shaped square on the road to just about everywhere.

Southward from Santa Maria Formosa runs the busy shopping street of ruga Giuffa, named after either a community of Armenian merchants from Julfa, or a band of thugs – *gagiuffos* in 13th-century dialect – who used to terrorise the area. The first turn to the left off this street leads to the grandiose 16th-century **Palazzo Grimani** (Castello 4854, ramo Grimani, 041 241 1507, www. polomusealeveneto.beniculturali. itmusei/musei/museo-di-palazzo-grimani), which film buffs may remember as the setting for the final gory scenes of Nicholas Roeg's film, *Don't Look Now*.

For more grandeur, head north to **campo Santi Giovanni e Paolo**. The Gothic red brick of the Dominican church is beautifully set off by the glistening marble on the trompe l'œil façade of the **Scuola Grande di San Marco** – now housing the civic hospital, but with a series of magnificent rooms open to the public – and the bronze of the equestrian monument to Bartolomeo Colleoni by Verrochio gazing down contemptuously. It's a short walk through narrow *calli* from Santi Giovanni e Paolo to the fondamenta Nove, where the northern lagoon comes into view.

Sights & museums

Museo della Fondazione Querini Stampalia

*Castello 5252, campo Santa Maria Formosa (041 271 1411, www. querinistampalia.it). Vaporetto Rialto. **Open** Museum 10am-8pm Tue-Sun. **Admission** €10; €8 reductions. **Map** p88 M9.*

This Renaissance *palazzo* and its art collection were bequeathed to Venice by Giovanni Querini, a 19th-century scientist, man of letters and silk producer from one of the city's most ancient families. Querini specified in his will that a library should be created here that would open 'particularly in the evenings for the convenience of scholars', and that the foundation should promote 'evening assemblies of scholars and scientists'. Today, the Querini Stampalia still exudes something of its founder's spirit: the first-floor library is a great place to study.

The ground floor and gardens, redesigned in the 1960s by Carlo Scarpa, offer one of Venice's few successful examples of modern architecture. On the second floor, the gallery contains some important paintings, including

Palma il Vecchio's portraits of Francesco and Paola Querini (for whom the palace was built in the 16th century), as well as a marvellous *Presentation in the Temple* by Giovanni Bellini, and a striking *Judith and Holofernes* by Vincenzo Catena. It also has a fascinating series of minor works, such as Gabriele Bella's 67 paintings of Venetian festivals, and a selection of Pietro Longhi's scenes of bourgeois life in 18th-century Venice. On the top floor is a gallery designed by Mario Botta, which hosts exhibitions of contemporary art.

♥ San Francesco della Vigna

*Castello, campo San Francesco della Vigna (041 520 6102). Vaporetto Celestia. **Open** 8am-12.30pm, 3-6pm daily. **Map** p88 Q8.*

San Francesco may be off the beaten track, but the long trek over to the down-at-heel area beyond the gasworks is worth it. In 1534, Jacopo Sansovino was asked by his friend Doge Andrea Gritti to design this church for the Observant Franciscan order. The Tuscan architect opted for a

San Francesco della Vigna

deliberately simple style to match the monastic rule of its inhabitants. The façade (1568-72) was a later addition by Andrea Palladio; it is the first example of his system of superimposed temple fronts.

The dignified, solemn interior consists of a single broad nave with side chapels. The Cappella Giustiniani on the left of the chancel holds a marvellous cycle of bas-reliefs by Pietro Lombardo and school, moved here from an earlier church on the same site. In the nave, the fourth chapel on the right has a *Resurrection* attributed to Paolo Veronese. In the right transept is a fruity, flowery *Madonna and Child Enthroned* (c1450), a signed work by the Greek artist Antonio da Negroponte.

From the left transept, a door leads into the Cappella Santa, which contains a *Madonna and Saints* (1507) by Giovanni Bellini (perhaps assisted by Girolamo da Santacroce). From here, it is possible to make a detour and visit two of the church's peaceful Renaissance cloisters.

Back in the church, the fifth chapel on the left is home to Paolo Veronese's first Venetian commission, the stunning *Holy Family with Saints John the Baptist, Anthony the Abbot and Catherine* (c1551). The third chapel has trompe l'œil frescoes in chiaroscuro by GB Tiepolo (1743, recently restored). The second chapel has three powerful statues of saints Roch, Anthony the Abbot and Sebastian (1565) by Alessandro Vittoria.

Santa Maria Formosa

Castello, campo Santa Maria Formosa (041 275 0462, www. chorusvenezia.org). Vaporetto San Zaccaria or Rialto. **Open** *10.30am-4.30pm Mon-Sat.* **Admission** *€3 (or Chorus; see p23). No cards.* **Map** *p88 M9.*

In the pre-Freudian seventh century, St Magnus, Bishop of Oderzo, had a vision in which the Virgin appeared as a buxom (*formosa*) matron, and a church was built in this bustling square to commemorate the fact. The present church was designed by Mauro Codussi in 1492 and has something fittingly bulgy about it. Codussi retained the Greek cross plan of the original in his Renaissance design. It has two façades, one on the canal (1542), the other on the campo (1604). The Baroque campanile has a grotesque mask, now recognised as a portrait of a victim of the disfiguring Von Recklinghausen's disease.

The first chapel in the right aisle has a triptych painted by Bartolomeo Vivarini, *Madonna of the Misericordia* (1473), which includes a realistic *Birth of the Virgin*. The altar in the right transept was the chapel of the Scuola dei Bombardieri, with an altarpiece of St Barbara, by Palma il Vecchio. Half-hidden by the elaborate high altar is one of the few works on show in Venice by a female artist: an 18th-century *Allegory of the Foundation of the Church, with Venice, St Magnus and St Maria Formosa* by Giulia Lama.

San Zaccaria

Castello, campo San Zaccaria (041 522 1257). Vaporetto San Zaccaria. **Open** *10am-noon, 4-6pm Mon-Sat; 4-6pm Sun.* **Map** *p88 N10.*
Founded in the ninth century, this church has always had close ties with the Doge's Palace. Eight Venetian rulers were buried in the first church on the site, one was killed outside and another died while seeking sanctuary inside. The body of St Zacharias, the father of John the Baptist, was brought to Venice in the ninth century; it still lies under the second altar on the right.

💜 Santi Giovanni e Paolo (San Zanipolo)

Castello, campo Santi Giovanni e Paolo (041 523 5913, www. basilicasantigiovanniepaolo.it). Vaporetto Ospedale or Fondamente Nove. **Open** *9am-6pm Mon-Sat; noon-6pm Sun.* **Admission** *€2.50, €1.25 reductions. No cards.* **Map** *p88 M7.*

Santi Giovanni e Paolo was founded by the Dominican order in 1246 but not finished until 1430. Between 1248 and 1778, 25 doges were buried here. The vast interior – 101 metres (331 feet) long – is a single spatial unit; the monks' choir was removed in the 17th century, leaving nothing to impede the view. Santi Giovanni e Paolo is packed with monuments to Venetian heroes as well as doges.

The entrance wall is dedicated to a series of funerary tributes to the Mocenigo family. The grandest – a masterpiece by Pietro, Tullio and Antonio Lombardo – belongs to Pietro Mocenigo, who died in 1476: the doge stands on his own sarcophagus, supported by three warriors representing the three ages of man. The religious reference above – the three Marys at the sepulchre – seems almost an afterthought.

The second altar on the right features an early polyptych by Giovanni Bellini (1465) in its original frame. Continuing down the right side of the church, the huge Baroque mausoleum by Andrea Tirali (1708) has two Valier doges and a *dogaressa* taking a bow before a marble curtain. Tirali

also designed the Chapel of St Dominic, notable for its splendid ceiling painting by Giovani Battista Piazzetta of *St Dominic in Glory* (c1727). The right transept has a painting of *St Antonine Distributing Alms* (1542) by Lorenzo Lotto. Above are splendid stained-glass windows, to designs by such Renaissance artists as Bartolomeo Vivarini and Cima da Conegliano (1470-1520).

On the right side of the chancel, with its Baroque high altar, is the Gothic tomb of Michele Morosini; opposite is the tomb of Doge Andrea Vendramin, by the Lombardo family.

The rosary chapel, off the left transept, was gutted by fire in 1867, just after two masterpieces by Titian and Bellini had been placed here for safe keeping. It now contains paintings and furnishings from suppressed churches. The ceiling paintings, *The Annunciation*, *Assumption* and *Adoration of the Shepherds*, are by Paolo Veronese. There is another Veronese, *Adoration* to the left of the door.

The current church was begun in 1444 but took decades to complete, making it a curious combination of Gothic and Renaissance. The interior is built on a Gothic plan – the apse, with its ambulatory and radiating cluster of tall-windowed chapels, is unique in Venice – but the architectural decoration is predominantly Renaissance. The façade is a happy mixture of the two styles.

Inside, every inch is covered with paintings, though of varying quality. Giovanni Bellini's magnificent *Madonna and Four Saints* (1505), on the second altar on the left, leaps out of the confusion. In the right aisle is the entrance to the Chapel of St Athanasius (admission €1), which contains carved 15th-century wooden stalls and *The Birth of St John the Baptist*, an early work by Tintoretto, and a striking *Flight into Egypt* by Giandomenico Tiepolo. The adjoining Chapel of St Tarasius was the apse of an earlier church that occupied this site; it has three altarpieces (1443) by Antonio Vivarini and Giovanni d'Alemagna – stiff, iconic works in elaborate Gothic frames.

The frescoed saints in the fan vault are by the Florentine artist Andrea del Castagno. Though painted a year before the altarpieces, they have a realistic vitality that is wholly Renaissance in spirit. In front of the altar are remains of the mosaic floor from the early Romanesque church; the tenth-century crypt below is usually flooded.

Scuola Grande di San Marco

Castello, campo Santi Giovanni e Paolo (041 529 4323, www. scuolagrandesanmarco.it). Vaporetto Ospedale or Fondamente Nove. **Open** *9.30am-5.30pm Tue-Sun.* **Admission** *free.* **Map** *p88 M7.* Once home to one of the six *scuole grandi* – the confraternities of

San Zaccaria p92

Venice (*see p127* Scuole Stories) – this is now occupied mainly by the city hospital. But late in 2013 some of the finest of the *scuola* rooms were opened to the public, beautifully restored.

The *scuola*'s façade by Pietro Lombardo and Giovanni Buora (1487-90) was completed by Mauro Codussi (1495). It features magnificent trompe l'oeil panels by Tullio and Antonio Lombardo representing two episodes from the life of St Mark and his faithful lion. Over the doorway is a lunette of *St Mark with the Brethren of the School* attributed to Bartolomeo Bon.

Inside, the immense column-punctuated entrance to the *scuola* is also the entrance to the hospital: surely one of the grandest hospital entrances in the world. At the top of a staircase designed by Mauro Codussi, the chapter house has a magnificent gilded coffered ceiling. Cases here contain ancient manuscripts pertaining to medical practice, and historical records of the Venetian hospital. On the walls are excellent reproductions of works done for the *scuola* but carried off over the centuries: Palma il Giovane's *Christ in Glory with St Mark* hangs over the altar, and around the walls are four magnificent scenes from the life of St Mark by the Tintoretto clan. The Sala dell'Albergo, which contains the hospital's ancient library, is dominated by a reproduction of *St Mark Preaching in Alessandria* by Giovanni and Gentile Bellini. Originals of some of the *scuola*'s art works can be seen in the Accademia gallery (*see p144*).

Restaurants

❤ Alle Testiere €€€
Castello 5801, calle del Mondo Novo (041 522 7220, www.osterialletestiere.it). Vaporetto Rialto. **Meals served** noon-2pm, 7-10.30pm Tue-Sat. Closed late Dec-mid Jan & late July-Aug. **Map** *p88 M9* ❶ *Seafood*

This tiny restaurant is today one of the hottest culinary tickets in Venice. There are so few seats that staff do two sittings each evening; booking for the later one (at 9pm) will ensure a more relaxed meal. Bruno, the chef, offers creative variations on Venetian seafood; *caparossoli* (local clams) sautéed in ginger and John Dory fillet sprinkled with aromatic herbs in citrus sauce are two mouth-watering examples. Sommelier Luca guides diners around a small but well-chosen wine list. The desserts, too, are spectacular.

❤ Al Portego €€
Castello 6015, calle Malvasia (041 522 9038). Vaporetto Rialto. **Open** 11.30am-3pm, 5.30-10pm daily. **No cards. Map** *p88 L8* ❷ *Bacaro*

With its wooden decor and happy drinkers in the *calle* outside, this rustic *osteria* is every inch the traditional Venetian *bacaro*. Alongside a big barrel of wine, the bar is loaded down with a selection of *cicheti*, from meatballs and stuffed squid to *nervetti* (veal cartilage) stewed with onions. In a second room, simple pasta dishes and soups and *secondi*, such as *fegato alla veneziana* (liver), are served up for early lunch and dinner. A glass and a plateful of *cicheti* at the bar should cost around €10-€15, sitting down more than double that.

Cafés, bars & gelaterie

Da Bonifacio
Castello 4237, calle degli Albanesi (041 522 7507). Vaporetto San Zaccaria. **Open** 6.30am-7.30pm Mon-Wed, Fri; 7.30am-7.30pm Sat, Sun. **No cards. Map** *p88 M10* ❶

In a narrow *calle* behind the Danieli Hotel, this is a firm favourite with Venetians, whom you'll find outside the entrance in great numbers, waiting to squeeze inside for a coffee, drink and something from the cake cabinet. As well as a tempting array of snacks and traditional cakes such as *mammaluchi* (deep-fried batter cakes with candied fruit), Da Bonifacio is famous for its creative *fritelle* (fried dough balls with wild berry, chocolate, almond or apple fillings), which appear in January and remain through Carnevale.

La Mascareta
Castello 5183, calle lunga Santa Maria Formosa (041 523 0744, www.ostemaurolorenzon.it). **Open** 7pm-2am daily. **Map** *p88 M8* ❷

Genial, bow-tied Mauro Lorenzon keeps hundreds of wines – including some rare vintages – in his cellars, serving them up by the bottle or glass along with plates

VizioVirtù

of cheeses, seafood, cold meats or *crostini*. His current kick is natural unfiltered wine – but you might prefer to insist on the more traditional stuff. At mealtimes, the pressure will be on to sit down and eat a proper meal, but though the food here is good, it's not exceptional and prices are high: it's better to stick with the drink and the personality-led Lorenzon experience.

Shops & services

I Tre Mercanti
Castello 5364, campo de la Guerra (041 522 2901, www.itremercanti. it). Vaporetto Rialto. **Open** *11am-7.30pm daily.* **Map** *p88 L9* ❶ *Food & drink*
There's an interesting selection here of seriously good Italian food and wine, much of it from local producers but some from further afield. Stock includes excellent olive oils, preserved vegetables, pastas and rice – none of them cheap but all of them chosen with an eye to quality. At a street-side window, passersby can pick up sandwiches and rolls: a choice of locally made breads with 30-odd fillings. And there are gourmet

variations on tiramisu to go as well. (A couple of perching-tables inside mean you can consume on the premises if you prefer.)

❤ Papier Mâché
Castello 5174B, calle lunga Santa Maria Formosa (041 522 9995, www.papiermache.it). Vaporetto Rialto. **Open** *9am-7.30pm Mon-Sat; 10am-7pm Sun.* **Map** *p88 M8* ❷ *Gifts & souvenirs*
This workshop uses traditional techniques to create contemporary masks inspired by the works of Klimt, Kandinsky, Tiepolo and Carpaccio. It stocks ceramics and painted mirrors too.

❤ VizioVirtù
Castello 5988, calle Forneri (041 275 0149, www.viziovirtu. com). Vaporetto Rialto. **Open** *10am-7.30pm daily.* **Map** *p88 L8* ❸ *Food & drink*
VizioVirtù serves up plenty of gluttonous pleasures. Here, you can witness chocolate being made while nibbling on a spicy praline or sipping an iced chocolate. This cornucopia of cocoa has unusual delights such as blocks of chocolate Parmesan, and cocoa tagliatelle (the chef recommends teaming it with game sauces).

Southern & eastern Castello

The low-rise, clustered buildings of working-class eastern Castello housed the employees of the Arsenale – Venice's docklands. Also here were Venice's foreign communities, as local churches testify: there's **San Giorgio dei Greci** (Greeks) and the **Scuola di San Giorgio degli Schiavoni** (Slavs), with its captivating cycle of paintings by Vittorio Carpaccio. The great promenade along the lagoon – the riva degli Schiavoni – was named after the same community.

Inland from the *riva* is the quaint Gothic church of **San Giovanni in Bragora** in the square of the same name. Antonio Vivaldi was born on this campo on 4 March 1678, and was choir master at the church of **La Pietà**. In calle della Pietà, alongside the church, is the **Piccolo Museo della Pietà**, dedicated to the Pietà (a foundling home) and the composer.

Crossing the bridge over the rio dell'Arsenale, you can see the grand Renaissance entrance to the **Arsenale** shipyard. Once a hive of empire-building industry, it's now an expanse of empty warehouses and docks, though parts have been beautifully restored and are used for Biennale-related events.

The *riva* passes the greenery of the **Giardini della Biennale** and ends in the sedately residential district of **Sant'Elena**. This, in Venetian terms, is a 'modern' district. In 1872, work began to fill in the *barene* (marshes) that lay between the edge of the city and the ancient island of Sant'Elena, with its charming Gothic church. Also tucked away here is Venice's football stadium, **Stadio PL Penzo** – though fans are hoping for a new mainland ground sometime in the not-too-distant future.

Sights & museums

❤ Arsenale
Castello, campo dell'Arsenale (www.comune.venezia.it/content/arsenale-di-venezia). Vaporetto Arsenale. **Map** p88 R10.
The word *arsenale* derives from the Arabic *dar sina'a*, meaning 'house of industry' – the industry, and efficiency, of Venice's Arsenale was legendary: the *arsenalotti* could assemble a galley in just a few hours. Shipbuilding activities began here in the 12th century; at the height of the city's power, 16,000 men were employed. Production expanded until the 16th century, when Venice entered its slow but inexorable economic decline.

Porta Magna, the imposing land gateway by Antonio Gambello (1460) in campo dell'Arsenale, is the first example of Renaissance classical architecture to appear in Venice, although the capitals of the columns are 11th-century Veneto-Byzantine. The winged lion gazing down from above holds a book without the traditional words *Pax tibi Marce* (Peace to you, Mark) – unsuitable in this military context. Outside the gate, four lions keep guard. Those immediately flanking the terrace were looted from Athens in 1687; the larger one stood at the entrance to the port of Piraeus and bears runic inscriptions on its side, hacked there in the 11th century by Norse mercenary soldiers in Byzantine service. The third lion, whose head is clearly less ancient than its body, came from Delos and was placed here to commemorate the recapture of Corfu in 1716.

Shipbuilding activity ceased in 1917, after which the complex remained largely unused navy property until 2013 when much of it returned to town council hands... not that they're entirely sure what to do with it now.

Arsenale

It is destined, authorities say, to become a 'scientific and cultural hub'. Exhibitions and performances will continue to be held in some of the cavernous spaces within its walls: the **Artiglierie** and the grandiose **Gaggiandre**, dockyards designed by Sansovino. In campo della Tana, on the other side of the rio dell'Arsenale, is the entrance to the **Corderie** (rope factory), an extraordinary building 316 metres (1,038 feet) long. This vast space is used to house large swathes of the Biennale (*see p101*). In May the **Mare Maggio** sea-, boat- and travel-themed festival (www.maremaggio.it) opens up much of the Arsenale to the curious.

Museo Storico Navale

*Castello 2148, campo San Biagio (041 244 1399, www.visitmuve. it/it/musei/museo-storico-navale-di-venezia/). Vaporetto Arsenale. Closed at time of writing. **Padiglione delle Navi**: Castello 2162, rio della Tana. **Open** 8.45am-5pm daily. **Admission** €5. **Map** p88 R12.*

This museum dedicated to ships and shipbuilding continues an old tradition: under the Republic, the models created for shipbuilders in the final design stages were kept in the Arsenale. Some of the models on display are from that collection. The museum was undergoing repairs as this guide went to press, but anyone yearning for a bit of naval exposure can visit the nearby **Padiglione delle Navi** ('ships pavilion'), a huge warehouse (worth a visit in its own right) housing a motley assortment of vessels from different eras.

❤ San Pietro in Castello

*Castello, campo San Pietro (041 275 0462, www.chorusvenezia. org). Vaporetto San Pietro. **Open** 10.30am-4pm Mon, 10.30am-4.30pm Tue-Sat. **Admission** €3 (or Chorus; see p23). No cards.*

Until 1807, San Pietro in Castello was the cathedral of Venice, and its remote position testifies to the determination of the Venetian government to keep the clerical authorities far from the centre of temporal power. There has probably been a church here since the seventh century, but the present building was constructed in 1557 to a design by Palladio.

The body of the first patriarch of Venice, San Lorenzo Giustiniani, is preserved in an urn elaborately supported by angels above the high altar, a magnificent piece of Baroque theatricality designed by Baldassare Longhena (1649). In the right-hand aisle is the so-called 'St Peter's Throne', a delicately carved marble work from Antioch containing a Muslim funerary stele and verses from the Koran. The Baroque Vendramin Chapel in the left transept was again designed by Longhena, and contains a *Virgin and Child* by the prolific Neapolitan Luca Giordano. Outside the entrance to the chapel is a late work by Paolo Veronese, *Saints John the Evangelist, Peter and Paul*.

❤ Scuola di San Giorgio degli Schiavoni
Castello 3259A, calle dei Furlani (041 522 8828). Vaporetto Arsenale or San Zaccaria. **Open** *2.45-6pm Mon; 9.15am-1pm, 2.45-6pm Tue-Sat; 9.15am-1pm Sun.* **Admission** *€5; €3 reductions. No cards.* **Map** *p88 P9.*

The *schiavoni* were Venice's Slav inhabitants, who had become so numerous and influential by the end of the 15th century that they could afford to build this *scuola* (or meeting house, *see p127* Scuole Stories) by the side of their church, San Giovanni di Malta. The *scuola* houses one of Vittore Carpaccio's two great Venetian picture cycles. In 1502, eight years after completing his St Ursula cycle (now in the Accademia, *see p144*), Carpaccio was commissioned to paint a series of canvases illustrating the lives of the Dalmatian saints George, Tryphone and Jerome. In the tradition of the

early Renaissance *istoria* (narrative painting cycle), there is a wealth of incidental detail, such as the decomposing virgins in *St George and the Dragon*, or the little dog in the painting of *St Augustine in his Study* (receiving the news of the death of St Jerome in a vision) – with its paraphernalia of humanism (astrolabe, shells, sheet music, archaeological fragments).

It's worth venturing upstairs to see what the meeting hall of a working *scuola* looks like. San Giorgio degli Schiavoni still provides scholarships, distributes charity and acts as a focal point for the Slav community. Opening hours are notoriously changeable.

Restaurants

Corte Sconta €€€
Castello 3886, calle del Pestrin (041 522 7024, www.cortescontavenezia. it). Vaporetto Arsenale. **Meals served** *12.30-2.30pm, 7-10pm Tue-Sat. Closed Jan & mid July-mid Aug.* **Map** *p88 Q10* ❸ *Seafood*

In the know
Well-heads through the ages

Until 1882-84, when pipes were laid to bring water from the mainland, Venice was supplied with fresh water through monumental well-heads located in *campi* throughout the city. Squares with wells at their centre were raised and angled towards drains, so that rain water could disappear into filtering systems and cisterns below. Today around 2,500 well-heads remain. The most ancient is in corte Correr (between San Zaccaria and Santa Maria Formosa), which dates from the ninth or tenth century; others include a late Gothic one in the courtyard of the Ca' d'Oro (*see p107*) and Renaissance examples in campo Santi Giovanni e Paolo and campo San Zaccaria.

This trailblazing seafood restaurant is such a firm favourite on the well-informed tourist circuit that it's a good idea to book well in advance. The main act is a procession of seafood antipasti. The pasta is home-made and the warm *zabaione* dessert is a delight. Decor is of the modern Bohemian *trattoria* variety, the ambience loud and friendly. In summer, try to secure one of the tables in the pretty, vine-covered courtyard.

Dai Tosi Piccoli €
Castello 738, secco Marina (041 523 7102, www.trattoriadaitosi.com). Vaporetto Giardini. **Meals served** *noon-2pm Mon, Tue, Thur; noon-2pm, 7-9.30pm Fri-Sun. Closed 2wks Aug.* **Map** *p88 U13* ④ *Pizzeria*
In one of Venice's most working-class areas, this pizzeria is a big hit with locals. Beware of another restaurant of the same name on the street: this place (at no.738) is better. The cuisine is humble but filling, the pizzas are tasty, and you can round the meal off nicely with a killer *sgropin* (a post-prandial refresher made with lemon sorbet, vodka and prosecco). In summer, angle for one of the garden tables.

Il Ridotto €€€€
Castello 4509, campo Santi Filippo e Giacomo (041 520 8280,www. ilridotto.com). Vaporetto San Zaccaria. **Meals served** *noon-2pm, 7-11pm Mon, Tue, Fri-Sun; 7-10pm Thur.* **Map** *p88 M10* ⑤
Modern Venetian
Gianni Bonaccorsi's restaurant is a natural stop-over for upcoming chefs passing through the lagoon city. Though expertise flows in both directions, Gianni's policy of using the freshest and best of local ingredients in unfussy ways to produce something remarkably sophisticated is adhered to with memorable results. The five-course taster menu (€70) gives the best scope for experiencing

Il Ridotto's range, which might include octopus on a broad bean purée with turnip tops, a superb *caciucco* fish soup or seabass served on a bed of creamed celeriac. The place – two narrow rooms – is tiny, the decor is ultra-simple and the service is warmly professional. There's a good lunch deal, at €28 for a selection of *cicheti* plus a fish or meat main. Be sure to book: gourmets whether local or visiting know that this is one of the city's best foody attractions.

Cafés, bars & gelaterie

Angiò
Castello 2142, ponte della Veneta Marina (041 277 8555). Vaporetto Arsenale. **Open** *7am-9pm Mon, Wed-Sun.* **Map** *p88 R12* ③
Angiò is the finest stopping point along one of Venice's most tourist-trafficked spots – the lagoon-front riva degli Schiavoni. Tables stretch towards the water's edge, with a stunning view across to San Giorgio Maggiore; ultra-friendly staff serve up pints of Guinness, freshly made sandwiches and interesting selections of cheese and wine. Closing time is pushed back to midnight or later in summer months, when music events are held on Saturday evenings.

El Refolo
Castello 1580, via Garibaldi (no phone). Vaporetto Giardini. **Open** *During Biennale 10.30am-midnight Tue-Sun. Rest of year 5.30pm-12.30am Tue-Sun.* **No cards.** **Map** *p88 S12* ④
If you want to settle at one of the high stools on the pavement outside this tiny bar, be prepared to wait. Because friendly El Refolo, with its well-priced wine (from €2.50 a glass), interesting and ever-changing selection of filled rolls and excellent salami and/or cheese platters, is everybody's favourite,

💙 La Biennale

*Information 041 521 8711, www. labiennale.org. **Date** May/June-Nov.*

Officially known as l'Esposizione internazionale d'arte della Biennale di Venezia, Venice's Biennale was responsible for putting the city on the map of international contemporary art back in 1895. Since then this massive exhibition has been 'invading' Venice throughout the summer of every odd year.

It was the first (its closest rival Sao Paolo didn't start until 1951), and to this day it remains one of the few to include national exhibits as part of a wider-ranging collective event.

In 1980, Biennale organisers decided to fill in even years with an architecture equivalent – a far lower-profile event to start off with but now as extravagant, sprawling and (almost as) well-attended as its arty sister.

From the start, the Biennale spread over the leafy **Giardini della Biennale** park in eastern Castello, where some 30 small national pavilions cluster around the far larger central pavilion – previously Italy's Biennale home but now renovated and called the **Palazzo delle Esposizioni**, housing the Biennale archive and part of the themed event.

Much more of the curated section of the Biennale now straggles into the glorious spaces of Venice's **Arsenale** (*see p97*), where each year an internationally renowned artist, architect, critic or expert selects exhibits around a theme of his or her choosing. And all over town, shows mounted by nations with no foothold in the Giardini and no space in the Arsenale occupy *palazzi*, galleries, gardens and other settings, opening up rarely glimpsed spaces to a curious public in a three-month art jamboree.

Unusually for Italy, the Biennale has a US-style financial model mixing sponsorship, public funds and income generated by ticket sales and merchandising. With money from sources other than the public purse, this organisation enjoys an autonomy from political manoeuvring envied by many.

Installation by Thu Van Tran at the 57th Biennale

especially when the area throngs with Biennale-goers (*see p101*). Over summer weekends, owner Massimiliano doesn't pull down the shutters until very late indeed.

Serra dei Giardini

Castello 1254, viale Garibaldi/ giardini pubblici (041 296 0360, www.serradeigiardini. org). Vaporetto Giardini. **Open** *10am-8pm Tue- Sun.* **Map** *p88 T13* ⑤

This gorgeous greenhouse has stood inside the *Giardini pubblici* since 1894, when its purpose was to provide winter shelter for the exotic plants brought out in summer to grace the national pavilions in the neighbouring Biennale gardens. Restored and run by a local cooperative, it now houses a plant shop, spaces for children's activities, parties and exhibitions, and a café/tea shop with garden tables when the weather permits. The setting is charming, and the coffee, juices and light meals on offer are good. The idyll can be slightly marred by less-than-charming staff.

Shops & services

💗 Banco Lotto N°10

Castello 3478B, salizada Sant'Antonin (041 522 1439, www. ilcerchiovenezia.it). Vaporetto Arsenale. **Open** *3.30-7.30pm Mon; 10am-1pm, 3.30-7.30pm Tue-Sat.* **Map** *p88 P10* ④ *Fashion/ accessories*

The quirky dresses, bags and accessories sold in this little outlet all hail from the workshops of Venice's women's prison on the Giudecca island. Many of the designs are one-offs, and there's a strong vintage flavour, and some interesting recycling goes on too.

Entertainment

Performances for the **Biennale di Venezia, danza-Musica-Teatro** (*see p58*) take place in two spectacular venues inside the Arsenale – the **Teatro alle Tese** ① and the smaller **Teatro Piccolo Arsenale** ②.

💗 La Pietà

Castello, riva degli Schiavoni (348 765 7154 mobile, www. ivirtuosiitaliani.eu, www. chiesavivaldi.it). Vaporetto San Zaccaria. **Shows** *8.30pm daily in season. Tickets €28; €23 reductions.* **Map** *p88 P11* ③

I Virtuosi Italiani perform early music concerts in what must surely be the easiest sell in Venice: Vivaldi in the Vivaldi church.

Dance Biennale

Santa Maria dei Miracoli

Cannaregio

Step out of Santa Lucia station and be prepared to be dazzled by the stunning sight of the Grand Canal. The walk to the centre along busy lista di Spagna, Cannaregio's main thoroughfare, is less grand. Concealed beyond, however, is a blissfully calm area of long canalside walks. Until the 19th century, the Cannaregio Canal was the main route into Venice from the mainland. It remains an impressive waterway that's worth exploring, with wide *fondamente* on each side and several imposing *palazzi*. It's spanned by two stately bridges, the ponte delle Guglie (1823) and the ponte dei Tre Archi (1688), the only three-arch stone bridge in Venice. Just beyond the ponte delle Guglie on the right-hand *fondamenta*, you pass the *sottoportico* leading to the Jewish Ghetto, where a thriving Jewish community creates a sudden burst of activity amid the quiet of this second-largest *sestiere*.

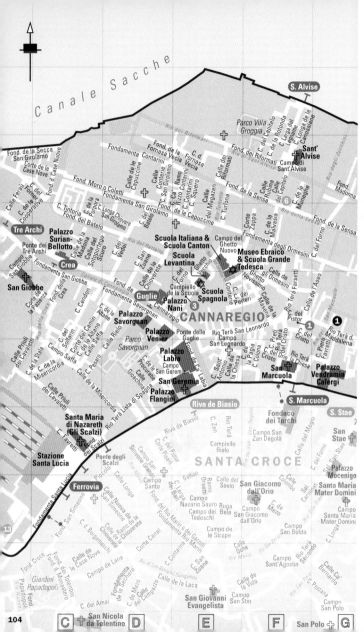

CANNAREGIO

Best for cultural history
Learn about the original Jewish ghetto at the Museo Ebraico (*p111*).

Best entertainment
There's classical music and dance at Teatro Malibran (*p110*), while Paradiso Perduto (*p116*) mixes seafood snacks with jazz and salsa.

Best shops
Vittorio Costantini (*p116*) creates the most intricate Venetian glass animals. Mori & Bozzi (*p110*) makes shoes to die for.

Best for foodies
Panificio Volpe Davide (*p111*) makes the best Jewish pastries in Venice. For a modern spin on Venetian classics, there's Anice Stellato (*p115*); for the best meatballs go to Alla Vedova Ca' D'Oro (*p109*).

Best churches
Head to Santa Maria dei Miracoli (*p108*) for a miracle of multicoloured marble. Madonna dell'Orto (*p113*) is where the Tintoretto clan let rip.

From Santa Lucia station to the Rialto

Heading away from the railway station towards the Rialto, the tourist-tack-filled lista leads to the large campo **San Geremia**, overlooked by the church of the same name. Once you've crossed the Cannaregio Canal – by way of ponte delle Guglie, a grandiose bridge with obelisks – the route assumes more character, taking in lively street markets.

Off to the right, in a square giving on to the Grand Canal, is the church of **San Marcuola**, which has a gleaming interior to set off a *Last Supper* by Tintoretto. A bit further on, the more picturesque church of **La Maddalena**, inspired by the Pantheon in Rome, stands in the small campo della Maddalena. Beyond this, wide strada Nova begins. Off to the left is the church of **San Marziale**, with whimsical

ceiling paintings; on the strada Nova itself stands the church of **Santa Fosca**, another mainly 18th-century creation. Down a *calle* to the right is the entrance to the **Ca' d'Oro**, Venice's most splendid Gothic *palazzo*.

The strada Nova ends by the church of **Santi Apostoli**; the route to the Rialto soon becomes narrow and crooked, passing the church of **San Giovanni Crisostomo**, which contains two great paintings by Bellini and del Piombo. The adjacent courtyard of the corte Seconda del Milion is where Marco Polo was born in 1256. Some of the Veneto-Byzantine-style houses in the courtyard date from that time. There's a plaque commemorating Marco Polo on the rear of the **Teatro Malibran**, formerly the Teatro di San Giovanni Crisostomo, one of Venice's earliest theatres. Just north-east of here is the miniature marvel of **Santa Maria dei Miracoli**.

Sights & museums

Ca' d'Oro (Galleria Franchetti)

Cannaregio 3932, calle Ca'
d'Oro (041 520 0345, www.
cadoro.org). Vaporetto Ca'
d'Oro. Open 8.15am-2pm Mon;
8.15am-7.15pm Tue-Sat; 9am-7pm
Sun. Admission €13; €6.50
reductions; price varies during
special exhibitions. No cards.
Map p104 J6.

In its 15th-century heyday, the façade of this pretty townhouse on the Grand Canal must have looked a psychedelic treat: the colour scheme was light blue and burgundy, with 24-carat gold highlights. Though the colour has worn off, the Grand Canal frontage of Ca' d'Oro – built for merchant Marin Contarini between 1421 and 1431 – is still the most elaborate example of the florid Venetian Gothic style besides the Doge's Palace.

Inside, little of the original structure and decor has survived. The pretty courtyard was reconstructed with its original 15th-century staircase and well-head a century ago by Baron Franchetti; the mosaic floor is a 19th-century imitation of the floors in San Marco. The baron also assembled the collection of paintings, sculptures and coins that is exhibited inside.

The highlight of the collection is Mantegna's *St Sebastian*, a powerful late work; the Palladian frame contrasts oddly with the saint's existential anguish. The rest is good in parts, though not necessarily the parts you would expect. A small medal of Sultan Mohammed II by Gentile Bellini (a souvenir of his years in Constantinople, being restored at the time of writing) is more impressive than the faded frescoes by Titian and Giorgione removed from the T Fondaco dei Tedeschi (*see p80*). There are some good Renaissance bronzes from deconsecrated churches, and small but vigorous plaster models by Bernini for the statues on the fountains in Rome's piazza Navona.

Ca' d'Oro

Gli Scalzi

*Cannaregio, fondamenta degli Scalzi
(041 822 4006, www.centroscalzi.it,
www.giardinomistico.it). Vaporetto
Ferrovia.* **Open** *7-11.50am, 4-7pm
daily.* **Map** *p104 C6.*

Officially Santa Maria di Nazareth,
this church is better known as Gli
Scalzi after the order of *Carmelitani
scalzi* (Barefoot Carmelites) to
whom it belongs. They bought
the plot in 1645 and subsequently
commissioned Baldassare
Longhena to design the church.
The fine façade (1672-80) is the
work of Giuseppe Sardi; it was
paid for by a newcomer to Venice's
ruling patrician class, Gerolamo
Cavazza, determined to make his
mark on the landscape.

The interior is striking for its
coloured marble and massively
elaborate baldachin over the high
altar. There are many fine Baroque
statues, including *St John of the
Cross* by Giovanni Marchiori in the
first chapel on the right and the
anonymous marble crucifix and
wax effigy of Christ in the chapel
opposite. An Austrian shell that
plummeted through the roof in 1915
destroyed the church's greatest
work of art, Tiepolo's fresco, *The
Transport of the House of Loreto*,
but later restored some of the artist's
lesser frescoes, *Angels of the Passion*
and *Agony in the Garden*, in the first
chapel on the left, and *St Theresa
in Glory*, which hovers gracefully
above a ham-fisted imitation of
Bernini's sculpture, *Ecstasy of St
Theresa*, in the second on the right.
In the second chapel on the left
lie the remains of the last doge of
Venice, Lodovico Manin.

❤ Santa Maria dei Miracoli

*Cannaregio, campo Santa Maria
dei Miracoli (041 275 0462, www.
chorusvenezia.org). Vaporetto
Fondamente Nove or Rialto.*
Open *10.30am-4.30pm Mon-Sat.*
Admission *€3 (or Chorus; see
p23). No cards.* **Map** *p104 L7.*

Santa Maria dei Miracoli

Arguably one of the most exquisite
churches in the world, Santa Maria
dei Miracoli was built in the 1480s
to house a miraculous image of
the Madonna, reputed to have
revived a man who had spent
half an hour underwater in the
Giudecca Canal, and also to have
cancelled all traces of a knife attack
on a woman. The building is the
work of the Lombardo family, early
Renaissance masons who fused
architecture, surface detail and
sculpture into a unique whole.

Pietro Lombardo may have been
a Lombard by birth but he soon
got into the Venetian way of doing
things, employing Byzantine spoils
left over from work on St Mark's
to create a work of art displaying
an entirely Venetian sensitivity

to texture and colour. There is an almost painterly approach to the use of multicoloured marble in the four sides of the church, each of which is of a slightly different shade. The sides have more pilasters than necessary, making the church appear longer than it really is.

Inside, the 50 painted ceiling panels by Pier Maria Pennacchi (1528) are almost impossible to distinguish without using binoculars. Instead, turn your attention to the church's true treasures: the delicate carvings by the Lombardos on the columns, steps and balustrade, with their exquisite, lifelike details.

Restaurants

La Bottega ai Promessi Sposi €€

Cannaregio 4367, calle dell'Oca (041 241 2747). Vaporetto Ca' d'Oro. **Meals served** *12-2.15pm Tue, Thur-Sun; 6.30-10.15pm Tue-Sun.* **No cards.** **Map** *p104 K6* ❶ *Venetian*

This pared-back *osteria* has a wooden counter groaning with excellent *cicheti* and a good selection of wines by the glass, to be sampled at the bar or mingling with the standing, chatting crowds that form in the narrow alley outside. In the back rooms are a few tables where diners can sample simple dishes – mainly but not exclusively seafood – with some twists on local stalwarts, such as fried *schie* (tiny grey prawns) on rocket with balsamic vinegar.

♥ Ca' D'Oro (Alla Vedova) €€

Cannaregio 3912, ramo Ca' d'Oro (041 528 5324). Vaporetto Ca' d'Oro. **Meals served** *11.30am-2.30pm, 6.30-10.30pm Mon-Wed, Fri, Sat; 6.30-11pm Sun. Closed Aug.* **No cards.** **Map** *p104 J6* ❷ *Venetian*

Officially Ca' D'Oro, this place is known by locals as Alla Vedova – the Widow's Place. The widow has joined her *marito* (husband), but her family still runs the show. The traditional decor remains, though the warmth of the welcome can vary. Tourists head for the tables (it's best to book), where tasty pasta dishes (like spaghetti in cuttlefish ink) and *secondi* are served; locals stay at the bar snacking on classic *cicheti*, including the best *polpette* (meatballs) in Venice.

Vini da Gigio €€

Cannaregio 3628, fondamenta San Felice (041 528 5140, www. vinidagigio.com). Vaporetto Ca' d'Oro. **Meals served** *noon-2.30pm, 7-10.30pm Wed-Sun. Closed 3wks Jan-Feb.* **Map** *p104 H5* ❸ *Venetian*

Vini da Gigio is strong on Venetian antipasti, including raw seafood; there are also a number of good meat and game options, like seared cuts of breaded lamb or tuna in a sesame seed crust. As the name suggests, wine is another forte, with good international and by-the-glass selections. The only drawback in this highly recommended restaurant is the unhurried service. Book well ahead.

Cafés, bars & gelaterie

Pasticceria Nobile

Cannaregio 1818, campiello de l'Anconeta (041 720 731, www. pasticcerianobile.it). Vaporetto San Marcuola. **Open** *6.40am-8.40pm daily.* **No cards.** **Map** *p104 F4* ❶

The bar at Boscolo's *pasticceria* is always packed; locals flock to enjoy an extra-strong *spritz al bitter* with one of the home-made *pizzette* (small pizza). There is also an excellent assortment of Venetian sweets: *frittelle* (fried dough balls) during Carnevale, as well as *zaleti* (polenta biscuits) and *pincia* (Veneto bread pudding, made with cornflour and raisins). Boscolo's range of chocolates in the form of interesting (and graphic) Kama Sutra positions has made this confectioner famous.

Santo Bevitore

*Cannaregio 2393A, campo Santa Fosca (041 717 560, www. ilsantobevitorepub.com). Vaporetto Ca' d'Oro or San Marcuola. **Open** 9.30am-1.30am Mon-Sat. **No cards**. Map p104 H4* ❷

This friendly pub-café on campo Santa Fosca, just off strada Nova, has consistently proved popular with both Venetian locals and visitors, who drop in to munch *cicheti* during the day or come to while away the evening over a craft beer.

Shops & services

❤ Mori & Bozzi

*Cannaregio 2367, rio terà Maddalena (041 715 261). Vaporetto San Marcuola. **Open** 9.30am-7.30pm daily. Closed Sun in July & Aug. Map p104 G4* ❶ *Shoes & accessories*

Women's shoes for the coolest of the cool: whatever the latest fad – pointy or square – it's here. There are enough trendy names and designer-inspired footwear to please the Carrie Bradshaw in us all. Also beautiful bags, clothes, hats and accessories of all kinds.

Entertainment

Giorgione Movie d'Essai

*Cannaregio 4612, rio terà dei Franceschi (041 522 6298). Vaporetto Ca' d'Oro. **No cards**. Map p104 K6* ❶ *Cinema*

This two-screener run by Circuito Cinema (*see p41* Entertainment) combines the usual fare with themed seasons and kids' films (on Saturday and Sunday at 3pm).

❤ Teatro Malibran

*Cannaregio 5873, calle dei Milion (041 965 1975, www.teatrolafenice. it). Vaporetto Rialto. **Map** p104 L8* ❷ *Classical music*

Inaugurated in 1678 as Teatro San Giovanni Crisostomo, this 900-seater was built on the site where Marco Polo's family *palazzo* once stood. The theatre now shares the classical music, ballet and opera season with La Fenice; in addition, it has its own chamber music season.

Il Ghetto

The word 'ghetto' is one that Venice has given to the world. It originally meant an iron foundry, a place where iron was *gettato* (cast). Until 1390, when the foundry was transferred to the Arsenale, casting was done on a small island in Cannaregio. In 1516, it was decided to confine the city's Jewish population to this island; here they remained until 1797. Venetian treatment of the Jews was by no means as harsh as in many European countries, but neither was it benevolent – restrictions were many and tough (*see p112* Living in the Ghetto).

With the arrival of Napoleon in 1797, Jews gained full citizenship rights; many chose to remain in the Ghetto. In the deportations during the Nazi occupation of Italy in 1943, 202 Venetian Jews were sent to the death camps. The Jewish population of Venice and Mestre now stands at about 500 (see www.jvenice.org for information). Only around a dozen Jewish families still live in the Ghetto, but it remains the centre of spiritual, cultural and social life for the Jewish community. Most of the city, including the Ghetto, is an eruv – an area in which activities that are normally forbidden in public on the Sabbath are permitted.

Monument of the Holocaust in Campo del Ghetto Nuovo (Arbit Blatas, 1979)

Sights & museums

♥ Museo Ebraico

Cannaregio 2902B, campo del Ghetto Nuovo (041 715 359, www.coopculture.it). Vaporetto Guglie or San Marcuola. **Open** *10am-5.30pm (7pm June-Sept) Mon-Fri, Sun. Guided tours (hourly) 10.30am-4.30pm Mon-Thur, Sun (5.30pm June-Sept); 10.30am-3.30pm Fri.* **Admission** *Museum only €8; €6 reductions. Museum & synagogues €12; €10 reductions.* **Map** *p104 E3.*

This well-run museum and cultural centre – founded in 1953 – has been spruced up in recent years, with a bookshop and a new section dedicated to the history and traditions of the various 'nations' that make up Venice's Jewish community, its relationship with the city after the 1797 opening of the Ghetto, some of its famous personages and the role of usury.

In the older rooms there are ritual objects in silver – Torah finials, Purim and Pesach cases, menorahs – sacred vestments and hangings, and a series of marriage contracts. The museum is best visited as part of a guided tour. This takes in three synagogues – the **Scuola Canton** (Ashkenazi rite), the **Scuola Italiana** (Italian rite) and the **Scuola Levantina** (Sephardic rite). Tours of the Jewish cemetery on the Lido also set out from here.

Cafés, bars & gelaterie

♥ Panificio Volpe Davide

Cannaregio 1143, calle del Ghetto Vecchio (041 715 178). Vaporetto Guglie. **Open** *7am-7.30pm Mon-Sat, 8.30am-12.30am Sun.* **No cards.** **Map** *p104 E4* ❸

In the heart of the Ghetto, this bakery produces excellent breads, biscuits and cakes... all kosher, as its location implies.

Living in the Ghetto

Creative solutions to cramped conditions

Today, pretty **campo del Ghetto Nuovo** gives little idea of the hardships suffered there through the centuries when it hosted the closed community of Jews. Note the houses on the southern and eastern sides of the campo: taller than any others in Venice, they bear witness to how the hopelessly cramped inhabitants, prevented from expanding horizontally, did so vertically. Similar upwards extensions on the other two sides of the square have since been demolished; in times past, however, the open space was hemmed in and towered over on all sides.

During the day, the *campo* would have buzzed with activity. Christians came to the Ghetto to visit not only the pawnbrokers and money-lenders but also the *strazzerie* (second-hand clothes sellers) and artisans. As successive waves of immigrants arrived, the Ghetto would have resounded with a babble of languages from around the Mediterranean, as well as the northern inflections of Polish and German.

At night, the gates were closed and guarded by armed boats that patrolled the canals circling the small island; the Jews themselves were forced to pay for this guard service.

The ground floors of the buildings around the *campo* were almost entirely devoted to commercial activities; everything else – residences, synagogues and schools – was located above. Ceilings were low and the staircases were narrow, to save space. For structural stability, the walls on the ground floor were reinforced and the interior structures made of wood. There are reports of floors collapsing under the feet of over-enthusiastic wedding parties.

Despite hardship and chronic overcrowding, these outwardly unassuming buildings manage to contain the splendid spaces of the synagogues. The **Scuola Canton** and the **Scuola Tedesca**, the earliest of the synagogues, are distinguished on the exterior only by the array of five windows and by the small wooden lantern in Scuola Canton; inside, however, architects created room for impressive devotional spaces, with rich carvings and decorations (again, all in wood). Clearly, religion played an enormous part in the lives of the inhabitants.

It has been calculated that when the population was at its height (and before the Jews were allowed to spill over into the adjoining areas of the Ghetto Vecchio and Ghetto Novissimo), overcrowding was such that the inhabitants had to take it in turns to sleep.

North & east

There's no better place for getting away from it all than northern Cannaregio. Built around three long parallel canals, it has no large animated squares and (with the exception of the Ghetto) no sudden surprises – just views over the northern lagoon. And, at night, a lively scene around a handful of restaurants and bars along fondamenta della Misericordia.

The area does, however, have its landmarks: on the northern-most canal (the rio della Madonna dell'Orto) are the churches of **Sant'Alvise** and **Madonna dell'Orto**, plus many fine palazzi; and at the eastern end of the fondamenta della Misericordia are the vecchia (old; 14th-century) and nuova (new; 16th-century) *scuole* of the same name. The 'new' one is a huge plan designed by Sansovino, with an unfinished façade. Across the Canale della Misericordia from here, eastern Cannaregio is more intriguingly closed in, with many narrow alleys (including the Venetian record holder: calle Varisco, which is 52 centimetres/20 inches wide at its narrowest point), charming courtyards and well-heads, but no major sights, with the exception of the spectacularly ornate church of **I Gesuiti** and the 13th-century **Oratorio dei Crociferi**.

Sights & museums

I Gesuiti

Cannaregio, salizada dei Spechieri (041 523 1610). Vaporetto Fondamente Nove. **Open** *10am-noon, 4-6pm daily.* **Map** *p104 L4.*
The Jesuits were never very popular in Venice, and it wasn't until 1715 that they felt secure enough to build a church

here. Even then they chose a comparatively remote plot on the edge of town. But once they made up their mind to go ahead, they went all out: local architect Domenico Rossi was given explicit instructions to dazzle. The result leaves no room for half measures: you love it or you hate it, and many people do the latter.

The exterior, with a façade by Gian Battista Fattoretto, is conventional enough; the interior is anything but. All that tassled, bunched, overpowering drapery is not the work of a rococo set designer gone berserk with luxurious brocades: it's plain old green and white marble. Bernini's altar in St Peter's in Rome was the model for the baldachin over the altar, by Fra' Giuseppe Pozzo. The statues above the baldachin are by Giuseppe Torretti, as are the rococo archangels at the corners of the crossing. Titian's *Martyrdom of St Lawrence* (1558-59), over the first altar on the left side, came from an earlier church on this site, and was one of the first successful night scenes ever to be painted.

❤ Madonna dell'Orto

Cannaregio, campo Madonna dell'Orto (041 719 933, www. madonnadellorto.org). Vaporetto Orto. **Open** *10am-5pm Mon-Sat; noon-5pm Sun.* **Admission** *€2.50. No cards.* **Map** *p104 H2.*
The 'Tintoretto church' was originally dedicated to St Christopher (a magnificent statue of whom stands over the main door), the patron saint of the gondoliers (who ran the ferry service to the islands from a nearby jetty). However, a cult developed around a large, unfinished and supposedly miraculous statue of the Madonna and Child that stood in a nearby garden. In 1377, the sculpture was transferred into the church (it's now in the chapel

Madonna dell'Orto

of San Mauro), and the church's name was changed to the Madonna dell'Orto – of the Garden.

The church was rebuilt between 1399 and 1473, and a monastery was constructed alongside. The false gallery at the top of the beautiful Gothic façade is unique in Venice; the sculptures are all fine 15th-century works. But it is the numerous works by Tintoretto that have made the Madonna dell'Orto famous. Tradition has it that the artist began decorating the church as penance for insulting a doge: in fact, it took very little to persuade Tintoretto to get his palette out, and the urgent sincerity of his work here speaks for itself.

Two colossal paintings dominate the side walls of the chancel. On the left is *The Israelites at Mount Sinai*; opposite is a gruesome *Last Judgement*. Tintoretto had no qualms about mixing religion and myth: note the classical figure of Charon ferrying

the souls of the dead. His paintings in the apse include *St Peter's Vision of the Cross* and *The Beheading of St Paul* (or Christopher, according to some), both maelstroms of swirling angelic movement. On the wall of the right aisle is the *Presentation of the Virgin in the Temple*. The Contarini Chapel, off the left aisle, contains the artist's beautiful *St Agnes Reviving the Son of a Roman Prefect*. It is the swooping angels in their dazzling blue vestments that steal the show. Tintoretto, his son Domenico and his artistically gifted daughter Marietta are buried in a chapel off the right aisle.

When the Tintorettos get too much for you, take a look at Cima da Conegliano's masterpiece *Saints John the Baptist, Mark, Jerome and Paul* (1494-95) over the first altar on the right. The saints stand under a ruined portico against a sharp, wintry light. There used to be a small *Madonna and Child* by Giovanni

Bellini in the chapel opposite, but it was stolen in 1993. The second chapel on the left contains, on the left-hand wall, a painting by Titian of *The Archangel Raphael and Tobias* (and dog) that has been moved here from the church of San Marziale. In a room beneath the bell tower, a small treasury contains reliquaries and other precious objects.

Restaurants

Algiubagiò €€
Cannaregio 5039, fondamenta Nove (041 523 6084, www. algiubagio.net). Vaporetto Fondamente Nove. **Open** 7am-midnight daily. Closed Jan. **Meals served** noon-3pm, 7-10.30pm Mon, Wed-Sun. **Map** p104 L5 ④ *European*
This busy spot has morphed from bar to full-on restaurant, now with a vast waterside terrace. The menu ranges from seafood, meat, salad and cheese antipasti, through pasta dishes such as tagliolini with duck and autumn greens, to Angus steak (the house speciality), prepared every which way. Vegetarians are well served, and there's a small but well-chosen wine list. Right by the Fondamente Nove vaporetto stop, this is the perfect place for a quick bite before heading out to the islands of the northern lagoon.

Alla Frasca €€
Cannaregio 5176, campiello della Carità (041 241 2585). Vaporetto Fondamente Nove. **Meals served** noon-2pm Tue, Thur-Sun, 7-10pm Tue-Sun. **Map** p104 L5 ⑤ *Seafood*
Alla Frasca is a pleasant *trattoria* with a good seafood menu: the *zuppa di pesce* (fish soup) and spaghetti with lobster are particularly fine. With outside tables on a tiny square just south of fondamente Nove, it is almost ridiculously picturesque.

❤ Anice Stellato €€
Cannaregio 3272, fondamenta della Sensa (041 720 744). Vaporetto Guglie or Sant'Alvise. **Meals served** 12.30-2pm, 7.30-10pm Wed-Sun. **Map** p104 F2 ⑥ *Venetian*
The bar in this friendly *bacaro* fills up with *cichetari* (snacking locals) in the hour before lunch and evening meals. Tables take up two simply decorated rooms, and spill out on to the canalside walk in summer. What emerges from the kitchen are mostly Venetian classics such as *bigoli in salsa* (pasta with onion and anchovies or sardines), some given a novel twist.

Da Rioba €€
Cannaregio 2553, fondamenta della Misericordia (041 524 4379, www.darioba.com). Vaporetto Orto. **Meals served** 12.30-2.30pm, 7.30-10.30pm Tue-Sun. Closed 3wks Jan & 3wks Aug. **Map** p104 H4 ⑦ *Venetian*
Taking its name from the iron-nosed stone figure of a turbaned merchant – known as Sior Rioba – set into a wall in nearby campo dei Mori, Da Rioba is a pleasant place for lunch on warm days, when tables are laid out along the canal. This nouveau-rustic *bacaro* attracts a predominantly Venetian clientele – always a good sign. The menu ranges from local standards like *schie con polenta* (shrimp with polenta) to forays such as red mullet fillets on a bed of artichokes with balsamic sauce.

Cafés, bars & gelaterie

Bar Puppa
Cannaregio 4800, calle del Spezier (041 476 1454). Vaporetto Fondamente Nove. **Open** 8am-11pm daily. **No cards**. **Map** p104 K5 ④
Blink and you might miss this small bar on a narrow street well removed from the main drag. It's

worth the detour: exceptionally friendly Bangladeshi host Masud makes a great classic spritz and a number of popular variations (try his *spritz bianco* with ginger and mint). The kitchen offers a selection of dishes (using fresh local ingredients with a non-Venetian twist – herbs and spices abound) at extremely reasonable prices, from seafood pasta to the chef's trademark hamburgers and vegetable samosas.

Vino Vero
Cannaregio 2497, fondamenta della Misericordia (041 275 0044). Vaporetto Orto. **Open** *11am-midnight Tue-Sun, 6pm-midnight Mon.* **Map** *p104 H4* ❺

A buzzy wine bar specialising in natural wines and *cicheti*, which can be enjoyed in a picturesque setting along the Misericordia canal. You'll have to get there early to secure one of the tables on the *fondamenta* outside, as locals flock here after work.

Shops & services
❤ Vittorio Costantini
Cannaregio 5311, calle del Fumo (041 522 2265, www.vittoriocostantini.com). Vaporetto Fondamenta Nove. **Open** *9.30am-1pm, 2.30-5.30pm Mon-Fri.* **Map** *p104 L6* ❷ *Glass*

Vittorio is internationally renowned as one of the most original Venetian glass workers (*see p159* Murano glass). His intricate animals, insects, fish and birds are instantly recognisable for their fine workmanship.

Entertainment
❤ Paradiso Perduto
Cannaregio 2540, fondamenta della Misericordia (041 720 581, http://ilparadisoperduto. wordpress.com). Vaporetto San Marcuola. **Open** *6pm-midnight Mon-Thur; noon-1am Fri, Sat; noon-midnight Sun.* **No cards.** **Map** *p104 H4* ❸ *Bar*

Probably the most famous Venetian haunt after Harry's Bar (*see p86*), this 'Paradise Lost' is well worth finding. Arty types of all ages take their places at the long *osteria* tables for the mix of seafood and succulent sounds (mainly jazz and salsa), although the city's stringent noise regulations occasionally throw a spanner in the works.

Glasswork by Vittorio Costantini

Glasswork by Vittorio Costantini

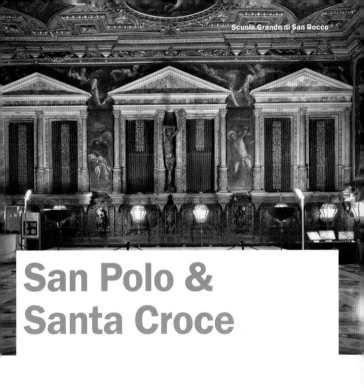

San Polo & Santa Croce

Within the bulge created by the great bend in the Grand Canal lie the *sestieri* of San Polo and Santa Croce. Working out where one stops and the other begins is an arduous task. The area ranges from the eastern portion, tightly clustered around the Rialto market – which was the city's ancient heart and where, despite the stalls selling trashy tourist-trinkets, you can still feel its steady throb, particularly in the bustling morning market – to a quieter, residential, more down-at-heel area in the far west, extending to the university zone by San Nicolò da Tolentino. Between the two extremes come the large open space of campo San Polo, the great religious complex of the Frari and the *scuole* of San Rocco and San Giovanni Evangelista.

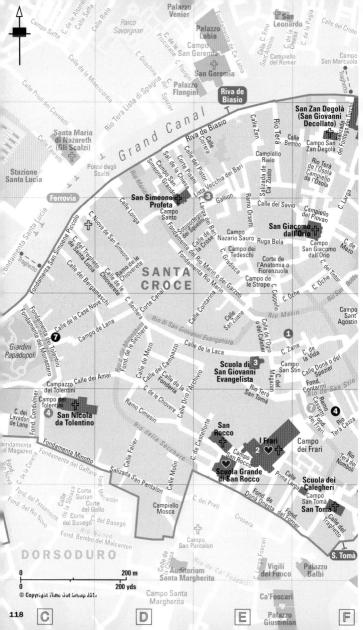

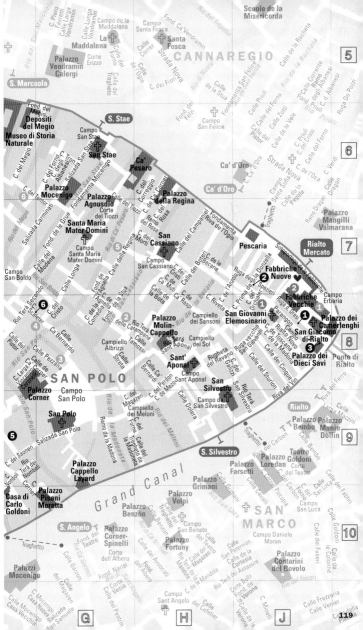

Best art & architecture
There's artistic overload in I Frari
(*p130*) and the neighbouring
Scuola Grande di San Rocco (*p129*).

Best local food
The Mercato di Rialto (*p122*) is the
source of all that's good and fresh
on Venetian plates. Nearby, don't
miss the buzzing market hole-in-
the-wall Al Mercà (*p121*). Antiche
Carampane (*p123*) is a simple,
timeless classic. Head to Da Fiore
(*p127*) for Michelin-starred local
cuisine.

Best classical music
Music to the ears... and the eyes at
the Basilica dei Frari (*p130*). The
Scuola Grande di San Giovanni
Evangelista (*p131*) offers ancient
music in a fabulous setting.

Best Venetian fashion
For magnificent jewellery, head to
Attombri (*p121*). Pair it with one of
Atelier Pietro Longhi's creations
(*p124*), and you'll be dressed to
impress.

Rialto

'Rialto', most experts agree,
derives from 'Rivoaltus' (high
bank). It was on this point of higher
ground at the midpoint along the
Grand Canal that one of the earliest
settlements was founded, in the fifth
century. The district has been the
commercial centre of the city since
the market was placed here in 1097.

Near the foot of the **Rialto bridge**
(*see p24*), the small church of **San
Giacomo di Rialto** is generally
agreed to be the oldest of the city's
churches. All around it stretch the
markets – the best places to buy your
fruit, veg and seafood.

Beyond the market extends
a warren of medieval low-rent
housing interspersed with
proud *palazzi*.

Sights & museums

San Giacomo di Rialto
*San Polo, campo San Giacomo
(041 522 4745). Vaporetto
Rialto or Rialto Mercato.* **Open**
9.30am-noon, 4-5pm Mon-Sat.
Map *p118 J8.*
The traditional foundation date for
this church is that of the city itself:
25 March 421. It has undergone

several radical reconstructions
since then, the last in 1601.
Nonetheless, the original Greek-
cross plan was always preserved, as
were its minuscule dimensions.

The special role of this church
in Venetian history was given
official recognition after 1532,
when Pope Clement VII bestowed
the patronage of the church on the
doge, effectively annexing it to the
Ducal Chapel of St Mark's.

Restaurants

Bancogiro €€
*San Polo 122, campo San Giacomo
di Rialto (041 523 2061, www.
osteriabancogiro.it). Vaporetto
Rialto Mercato.* **Meals served**
noon-11pm daily. **Map** *p118 J8* ①
Venetian
The location of this updated *bacaro*
is splendid: the main entrance
gives on to the busy Rialto square of
San Giacomo, while the back door
leads to a prime bit of Grand Canal
frontage, with (hotly contested)
tables from which to soak in
the view. Bancogiro dispenses
excellent wines and *cicheti* to an
appreciative crowd downstairs;
upstairs, the restaurant has creative
seafood dishes.

Cafés, bars & gelaterie

Alla Ciurma

San Polo 406, calle Galeazza (041 523 9514). Vaporetto Rialto or Rialto Mercato. **Open** *8am-3pm, 5.30-9pm Mon-Sat.* **No cards.** **Map** *p118 J8* ❶

Packed, loud and casually friendly, Alla Ciurma mixes market stallholders with locals and tourists in a happy confusion around a high counter packed with *cicheti* (snacks) of all kinds, including skewers of deep-fried seafood and – their speciality – king prawns wrapped in bacon. Alcohol here is consumed throughout daylight hours here by stallholders whose day begins before dawn.

❤ Al Mercà

San Polo 213, campo Cesare Battisti già Bella Vienna (347 100 2583 mobile). Vaporetto Rialto or Rialto Mercato. **Open** *9am-3pm, 6-9pm Mon-Sat; 6-9pm Sun.* **No cards.** **Map** *p118 J7* ❷

Quite literally a hole in the wall, with standing room only in this *campo* in the market, Al Mercà (or Al Marcà, the spelling varies) has been serving Rialto marketgoers since 1918. Today's owners dispense the usual choice of wine, and a decent spritz, plus snacks – meatballs, artichoke hearts and mini-sandwiches, in addition to numerous options for panini toppings.

Shops & services

❤ Attombri

San Polo 65, sottoportego degli Orafi (041 521 2524, www.attombri. com). Vaporetto Rialto or Rialto Mercato. **Open** *10am-1pm, 2.30-7pm Mon-Sat.* **Map** *p118 J8* ❶ *Jewellery*

Underneath the arches at the north-western foot of the Rialto, Stefano and Daniele Attombri

peddle their sumptuous creations. Intricate, unique pieces combine metal-wire and antique Venetian glass beads, or blown glass cameos of their own designs. They also produce interior design pieces, including mirrors and lamps.

Drogheria Mascari

San Polo 381, ruga degli Spezieri (041 522 9762). Vaporetto Rialto Mercato or San Silvestro. **Open** *8am-1pm, 4-7.30pm Mon-Sat.* **No cards.** **Map** *p118 J7* ❷ *Food & drink*

Dry-goods stores like Mascari are a rarity these days, which makes a visit to this old-fashioned emporium such a treat. It's overflowing with Venetian goodies (bigoli pasta, buranei biscuits) and with teas, coffees, herbs and spices from all over the world: a reminder that Venice was once a major centre of international trade.

Piedàterre

San Polo 60, sottoportego degli Orafi (041 528 5513, www. piedaterre-venice.com). Vaporetto Rialto or Rialto Mercato. **Open** *10am-12.30pm, 2.30-7.30pm Mon-Sat.* **Map** *p118 J8* ❸ *Shoes*

Furlane (or *friulane*) are those traditional slipper-like shoes that you'll see on the feet of many gondoliers. In this little shop at the foot of the Rialto Bridge, brilliantly coloured bundles of them line the walls. The design is traditional, as is the use of recycled materials such as old tyres to make the soles. But the colours and textiles are eye-catchingly modern.

West from the Rialto

The route to campo San Polo traverses a series of busy shopping streets, passing the Renaissance church of **San Giovanni Elemosinario** and the deconsecrated church of **Sant'Aponal**, which has fine Gothic sculpture on its façade.

❤ Mercato di Rialto

West of the Rialto Bridge (*see p24*) and all around the church of San Giacometto (*see p120*) stretch the stalls of the Rialto market – the best place in Venice to buy seasonal fruit, veg and seafood. It's the heartbeat of this quintessentially mercantile city, where locals have been mingling and trading goods for almost a thousand years. The market specialises in food from the lagoon and its islands: delicacies such as *castraure* (the first tender artichoke buds), sweet green peas and white asparagus, or extraordinarily fresh seafood, including *moeche* (soft-shell crab), *schie* (tiny grey shrimp) and *sepe* (cuttlefish). Venetians and tourists converge in front of the fish stalls of the **Pescaria** from early morning, lured in by the sellers' colourful clamour and by sea monster-like offerings from the Venetian lagoon. (The more recognizable fish, such as sea bass and swordfish, tend

to come from the Adriatic and Atlantic.) A historic plaque on the side of the neo-Gothic arcade lists the minimum size that each fish should measure in order to be sold. In recent years, this area has taken on a new lease of life as a centre of Venetian nightlife, with a number of bars opening under the porticos of the Renaissance **Fabbriche Vecchie** building (Scarpagnino, 1520-22), including some on **campo Erbaria**. The name Erbaria denotes the fact that vegetables are sold here; there are other examples of such names in the streets and squares nearby (Naranzeria – oranges; Casaria – cheese; Speziali – spices), while the narrower alleys mostly bear the names of ancient inns and taverns – some still in operation – such as 'the Monkey', 'the Two Swords', 'the Two Moors', 'the Ox' and 'the Bell'. Then, as now, market traders hated to be too far from liquid refreshment.

To the south of this route, towards the Grand Canal, stands **San Silvestro**, which holds a Tintoretto, while to the north is a fascinating network of little-visited alleys and courtyards.

After the shadowy closeness of these *calli*, the open expanse of **campo San Polo** – home to the church of the same name – comes as a sunlit surprise. It's the largest square on this side of the Grand Canal.

The curving line of *palazzi* on the east side of the square is explained by the fact that these buildings once gave on to a canal, which was subsequently filled in. From the south-west of the square, salizada di San Polo leads to **Palazzo Centani**, the birthplace of the prolific Venetian playwright Carlo Goldoni, which contains a small theatre studies museum and library: the **Casa di Carlo Goldoni** (San Polo 2794, calle dei Nomboli, 041 275 9325, www.visitmuve.it).

Sights & museums

San Polo
San Polo, campo San Polo (041 275 0462, www.chorusvenezia. org). Vaporetto San Silvestro or San Tomà. **Open** *10.30am-4.30pm Mon-Sat.* **Admission** *€3 (or Chorus; see p23). No cards.* **Map** *p118 G9.*
The church of San Polo (Venetian for Paolo, or Paul) faces away from the square, towards the canal, although later buildings have deprived it of its façade and water entrance. The campanile (1362) has two 12th-century lions at the base, one brooding over a snake and the other toying with a human head, which Venetians like to think of as that of Count Carmagnola, who was beheaded for treachery in 1402. The Gothic church was extensively altered in the 19th century, when a neoclassical look was imposed

on it. Some of this was removed in 1930, but the interior remains a rather awkward hybrid.

Paintings include a *Last Supper* by Tintoretto, to the left of the entrance, and a Tiepolo: *The Virgin Appearing to St John of Nepomuk*. Giambattista Tiepolo's son, Giandomenico, is the author of a brilliant cycle of Stations of the Cross in the Oratory of the Crucifix. He painted these, as well as the ceiling paintings, at the age of 20.

Restaurants

❤ Antiche Carampane €€€
San Polo 1911, rio terà delle Carampane (041 524 0165, www.antichecarampane.com). Vaporetto San Silvestro. **Meals served** *12.30-2.30pm, 7.30-11pm Tue-Sat. Closed Aug.* **Map** *p118 G8* ❷ *Seafood*
Fiendishly difficult to find, Antiche Carampane is a Venetian classic but be warned: there are a lot of tables packed into a very small space so don't expect privacy; and demand is so great that there are two evening sittings – at 7.30pm and 9.30pm – arrive later than you booked and your table will be given away. What eager diners pile in here for is fine (though not cheap) seafood that goes beyond the ubiquitous standards with recherché local specialities such as *spaghetti in cassopipa* (a spicy sauce of shellfish and crustaceans). Leave room for an unbeatable *fritto misto* (mixed seafood fry-up) and their delicious desserts. Inside is cosy; outside is better.

Birraria La Corte €€
San Polo 2168, campo San Polo (041 275 0570, www.birrarialacorte. it). Vaporetto San Silvestro or San Tomà. **Meals served** *noon-3pm, 6-10.30pm daily.* **Map** *p118 G8* ❸ *Pizzeria*

The outside tables of this huge, no-nonsense pizzeria are a great place to observe life in the *campo* – and a boon for parents with small children, who can chase pigeons while mum and dad tuck into a decent pizza. The restaurant occupies a former brewery, and beer still takes pride of place over wine. There's also a regular menu with decent pasta options and some good grilled-meat *secondi*.

Shops & services

❤ Atelier Pietro Longhi
San Polo 2608, rio terà dei Frari (041 714 478, www.pietrolonghi. com). Vaporetto San Tomà. **Open** *9.30am-3.30pm Mon-Fri.* **Map** *p118 F9* ❹ *Costumes*
This atelier makes exquisite period costumes and accessories for rent or purchase. Prices vary greatly, but renting something simple will cost about €160 for the first day, and less for subsequent days.

Gilberto Penzo
San Polo 2681, calle II dei Saoneri (041 719 372, www.veniceboats. com). Vaporetto San Tomà. **Open** *8.30am-12.30pm, 3-6pm Mon-Sat.* **Map** *p118 F9* ❺ *Model boats*
Gilberto Penzo creates astonishingly detailed models of gondolas, *sandolos*, *topos* and vaporetti. Inexpensive kits

---

In the know
Dubious denizens

North-west of campo Sant'Aponal is one of Venice's early red-light zones; the district of Ca' Rampana passed on its own name (*carampana* means 'slut') to the Italian language. Just round the corner is the ponte delle Tette (Tits Bridge), where prostitutes were allowed to display their wares with the aim of saving Venetian men from 'less acceptable' vices.

---

are also on sale – if you would like to practise the fine art of shipbuilding yourself.

North-west from the Rialto

Yellow signs pointing to 'Ferrovia' mark the zigzagging north-western route from the Rialto, past the fish market, and on past **campo San Cassiano**. The plain exterior of the church here gives no clue as to its heavily decorated interior.

Across a bridge is **campo Santa Maria Mater Domini** with its Renaissance church. Before entering the *campo*, stop on the bridge to admire the view of the curving Grand Canal-facing marble flank of **Ca' Pesaro**, the seat of the **Museo Orientale and Galleria d'Arte Moderna**. On the far side of the square, the yellow road sign indicates that the way to the station is to the left and to the right. Take your pick.

The quieter route to the right curls parallel to the Grand Canal. Many of the most important sights face on to the Grand Canal (*see p24*), including the 18th-century church of **San Stae** and the Fondaco dei Turchi (Warehouse of the Turks), home to the **Museo di Storia Naturale**.

On the wide road leading towards San Stae is **Palazzo Mocenigo**, with its collection of perfumes, textiles and costumes. Near to the Fondaco is the quiet square of **San Zan Degolà** (San Giovanni Decollato), with a well-preserved 11th-century church. From here, a series of narrow roads leads past the church of **San Simeone Profeta** to the foot of the Scalzi bridge across the Grand Canal.

Leave campo Santa Maria Mater Domini by the route to the left, on the other hand, and you'll make your way past the near-legendary

Da Fiore restaurant to the house (no. 2311) where Aldus Manutius set up the Aldine Press in 1490, and where the humanist Erasmus came to stay in 1508. To the right, the rio terà del Parrucchetta leads to the large leafy **campo San Giacomo dell'Orio**.

Sights & museums

Ca' Pesaro – Galleria Internazionale d'Arte Moderna & Museo Orientale

Santa Croce 2076, fondamenta Ca' Pesaro (041 524 0695, www. visitmuve.it). Vaporetto San Stae. **Open** *10am-6pm Tue-Sun.* **Admission** *(incl Museo Orientale) €14; €11.50 reductions; see also p21 Visitor Passes.* **Map** *p118 H6.*
This grandiose *palazzo* was built in the second half of the 17th century for the Pesaro family, to a project by Baldassare Longhena. When Longhena died in 1682, the family called in Gian Antonio Gaspari who finished it in 1710.

Its last owner, Felicita Bevilacqua La Masa, bequeathed it to the city – into it went the city's collection of modern art, gleaned from the Biennale (*see p101*). The museum now covers a century of mainly Italian art, from the mid 19th century to the 1950s. The stately ground floor is used for temporary shows.

The first rooms on the *piano nobile* contain atmospheric works by 19th-century painters and some striking sculptures by Medardo Rosso. In the central hall are works from the early Biennali (up to the 1930s), including pieces by Gustav Klimt and Vassily Kandinsky, alongside more conventional, vast-scale 'salon' paintings. Room 4 holds works by Giorgio Morandi, Joan Mirò and Giorgio De Chirico. After rooms devoted to international art from the 1940s and '50s, the collection finishes up with works by notable post-war Venetian experimentalists such as Armando Pizzinato, Giuseppe Santomaso and Emilio Vedova.

Also in the *palazzo* is the oriental museum, which contains an eclectic collection of Japanese art and weaponry of the Edo period (1600-1868).

Museo di Storia Naturale

Santa Croce 1730, salizada del Fondaco dei Turchi (041 275 0206, www.visitmuve.it). Vaporetto San Stae. **Open** *10am-5pm Tue-Fri, 10am-6pm Sat, Sun.* **Admission** *€8; €5.50 reductions; see also p21 Visitor Passes.* **Map** *p118 F6.*
The Natural History Museum is housed in the Fondaco dei Turchi, a Venetian-Byzantine building leased to the Turks in the 17th century as a residence and warehouse. The Acquario delle Tegnue is devoted to the aquatic life of the northern Adriatic, and the Sala dei Dinosauri contains a state-of-the-art exhibition chronicling the Ligabue expedition to Niger (1973), which unearthed a fossil of the previously unknown *Auronosaurus nigeriensis* and a giant crocodile. With vast storerooms holding some two million items from scientific collections put together over the centuries, this museum is a hive of scientific activity.

Palazzo Mocenigo

Santa Croce 1992, salizada San Stae (041 721 798, www.visitmuve. it). Vaporetto San Stae. **Open** *10am-5pm Tue-Sun.* **Admission** *€8; €5.50 reductions. No cards.* **Map** *p118 G6.*
Palazzo Mocenigo is a rather splendid showcase for life of the aristocracy in 18th-century Venice. Already extant in an earlier form by 1500, this predominantly 17th-century *palazzo* was the home of the Mocenigo family, which provided the Republic with seven doges. A collection

SAN POLO & SANTA CROCE

of period costumes is displayed among fine furniture and fittings, in rooms with walls now covered with exquisite Rubelli (*see p39* Material Makers) reproductions of the original fabrics. Added to the museum during the restoration is a fascinating section on perfumes and perfumery, with intriguing essences in lovely glass jars to explore and sniff.

San Cassiano

San Polo, campo San Cassiano (041 721 408). Vaporetto Rialto Mercato or San Stae. **Open** *9am-noon, 5-7pm Mon-Sat.* **Map** *p118 H7.*
This church has a singularly dull exterior and a heavily decorated interior, with a striking ceiling by the Tiepolesque painter Constantino Cedini.

The chancel contains three major Tintorettos: *Crucifixion*, *Resurrection* and *Descent into Limbo*. The *Crucifixion* is particularly interesting for its viewpoint. As Ruskin puts it, 'The horizon is so low, that the spectator must fancy himself lying full length on the grass, or rather among the brambles and luxuriant weeds, of which the foreground is entirely composed.'

On the wall opposite the altar is a painting by Antonio Balestra, representing *The Martyrdom of St Cassian*, a teacher who was murdered by his pupils with their pens. This, of course, makes him the patron saint of schoolteachers.

San Giacomo dell'Orio

Santa Croce, campo San Giacomo dell'Orio (041 275 0462, www. chorusvenezia.org). Vaporetto Riva di Biasio. **Open** *10.30am-4.30pm Mon-Sat.* **Admission** *€3 (or Chorus; see p23). No cards.* **Map** *p118 F7.*
The main entrance of San Giacomo dell'Orio faces the canal rather than the *campo*. The interior is a fascinating mix of architectural

and decorative styles. Most of the columns have 12th- or 13th-century Veneto-Byzantine capitals; one has a sixth-century flowered capital and one is a solid piece of smooth verd-antique marble, perhaps from a Roman temple sacked during the Fourth Crusade. Note, too, the fine 14th-century ship's-keel roof. Among the paintings in the Sacrestia Nuova is *St John the Baptist Preaching* by Francesco Bassano, which includes a portrait of Titian (in the red hat).

Behind the high altar is a *Madonna and Four Saints* by Lorenzo Lotto, one of his last Venetian paintings. In the left transept, a central altarpiece by Veronese and two fine early works by Palma il Giovane hang in the San Lawrence chapel.

San Stae

Santa Croce, campo San Stae (041 275 0462, www.chorusvenezia. org). Vaporetto San Stae. **Open** *1.45-4pm Mon; 1.45-4.30pm Tue-Sat.* **Admission** *€3 (or Chorus; see p23). No cards.* **Map** *p118 G6.*
Stae is the Venetian version of Eustachio or Eustace, a martyred saint who was converted to Christianity by the vision of a stag with a crucifix between its antlers. This church on the Grand Canal has a dramatic late-Baroque façade (1709) by Swiss-born architect Domenico Rossi. On the side walls of the chancel, all the leading painters operating in Venice in 1722 were asked to pick an apostle. The finest of these are: Tiepolo's *Martyrdom of St Bartholomew* and Sebastiano Ricci's *Liberation of St Peter*, perhaps his best work (both left wall, lower row); Pellegrini's *Martyrdom of St Andrew* and Piazzetta's *Martyrdom of St James*, a disturbingly realistic work showing the saint as a confused old man in the hands of a loutish youth (both right wall, lower row).

Scuole Stories

Venice's confraternities were part of a complicated social system

Scuole – a blend of art-treasure house and social institution – are uniquely Venetian establishments. Essentially, they were devotional lay brotherhoods, subject to the state rather than the church. In Venice's complicated system of social checks and balances (*see p78* Machinery of State), they gave citizens of wealth – but with no hope of ever entering the ruling elite – a place to feel they exerted some influence.

The earliest were founded in the 13th century; by the 15th century, there were six *scuole grandi* and as many as 400 minor *scuole*. The six *scuole grandi* had annually elected officers drawn from the 'citizen' class (sandwiched between the governing patriciate and the unenfranchised *popolani*). While members of the *scuole grandi*

– such as the **Scuola Grande di San Rocco** (*see p129*), the recently restored **Scuola Grande di San Marco** (*see p94*) and **Scuola Grande di San Giovanni Evangelista** (*see p131*) – were mainly drawn from the wealthier professional classes, the humbler *scuole piccole* were exclusively devotional groups, trade guilds or confraternities of foreign communities (such as the **Scuola di San Giorgio degli Schiavoni**; St George of the Slavs, *see p99*).

The wealthier confraternities devoted a great deal of time and expense to beautifying their meeting houses (the *scuole* themselves), sometimes hiring one major painter to decorate the whole building; this was the case with Tintoretto at San Rocco and Carpaccio at San Giorgio degli Schiavoni.

Restaurants

❤ Da Fiore €€€€
San Polo 2202, calle del Scaleter (041 721 308, www.dafiore.net). Vaporetto San Stae or San Tomà. **Meals served** *12.30-2.30pm, 7.30-10.30pm Tue-Sat.* **Map** *p118 G8* ④
Venetian

Michelin-starred Da Fiore is considered by many to be Venice's best restaurant. Host Maurizio Martin treats his guests with egalitarian courtesy, while his wife Mara concentrates on getting the food right. Raw fish and seafood is a key feature of the antipasti; *primi* are equally divided between pasta dishes and a series of faultless risottos. *Secondi* are all about bringing out the flavour of the fish without smothering it in sauce. There's a

choice of €50 set lunch menus, and taster menus at €120 and €140 in the evening.

Vecio Fritolin €€€
Santa Croce 2262, calle della Regina (041 522 2881, www. veciofritolin.it). Vaporetto San Stae. **Meals served** *12.30-2.30pm, 7-10.30pm Mon, Thur-Sun; 7-10.30pm Wed.* **Map** *p118 G7* ⑤
Modern Venetian

Wooden beams, sturdy tables and the long bar at the back of the main dining room set the mood in this old-style *bacaro*. But the seasonally-changing menu is more creative than the decor might lead you to expect, with dishes such as cocoa tagliatelle with squid, or a main course of turbot in a crust of black rice with sautéed baby artichokes.

La Zucca €€

*Santa Croce 1762, ponte del Megio (041 524 1570, www.lazucca.it). Vaporetto San Stae. **Meals served** 12.30-2.30pm, 7-10.30pm Mon-Sat. **Map** p118 F6* 6 *Modern Italian*

One of Venice's first 'alternative' *trattorias* and still one of the best – not to mention one of the best value. By a pretty bridge, the vegetarian-friendly Pumpkin offers a break from all that seafood. The menu is equally divided between meat (ginger pork with pilau rice) and vegetables (pumpkin and seasoned ricotta quiche). Always book ahead, especially in summer for one of the few outside tables.

Cafés, bars & gelaterie

Alaska Gelateria-Sorbetteria

*Santa Croce 1159, calle larga dei Bari (041 715 211). Vaporetto Riva de Biasio. **Open** 11am-9pm daily. Closed Dec-Jan. **No cards**. **Map** p118 E6* 3

The jury is out about Alaska's gelato: some find the fruit flavours insufficiently creamy, others object to the fact that novelty flavours (celery anyone?) are hardly sweet. But to those who appreciate the eccentricities, Carlo Pistacchi's ice-cream is some of Venice's best.

Shops & services

Monica Daniele

*San Polo 2235, calle Scaleter (041 524 6242, www.monicadaniele. com). Vaporetto San Silvestro or San Stae. **Open** 9am-12.30pm, 2.15-6pm Mon-Sat. **Map** p118 F8* 6 *Fashion*

Monica Daniele has single-handedly brought the *tabarro* – that sweeping cloak seen in many an 18th-century Venetian print – back into vogue: a heavy woollen one will cost €500 or more. But this odd little shop also has a range of hats, from panamas to stylish creations by the shop's owner.

Entertainment

Palazzetto Bru Zane

*San Polo 2368, campiello Forner (041 521 1005, www.bru-zane.com). Vaporetto San Tomà. **Shows** vary. Tickets €15; €5 reductions. **Map** p104 E8* 1

Stuccoed and frescoed Palazzo Bru Zane is home to the Centre for French Romantic Music, a busy research and performance institute which hosts concerts, operas, seminars and special musical events for children where under-12s go free and their parents pay €10. There are free tours of the *palazzo* every Thursday, at 2.30pm (Italian), 3pm (French) and 3.30pm (English). Check the website for programme details.

From the Frari to piazzale Roma

At the heart of the western side of the two *sestieri* of San Polo and Santa Croce lies the great gothic bulk of **Santa Maria Gloriosa dei Frari** (aka I Frari; p130), with its 70-metre (230-foot) campanile, matched by the Renaissance magnificence of the *scuola* and church of **San Rocco** (*see* p129). These buildings contain perhaps the greatest concentration of influential works of art in the city outside piazza San Marco and the Accademia. Beyond the Frari is the **Scuola di San Giovanni Evangelista**, one of the six *scuole grandi*.

South-west of the Frari is the quiet square of **San Tomà**, with a church on one side and the **Scuola dei Calegheri** ('of the cobblers') opposite.

Heading west from the Frari, past the church and *scuola* of San Rocco, the route ends in a bland area of 19th-century housing. At the edge of this stands the Baroque church of **San Nicolò dei Tolentini**.

💜 Scuola Grande di San Rocco

San Polo 3054, campo San Rocco (041 523 4864, www. scuolagrandesanrocco.it). Vaporetto San Tomà. Open 9.30am-5.30pm daily. Admission €10; €8 reductions. Map p118 E9.

The Archbrotherhood of St Roch was the richest of the six *scuole grandi* in 15th-century Venice. It was dedicated to Venice's other patron saint, the French plague protector and dog-lover St Roch (also known as St Rock or San Rocco), whose body was brought here in 1485.

The architecture, by Bartolomeo Bon and Scarpagnino, is far less impressive than the interior decoration, which was entrusted to Tintoretto in 1564. In three intensive sessions spread out over the following 23 years, San Rocco

became his epic masterpiece. To follow the development of Tintoretto's style, pick up the free explanatory leaflet and the audio guide and begin in the smaller upstairs hall – the Albergo. Here, filling up the whole of the far wall, is the *Crucifixion* (1565).

Tintoretto began work on the larger upstairs room in 1575, with Old Testament stories on the ceiling and a *Life of Christ* cycle around the walls.

Finally, in the ground-floor hall – which the artist decorated between 1583 and 1587, when he was in his sixties – the paintings reach a visionary pitch. *The Annunciation*, with its domestic Mary surprised while sewing, and *Flight into Egypt*, with its verdant landscape, are among the painter's masterpieces.

SAN POLO & SANTA CROCE

❤ I Frari

*San Polo, campo dei Frari (041 275 0462, www.chorusvenezia. org). Vaporetto San Tomà. **Open** 9am-6pm Mon-Sat; 1-6pm Sun. **Admission** €3 (or Chorus; see p23). No cards. **Map** p118 E9* ❷

This gloomy Gothic barn, known officially as Santa Maria Gloriosa dei Frari, is one of the city's most significant artistic storehouses. It's also one of the best places for catching high-standard performances of sacred music. The church is 98m (320ft) long, 48m (158ft) wide at the transept and 28m (92ft) high – just slightly smaller than the Dominicans' Santi Giovanni e Paolo (*see p93*) – and has the second highest campanile in the city.

On the right side of the **nave**, a loud monument marks the spot where Titian is believed to be buried. He was the only victim of the 1575-76 plague who was allowed a city burial. A much finer memorial can be found on the third altar on this side: Alessandro Vittoria's statue of St Jerome.

Continuing round into the **right transept**, to the right of the sacristy door is the tomb of the Blessed Pacifico, attributed to Nanni di Bartolo and Michele da Firenze (1437); the sarcophagus is surrounded by a splendidly carved canopy in the florid Gothic style. The third chapel on the right side of this transept has an altarpiece by Bartolomeo Vivarini, in its original frame, while the Florentine Chapel, next to the chancel, contains the only work by Donatello in the city: a striking wooden statue of a stark, emaciated St John the Baptist.

The sacristy itself contains one of Giovanni Bellini's greatest paintings for the Pesaro family:

Altarpiece by Bartolomeo Vivarini

the *Madonna and Child with Saints Nicholas, Peter, Benedict and Mark* (1488), still in its original frame.

In the **chancel**, the high altar is dominated by Titian's *Assumption*, a work that seems to open the church up to the heavens. The left wall hosts one of the finest Renaissance tombs in Venice, the monument to Doge Niccolò Tron, by Antonio Rizzo (1473).

The **choir** has wooden stalls carved by Marco Cozzi (1468), inlaid with superb intarsia decoration.

In the **left transept**, the third chapel has an altarpiece by Bartolomeo Vivarini and Marco Basaiti; a slab on the floor marks the grave of composer Claudio Monteverdi. The Corner Chapel, at the end, contains a mannered statue of St John the Baptist by Sansovino.

Back in the **nave**, another magnificent Titian hangs to the left of the Emiliani chapel. The *Madonna di Ca' Pesaro* celebrates victory in a naval expedition against the Turks in 1502, and it revolutionised altar paintings in Venice. Titian dared to move the Virgin from the centre of the composition; but the real innovation was the rich humanity of the work.

The whole of the next bay, around the side door, is occupied by the mastodontic mausoleum of Doge Pesaro (d.1659), attributed to Longhena, with sculptures by Melchior Barthel of Dresden. The penultimate bay has a monument to Canova; his body is buried in his native town of Possagno, but his heart is here.

♥ Scuola Grande di San Giovanni Evangelista

San Polo 2454, campiello della Scuola (041 718 234, www. scuolasangiovanni.it). Vaporetto San Tomà. **Open** *9am-2pm, 2.30-5.15pm daily. Closed during conferences.* **Admission** *€8; €6 reductions. No cards.* **Map** *p118 E8* ❸

Used frequently during the day for conferences and in the evening for concerts, the Scuola Grande di San Giovanni Evangelista is one of the six *scuole grandi* (*see p127* Scuole Stories). Founded in 1261, it is the most ancient of the extant *scuole* and is one of the city's most magnificent structures. Originally attached to the church of Sant'Aponal, the *scuola* moved to its present premises in 1340. It grew in size and prestige, especially after the acquisition (1396) of a fragment of the True Cross; the fragment is housed in a tabernacle in the Oratorio della Croce, but is rarely on display.

The *scuola* stands in a small courtyard, at the entrance of which is a screen with a superb eagle pediment carved by Pietro Lombardo. The ground floor, was used as a space where members and pilgrims could gather.

The upper floor of the *scuola* is accessed by a magnificent double staircase, a masterpiece by the Renaissance architect Mauro Codussi.

The decoration in the Sala Capitolare is mainly 18th century. The floor is especially fine, with its geometrical patterns of multicoloured marbles that mirror the arrangement of the ceiling paintings, which include small but vivid scenes by Giandomenico Tiepolo. The walls are hung with 17th- and 18th-century paintings recounting the life of St John the Evangelist, by Domenico Tintoretto and others.

SAN POLO & SANTA CROCE

Scuola Grande di San Giovanni Evangelista

The Sala dell'Albergo contains a series of paintings by Palma il Giovane. The most spirited of these is *St John's Vision of the Four Horsemen*, recently restored.

Restaurants

Frary's €€

San Polo 2558, fondamenta dei Frari (041 720 050, www.frarys. it). Vaporetto San Tomà. **Meals served** *11.30am-3pm, 6-11pm Mon, Wed-Sun.* **Map** *p118 F9* ⑦ *Middle Eastern*

A friendly, reasonably- priced spot specialising in Arab cuisine, though there are some Greek and Kurdish dishes too, plus gluten-free options. Couscous comes with a variety of sauces: vegetarian, mutton, chicken or seafood. The *mansaf* (rice with chicken, almonds and yoghurt) is good.

Cafés, bars & gelaterie

Da Lele

Santa Croce 183, campo dei Tolentini (no phone). Vaporetto Piazzale Roma. **Open** *6am-8pm Mon-Fri; 6am-2pm Sat.* **No cards.** **Map** *p118 C9* ④

Gabriele's (Lele's) place is the first authentic *osteria* for those arriving in Venice – look for the two barrels outside and the crowds of people milling – and you've found this Venetian institution. It's so small in here, there isn't even room for a coffee machine, but there are local wines from Piave, Lison and Valdobbiadene on offer, as well as rolls that are filled to order with meat and/or cheese. A basic but good glass of chardonnay costs just 60c, a mini-*panino* 90c.

Shops & services

Mare di Carta

Santa Croce 222, fondamenta dei Tolentini (041 716 304, www.maredicarta.com). Vaporetto Piazzale Roma. **Open** *9am-1pm, 3.30-7.30pm Mon-Wed; 9am-7.30pm Thur-Fri; 9am-12.30pm, 3-7.30pm Sat.* **Map** *p118 C8* ⑦ *Books*

A small but well-stocked bookshop specialising in all things nautical: naval history, fishing techniques, water sports and pretty much anything aquatic.

Entertainment

The lofty Gothic **Basilica dei Frari** (*see p130*) is one of the best venues in Venice for catching high-standard performances of sacred music. For details, call 041 272 8611, or see www.basilicadeifrari.it/ calendario-concerti. Concerts of ancient music are performed in the **Scuola Grande di San Giovanni Evangelista** (*see p131*) by Società Veneziana Concerti (venicechambermusic. org) and by the Venetia Antiqua ensemble (www. venicemusicproject.it).

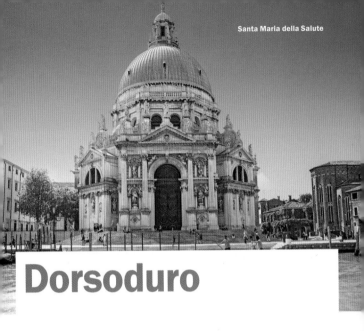

Santa Maria della Salute

Dorsoduro

Cradling the southern flank of Venice proper, Dorsoduro – literally 'hard back' – stretches from its smart, artsy eastern district of elegant *palazzi* and quiet *campielli* to the little-visited docks and university area in the *sestiere*'s far western reaches. The concentration of art – from the very contemporary at the Punta della Dogana through the modern at the Peggy Guggenheim Collection to the grand masters at the Gallerie dell'Accademia – is amazing. But there are fine churches here too, including the magnificent Santa Maria della Salute. In between the geographical and social extremes comes the democratic and buzzing campo Santa Margherita, around which much of the city's nightlife action takes place.

Unmissable sights

Santa Maria della Salute (*p146*) is a Venice icon. The Gallerie dell'Accademia (*p144*) holds one of the world's great art collections.

Best places to eat on a budget

Orient Experience (*p139*) for cheerful ethnic fare, or Cantinone (già Schiavi) (*p149*) for an *ombra* by a picturesque canal.

Best entertainment

Venice Jazz Club (*p141*) is one of the coolest live music venues in the city.

Best shops

Head to Signor Blum for jigsaws (*p141*) and to Libreria Marco Polo for books (*p141*).

Best galleries

Aside from the Gallerie dell'Accadmia, don't miss the Peggy Guggenheim Collection (*p143*) and the Punta della Dogana (*p147*).

Best places for fancy dining

Estro Vino e Cucina (*p139*) is an edgy gourmet wine bar. For creative luxury in a spectacular setting, head to Riviera (*p135*).

West

This was one of the first areas in the lagoon to be settled. Locals have never been in the top income bracket (in the past, they were mostly fishermen or salt-pan workers) and the area around the church of **San Nicolò dei Mendicoli** is still noticeably less sleek than the centre, although fishing was superseded as a source of employment by the port long ago, and subsequently by the Santa Marta cotton mill – now stunningly converted into the **Istituto Universitario di Architettura di Venezia (IUAV)**.

Moving eastwards, the atmosphere remains unpretentious around the churches of **Angelo Raffaele** and **San Sebastiano**. Head into the first to admire the paintings of *Tobias and the Angel* (Giovanni Antonio Guardi, 1750-53) on the organ loft, as featured in Sally Vickers' novel *Miss Garnet's Angel* (2000). Northwards from here, on the rio di Santa Margherita, are some grander *palazzi*, including **Palazzo Ariani** and **Palazzo Zenobio**.

On the southern shore, the final and widest stretch of the **Zattere** passes several notable *palazzi*, including the 17th-century façade of the **Scuola dei Luganegheri** (sausage-makers' school).

Sights & museums

San Nicolò dei Mendicoli

Dorsoduro, campo San Nicolò (041 275 0382). Vaporetto San Basilio or Santa Marta. **Open** *10am-noon, 3-5.30pm Mon-Sat; 9am-noon Sun.* San Nicolò is one of the few Venetian churches to have maintained its 13th-century Veneto-Byzantine structure, despite numerous refurbishments over the years. When the church underwent a thorough restoration in the 1970s, traces of the original foundations were uncovered, confirming the church's seventh-century origins. The 15th-century loggia at the front is one of only two extant examples of a once-common architectural feature; it originally served as a shelter for the homeless.

The church's interior contains a marvellous mishmash of architectural and decorative styles spanning the 12th to 17th centuries.

San Sebastiano

Dorsoduro, fondamenta di San Sebastiano (041 275 0462, www. chorusvenezia.org). Vaporetto San Basilio. **Open** *10.30am-3.45pm Mon; 10.30am-4.15pm Tue-Sat.* **Admission** *€3 (or Chorus; see p23). No cards.* **Map** *p136 C13.*
This contains perhaps the most brilliantly colourful church interior in Venice, and it's all the work of one man: Paolo Veronese. His first commission was for the sacristy. From then on, there was no stopping him: between 1556 and 1565 he completed three large ceiling paintings for the nave of the church, frescoes along the upper parts of the walls, organ shutters, huge narrative canvases for the chancel, and the painting on the high altar.

The ceiling paintings depict scenes from the life of Esther and are full of sumptuous pageantry: no painter gets more splendidly shimmering effects out of clothing.

The enormous canvases on the side walls of the chancel depict St Sebastian. Other paintings in the church include *St Nicholas*, a late painting by Titian, in the first altar on the right. Paolo Veronese and his brother Benedetto are buried here.

Paintings in the sacristy are among Veronese's earliest works in Venice (1555).

Restaurants

❤ Riviera €€€€

Dorsoduro 1473, fondamenta Zattere Ponte Longo (041 522 7621). Vaporetto San Basilio or Zattere. **Meals served** *12.30-3pm, 7-10.30pm Mon-Tue, Fri-Sun.* **Map** *p136 C13* ① *Seafood*
Riviera is rarely less than an experience. The setting is spectacular to start with: in warm weather tables on the *fondamenta* afford views across the splendid Giudecca Canal to San Giorgio Maggiore and the Redentore. What's on the plate – mainly but not solely seafood-based dishes – is creative, excellent... and pricey: this is a place for special occasions.

North & centre

A long, irregular-shaped campo with churches at both ends, **campo Santa Margherita** buzzes day and night. There are several ancient *palazzi* around the square. Isolated in the middle is the **Scuola dei Varoteri**, the School of the Tanners. At the north end is the former church of Santa Margherita, long used as a cinema and now beautifully restored as a conference hall for the university. Behind it, to the north, is **Campo San Pantalon**.

At the other end of the square are the **scuola** and **church of the Carmini**. Leaving campo Santa Margherita south from here, you reach the charming rio di San Barnaba. At the eastern end of the *fondamenta* is the entrance to **Ca' Rezzonico**, now the museum of 18th-century Venice.

The middle of the three bridges across the canal is **ponte dei Pugni**, with white marble footprints indicating that this was one of the bridges where punch-ups were held between the rival factions of the *nicolotti*, from the western quarters of the city, and the *castellani*, from the east. These violent brawls were tolerated by the authorities, who saw them as a chance for the working classes to let off steam in a way that was not disruptive to the state. They were banned, however, in 1705, after a particularly bloody fray.

Across the bridge is **campo San Barnaba**. The church of San Barnaba has a picturesque 14th-century campanile; the campo is a fine place for sitting outside a bar and watching the world go by.

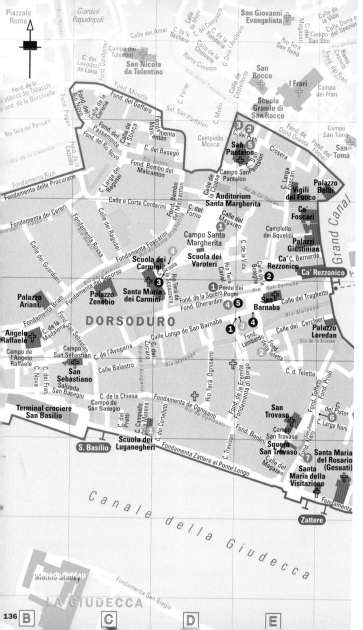

Piazzale Roma

Giardini Papadopoli

San Giovanni Evangelista

Calle de Mezo

C. de Magazen

Calle de la Vida

Calle Dona o Calle

Campo de lo Spezier

Fond. del Magazen

Calle dei Amai

C. de la Fondaria

Rio Tera San Tomà

Fond. di le Sechere

C. de la Chiovere

Campo dei Frari

Campo dei Tolentini

San Nicola da Tolentino

Ramo Cimesin

Rio delle Sezzocin

San Rocco

I Frari

Scuola Grande di San Rocco

Fond. de la Fabrica dei Tabacchi

Fond. de le Burchielle

Fond. Minotto

C. del Gaffaro

C. de la Cereria

Fond. del Gaffaro

Calle Faller

C. Molin

Calle di Castelfonte

Fond. di Donà Onesta

Campo San Tomà

Palazzo

San Tomà

Rio Terà dei Pensieri

Fond. del Rio Novo

Fond. del Gaffaro

Fond. dei Pagan

Fond. de la Cazziola

Rio Tè la Cazziola

Fondamenta Rizzi

Fondamenta delle Procuratie

Fond. Tolentini

Fond. de la Salbta

C. de la Sbiaca

Fondamenta Anton

Fond. Minotto

Sal. San Pantalon

Campiello Mosca

San Pantalon

3 C. dei Preti

5 San Pantalon

Crosera

Vigili del Fuoco

Palazzo Balbi

Grand Canal

C. Larga dei Ragusei

Fond. del Rio Novo

Fond. Bembo del Malcanton

Rio Novo

Calle de la Chiesa

Campo San Pantalon

Rio de la Trevisa

Ca' Foscari

Fondamenta dei Cereri

Calle e Corte Contarini

C. del Forno

Auditorium Santa Margherita

Calle del Magazen

Campiello dei Squelini

Palazzi Giustinian

Fondamenta dei Cereri

Fondamenta Rossa

Calle dei Ragusei

Campo Santa Margherita

Calle de la Vida

Ca' Bernardo

Ca' Rezzonico

Calle de Guardiani

Fondamenta Foscarini

4 Scuola dei Carmini

Scuola dei Varoteri

Palazzo Giustinian Rezzonico

2 Ca' Rezzonico

Calle del Socorso

Rio de la Scoazzera

Rio Terà Canal

Rio Terà Canal

Ponte dei Pugni

San Barnaba

Calle del Traghetto

Rio San Barnaba

Palazzo Ariani

Fondamenta Briati

3 Santa Maria dei Carmini

Palazzo Zenobio

1 Ponte dei Pugni

5 Fond. de la Squero

San Barnaba

Fond. Gherardini

1 3 4

Rio Malpaga

Calle dei Cercheri

Palazzo Loredan

Angelo Raffaele

Fondamenta Briati

C. de la Madalena

C. San Sebastian

Calle Longa de San Barnaba

2 Fond. Lombardo

Fond. Toletta

Rio de la Toletta

DORSODURO

Campo de l'Angelo Raffaele

Campo San Sebastian

C. de l'Avogaria

Rie Marzso

Rio Terà Ognisanti

C. de Nova

C. dei Frati

San Sebastiano

Calle Balastro

Fondamenta de Ognisanti

Rio de Ognisanti

C. d. Teletta

Fond. Priuli

Terminal crociere San Basilio

Salizada San Basegio

Campo de San Basegio

C. de la Chiesa

Fond. de le Eremite

Fondamenta di Borgo

San Trovaso

C. del Pistor

6

Santa Maria del Rosario (Gesuati)

S. Basilio

Scuola dei Luganegheri

C. dei Preti

Campiello della Masena

C. Corfellotti

Fondamenta Zattere al Ponte Longo

Fond. Trevisan

Fond. Bonlini

Campo San Trovaso

Squero San Trovaso

7

Fond. Nani

C. Larga Nani

Santa Maria della Visitazione

Fondamenta

Mulino Stucky

Canale della Giudecca

Fondamenta San Biagio

LA GIUDECCA

Zattere

B   C   D   E

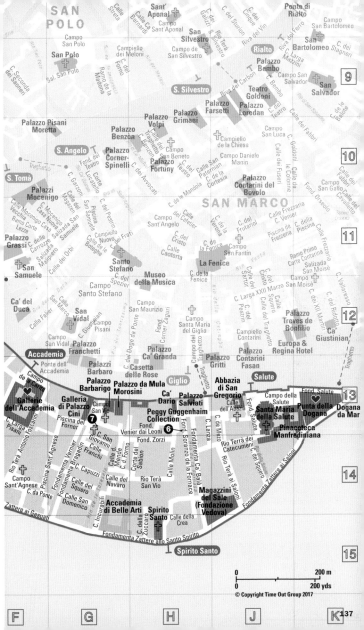

From here, a busy route leads towards the Accademia.

On the campo of the same name is the church of **San Trovaso**; backing on to the campo is a picturesque *squero*, one of the few remaining yards where gondolas are made (*see p150* Gondolas).

Sights & museums

Ca' Rezzonico

(Museo del Settecento Veneziano) *Dorsoduro 3136, fondamenta Rezzonico (041 241 0100, www. visitmuve.it). Vaporetto Ca' Rezzonico.* **Open** *10am-6pm Mon, Wed-Sun.* **Admission** *€10; €7.50 reductions (see also p21 Visitor Passes).* **Map** *p136 E11.*
The Museum of 18th-century Venice is a gleaming (if somewhat chilly) showcase for the art of the Republic's twilight years. For most visitors, the paintings on display here will appear less impressive than the *palazzo* itself, an imposing Grand Canal affair designed by Baldassare Longhena for the Bon family in 1667. Bon ambitions exceeded Bon means, and the unfinished palace was sold on to the Rezzonico family – rich Genoese bankers who bought their way into Venice's nobility. The Rezzonicos' bid for stardom was crowned in 1758 by two events: the election of Carlo Rezzonico as Pope Clement XIII, and the marriage of Ludovico Rezzonico into one of Venice's oldest noble families, the Savorgnan.

Giambattista Tiepolo was called upon to celebrate the marriage on the ceiling of the Sala del Trono; he replied with a composition so playful it's easy to forget that it's all about purchasing rank and power. Together with the Murano chandeliers and intricately carved furniture by Andrea Brustolon, they provide an accurate record of the lifestyles of the rich and famous.

A staircase at the far end of the entrance hall leads to the 'Mezzanino Browning', where the poet Robert Browning died in 1889.

San Pantalon

Dorsoduro, campo San Pantalon (041 523 5893). Vaporetto San Tomà. **Open** *10am-noon, 1-3pm Mon-Sat.* **Map** *p136 E10.*
The dedicatee of this church is St Pantaleon, a court physician to Emperor Galerius, who was arrested, tortured and finally beheaded during Diocletian's persecution of the Christians in the late third century. The saint's story is depicted inside the church in an extraordinary ceiling painting – a huge illusionist work, painted on 40 canvases, by the Cecil B De Mille of the 17th century, Gian Antonio Fumiani. It took him 24 years to complete the task (1680-1704), and at the end of it all he fell with choreographic grace from the scaffolding to his death. Veronese depicts the saint in less melodramatic fashion in the second chapel on the right, in what is possibly his last work, *St Pantaleon Healing a Child*.

Scuola dei Carmini

Dorsoduro 2617, campo dei Carmini (041 528 9420, www. scuolagrandecarmini.it). Vaporetto Ca' Rezzonico or San Basilio. **Open** *11am-5pm daily.* **Admission** *€5; €4 reductions. No cards.* **Map** *p136 D11.*
Begun in 1670 to plans by Baldassare Longhena, the building housing this *scuola* (*see p127* Scuole Stories) run by the Carmelite order was spared the Napoleonic lootings that dispersed the fittings of most other *scuole*. So we have a good idea of what an early 18th-century Venetian confraternity HQ must have looked like, from the elaborate Sante Piatti altarpiece to the staircase with its excrescence of gilded cherubs.

In the main hall of the first floor is one of the most impressive of Giambattista Tiepolo's Venetian ceilings: the airy panels were painted from 1740 to 1743.

Restaurants

Ai Artisti €€

Dorsoduro 1169A, fondamenta della Toletta (041 523 8944, www. enotecaartisti.com). Vaporetto Accademia or Ca' Rezzonico. Meals served 12.45-2.30pm, 7-11pm Mon-Sat. Closed 3wks Dec-Jan. Map p136 E12 ❷ *Italian*

This tiny *trattoria* expands out on to the pretty canal-side walk in the warmer months, which is good because the demand is overwhelming: you are advised to book. In the kitchen, Francesca prepares everything from scratch, from a menu that changes day by day depending on what's good in the market. On Monday, meat dominates because the boats don't go out on Sunday; other days, you might find delicious prawn-stuffed squid, or a fillet of John Dory lightly pan-fried with artichokes. If prices seem to be on the high-ish side, bear in mind that main courses have vegetables included (unusual in Italy).

La Bitta €€

Dorsoduro 2753A, calle lunga San Barnaba (041 523 0531). Vaporetto Ca' Rezzonico. Meals served 6.30-10.30pm Mon-Sat. Map p136 E12 ❸ *Italian*

La Bitta, a warm and rustic *osteria* with a small courtyard, stands out by having virtually no fish on the menu. Dishes like *straccetti di pollo ai finferli* (chicken strips with chanterelle mushrooms) or *oca in umido* (stewed goose) make a welcome change. There's also a good selection of cheeses, served with honey or chutney, and intelligent by-the-glass wine options.

❤ ### Orient Experience €€

Dorsoduro 2920, campo Santa Margherita (041520 0217). Vaporetto Ca' Rezzonico. Open 11am-11.30pm daily. Map p136 D11 ❹ *Middle Eastern*

A welcome break from Venice-as-usual for both the palate and the wallet. This fast-expanding ethnic joint, which today counts a takeaway and restaurant in Santa Margherita and a second sit-down branch in Cannaregio, offers up a choice of dishes from the Middle East and Central Asia (falafel, rice recipes from Syria and Iran, spicy vegetable and meat sides) that channel the culinary heritage of its genial founders and staff.

Cafés, bars & gelaterie

Caffè Rosso

Dorsoduro 2963, campo Santa Margherita (041 528 7998, www. cafferosso.it). Vaporetto Ca' Rezzonico. Open 7am-1am Mon-Sat. No cards. Map p136 D11 ❶

Laid back and eclectic, the campo's oldest bar says 'Caffè' over the door, but it's universally known as 'Caffè Rosso' — perhaps for the decor, or for the political leanings of its boho-chic clientele. It attracts a mixed crowd of all ages who spill out from its single room to sip a spritz in the campo or to choose from the impressive wine list.

❤ ### Estro Vino e Cucina

Dorsoduro 3778, calle Crosera (041 476 4914, www.estrovenezia.com), Vaporetto San Tomà. Open noon-2.30pm, 7-10.30pm Wed-Mon. Map p136 E10 ❷

This bustling *bacaro*, founded in 2014 by two brothers from Murano, offers up a refreshing blend of traditional and contemporary Venetian styles, and is a favourite with young gourmands. Perch at the high wooden tables (crafted from

Estro Vino e Cucina p139

lagoon marker-posts) by the bar and sample a selection of tasty snacks and quality wines from small Italian producers, or stay for a sit-down meal that gives a novel, unorthodox take on local recipes.

Malvasia all'Adriatico Mar
Dorsoduro 3771, calle Crosera (041 476 4322), Vaporetto San Tomà. **Open** *10am-10pm Tue-Sun, 5-10pm Mon.* **Map** *p136 E10* ❸
For a different take on the spritz, as well as a good selection of wines, duck into this friendly, nautically themed watering hole, which has rejected 'industrial' brands Aperol and Campari in favour of Rosso and Rabarbaro (rhubarb) Nardini, from the historic distillery in Bassano. A door opposite the bar opens onto a small jetty providing cool and picturesque relief in warmer months, if you're lucky enough to bag a spot.

Osteria ai Pugni
Dorsoduro 2836, fondamenta Gherardini (346 960 7785 mobile, www.osteriaaipugni.com). Vaporetto Ca' Rezzonico. **Open** *8am-12.30am Mon-Sat, 11am-11pm Sun.* **No cards.** **Map** *p136 D12* ❹
There's always a warm welcome at this friendly bar at the foot of the Pugni Bridge, where locals and students pile in from breakfast

time until late at night for time-appropriate beverages and snacks. As the day wears on, a selection of good sandwiches and *cicheti* appears on the counter.

Tonolo
Dorsoduro 3764, calle San Pantalon (041 523 7209). Vaporetto San Tomà. **Open** *7.45am-8pm Tue-Sat; 7.45am-1pm Sun. Closed Aug.* **No cards.** **Map** *p136 E10* ❺
This Venice institution has been operating in the same spot since 1953. The coffee is exceptional. On Sundays, the place fills up with locals buying sweet offerings to take to lunch – don't be shy about asserting your rights or you may never get served. All the delectable pastries come in miniature sizes to make sampling a little bit easier.

Shops & services

Annelie
Dorsoduro 2748, calle lunga San Barnaba (041 520 3277). Vaporetto Ca' Rezzonico. **Open** *9.30am-12.30pm, 4-7pm Mon-Sat.* **Map** *p136 E12* ❶ *Homewares/ children's*
A delightful shop run by a delightful lady who has a beautiful selection of sheets, tablecloths, curtains, shirts and baby clothes,

either fully embroidered or with lace detailing. Antique lace is also stocked.

Ca' Macana

Dorsoduro 3172, calle delle Botteghe (041 520 3229, www.camacana. com). Vaporetto Ca' Rezzonico. **Open** *10am-7.30pm daily.* **Map** *p136 E11* ❷ *Carnival masks*
This workshop packed with traditional papier-mâché masks from the commedia dell'arte theatre tradition makes all its own products, unlike so many of the carbon-copy shops that plague the city. This is where Stanley Kubrick came to stock up when making *Eyes Wide Shut*.

❤ Libreria Marco Polo

Dorsoduro 2899, rio Terà Canal (041 822 4843, www. libreriamarcopolo.com). Vaporetto Ca' Rezzonico. **Open** *10am-10pm Mon-Sat; 11am-8pm Sun.* **Map** *p136 D11* ❸ *Books & music*
Claudio Moretti's quirky bookshop is a labour of love. Selling books for adults and children from independent publishers in Italian, English and other languages, it moved to the area a few years ago and has benefited from the resulting influx of culture-hungry locals and university students. There are book presentations, meetings with writers and events of all kinds.

Madera

Dorsoduro 2762, campo San Barnaba (041 522 4181, www. maderavenezia.it). Vaporetto Ca' Rezzonico. **Open** *10am-1pm, 3.30-7.30pm Tue-Sat.* **Map** *p136 E12* ❹ *Homewares/accessories*
Fusing minimalist design with traditional techniques, the young architect and craftswoman behind Madera creates unique objects in wood. She also sells exceptional lamps, ceramics, jewellery and textiles by other craftspeople, many of them Venice-based. Some of the homeware is now just down the road in calle Lunga San Barnaba (2729).

❤ Signor Blum

Dorsoduro 2840, campo San Barnaba (041 522 6367, www. signorblum.com). Vaporetto Ca' Rezzonico. **Open** *9.45am-1.30pm, 2.45-7.15pm daily.* **Map** *p136 E12* ❺ *Jigsaw puzzles*
Mr Blum's colourful handmade wooden puzzles of Venetian *palazzi*, gondolas and animals make great gifts for children and adults alike. **Other locations** Castello 5786B, calle del Mondo Nuovo (041 523 3056); Cannaregio 1370, rio terà San Leonardo (041 719 695).

Entertainment

❤ Venice Jazz Club

Dorsoduro 3102, fondamenta dei Pugni (340 150 4985, www. venicejazzclub.com). Vaporetto Ca' Rezzonico. **Open** *7pm-2am Mon-Wed, Fri, Sat.* **Admission** *€20 incl first drink.* **Map** *p104 D12* ❶ *Live music*
The intimate setting and nightly live music make this club, just behind campo Santa Margherita, a perfect place for a night out for fans of high-quality jazz. Concerts start at 9pm, and some food is served.

East

The eastern reaches of Dorsoduro, from the rio di San Trovaso, past the **Gallerie dell'Accademia** and the **Salute** to the punta della Dogana, is an area of elegant, artsy prosperity. Ezra Pound spent his last years in a small house near the Zattere, and Peggy Guggenheim hosted her collection of modern art in her truncated palazzo on the Grand Canal (now the **Peggy Guggenheim Collection**). Today, artists use the vast spaces of the old warehouses on the Zattere as studios, and on Sunday mornings, British expats home in on the Anglican church of St George on campo San Vio.

It is a district of quiet canals and cosy *campielli*. But all that money has driven out the locals: nowhere in Venice are you further from a simple *alimentari* (grocery store).

The colossal magnificence of Longhena's church of **Santa Maria della Salute** brings the residential area to an end. Beyond is the old Dogana da Mar (Customs House). Debate about redeploying this empty space raged for years, but with the **Punta Della Dogana** gallery open and building work over, it is once again possible to stroll around the *punta*, with its spectacular view across the water towards St Mark's.

South from punta della Dogana, the mile-long stretch of **Le Zattere**, Venice's finest promenade after the riva degli Schiavoni, leads westwards to the San Nicolò zone. This long promenade bordering the Giudecca Canal is named after the *zattere* (rafts) that used to moor here.

The eastern end is usually quiet, with the occasional flurry of activity around the rowing clubs now occupying the 14th-century salt warehouses, one of which hosts the **Fondazione Vedova** gallery (Dorsoduro 50, fondamenta zattere ai Saloni, 041 522 6626, www.fondazionevedova.org).

Westward from these are the new premises of the **Accademia di Belle Arti**, the church of **Spirito Santo** and the long 16th-century façade of the grimly named **Ospedale degli Incurabili**.

The liveliest part of the Zattere is around the church of **I Gesuati**. Venetians flock here at weekends and on warm evenings to savour ice-cream or sip drinks at canalside tables.

Sights & museums

Galleria Palazzo Cini
Dorsoduro 864, piscina del Forner (041 2710217, www.palazzocini. it). Vaporetto Accademia. **Open** *Apr-Nov 11am-7pm Mon, Wed-Sun. Closed Dec-Mar.* **Admission** *€10; €8 reductions.* **Map** *p136 G13.* This lovely house-turned-museum showcases a stunning private collection of Ferrarese and Tuscan art, assembled by industrialist Vittorio Cini. Cini is better known for his restoration of the monastic complex on the island of San Giorgio Maggiore (*see p155*) as a cultural foundation, but this smaller project is well worth a visit.

Among the pieces on display are a few gems, including a collection of Tuscan primitives, the unfinished Pontormo double *Portrait of Two Friends* (on the first floor) and Dosso Dossi's *Allegorical Scene* (on the second), a vivacious character study from the D'Este Palace in Ferrara.

As you explore, take time to appreciate the oval spiral staircase and the dining room, designed by architect Tommaso Buzzi.

💙 Peggy Guggenheim Collection

Dorsoduro 701, fondamenta Venier dei Leoni (041 240 5411, www.guggenheim-venice.it). Vaporetto Accademia or Salute. **Open** *10am-6pm Mon, Wed-Sun.* **Admission** *€15; €9-€13 reductions.* **Map** *p136 H13.*

This remarkable establishment, tucked behind a high wall off a quiet street (but with a Grand Canal frontage), is the third most visited museum in the city. It was founded by one of Venice's most colourful expat residents, Peggy Guggenheim.

She turned up in the lagoon city in 1949 looking for a home for her already sizeable art collection. A short-sighted curator at the Tate Gallery in London had described her growing pile of surrealist and modernist works as 'non-art'. Venice, still struggling to win back the tourists after World War II, was less finicky, and Peggy found a perfect, eccentric base in Palazzo Venier dei Leoni, a truncated 18th-century Grand Canal *palazzo*.

There are big European names in her art collection, including Picasso, Duchamp, Brancusi, Giacometti and Max Ernst, plus a few Americans such as Calder and Jackson Pollock. Highlights include the beautifully enigmatic *Empire of Light* by Magritte and Giacometti's disturbing *Woman with Her Throat Cut*. The flamboyant *Attirement of the Bride*, by Peggy's husband, Max Ernst, often turns up as a Carnevale costume. But perhaps the most startling exhibit of all is the rider of Marino Marini's *Angel of the City* out on the Grand Canal terrace, who thrusts his manhood towards passing vaporetti. (Never the shrinking wallflower, Peggy took delight in unscrewing the member and pressing it on young men she fancied.) The gallery has a pleasant garden and café.

💗 Gallerie dell'Accademia

Dorsoduro 1050, campo Carità (041 520 0345, www.gallerieaccademia. org). Vaporetto Accademia. **Open** *8.15am-2pm Mon; 8.15am-7.15pm Tue-Sun.* **Admission** *€12; €6 reductions; under-18s free; price varies for special exhibitions. Audio guide €6.* **Map** *p136 F13.*

The Accademia is the essential one-stop shop for Venetian painting, and one of the world's greatest art treasure houses. It was Napoleon who made the collection possible: first, by suppressing hundreds of churches, convents and religious guilds, confiscating their artworks for the greater good of the state; and second, by moving the city's Accademia di Belle Arti art school here, with the mandate both to train students and to act as a gallery and storeroom for all the evicted artworks, which were originally displayed as models for pupils to aspire to. The art school moved to a new site on the nearby Zattere in 2004, leaving the freed-up space for a long-awaited gallery extension that opened in 2015. The Accademia galleries now incorporate parts of the church and Scuola della Carità (the oldest of the Venetian *scuole*, founded in the 13th century) and the 12th-century monastery of the Lateran Canons, which was remodelled by Andrea Palladio. (His superb oval staircase is now on view.) Note that the arrangement of art in the galleries may alter as restoration work continues.

The collection is arranged roughly chronologically, with the exception of the 15th- and 16th-century works in rooms 19-24 at the end. It opens with 14th- and 15th-century devotional works by Paolo Veneziano and others – stiff figures against gold backdrops in the Byzantine tradition. This room was the main hall of the *scuola grande*: note the original ceiling of gilded cherubim. Rooms 2 and 3 have devotional paintings and altarpieces by Carpaccio, Cima da Conegliano and Giovanni Bellini (a fine *Enthroned Madonna with Six Saints*).

In Room 4 are works by Bellini and Giorgione's *Old Woman*, while room 5 exhibits works from the museum's archives. In Room 6, two of the greats of 16th-century Venetian painting – Tintoretto and Veronese – are first encountered. But the battle of the giants gets under way in earnest in Room 10, where they are joined by Titian. Tintoretto's ghostly chiaroscuro *Transport of the Body of St Mark* vies for attention with Titian's moving *Pietà* – his last painting – and Veronese's huge *Christ in the House of Levi*.

Room 11 covers two centuries, with canvases by Tintoretto (the exquisite *Madonna dei Camerlenghi*), Bernardo Strozzi and Tiepolo. The series of rooms beyond brings the plot up to the 18th century, with all the old favourites: Canaletto, Guardi, Longhi and soft-focus, bewigged portraits by female superstar Rosalba Carriera.

Rooms 19 and 20 take us back to the 15th century; the latter has the rich *Miracle of the Relic of the Cross* cycle, a collaborative effort by Gentile Bellini, Carpaccio and others, which is packed with telling social details; there's even a black gondolier in Carpaccio's *Miracle of the Cross at the Rialto*.

An even more satisfying cycle has Room 21 to itself (closed for restoration during 2017). Carpaccio's *Life of St Ursula* (1490-95) tells the story of the legendary Breton princess who embarked on a pilgrimage to Rome with her betrothed so that he could be baptised into the true faith. All went swimmingly until Ursula and all the 11,000 virgins accompanying her were massacred by the Huns in Cologne (the initial 'M' – for martyr – used in one account of the affair caused the multiplication of the number of accompanying maidens from 11 to 11,000, M being the Roman numeral for 1,000). More than the ropey legend, it's the architecture, the ships and the pageantry in these meticulous paintings that grab the attention. Perhaps most striking, amid all the closely thronged, action-packed scenes, is the rapt stillness and solitude of *The Dream of St Ursula*.

Room 23 is the former church of Santa Maria della Carità: here are Giorgione's *The Tempest*, devotional works by Vivarini, the Bellinis and others.

Room 24 – the Albergo room (or secretariat) of the former *scuola* – contains the only work in the whole gallery that is in its original site: Titian's magnificent *Presentation of the Virgin*.

Christ in the House of Levi (Paolo Veronese, 1573)

I Gesuati

Dorsoduro, fondamenta Zattere ai Gesuati (041 275 0642, www.chorusvenezia.org). Vaporetto Zattere. **Open** *10.30am-4.30pm Mon-Sat.* **Admission** *€3 (or Chorus; see p23). No cards.* **Map** *p136 F14.*

This church is officially Santa Maria del Rosario, but it is always known as the Gesuati, after the minor religious order that owned the previous church here. The order merged with the Dominicans – the present owners – in 1668. I Gesuati is a great piece of teamwork by a trio of remarkable rococo artists: architect Giorgio Massari, painter Giambattista Tiepolo and sculptor Giovanni Morlaiter.

The façade deliberately reflects the Palladian church of the Redentore opposite, but the splendidly posturing statues give it that typically 18th-century touch of histrionic flamboyance. Plenty more theatrical sculpture is to be found inside the church, all by Morlaiter. Above is a magnificent ceiling by Tiepolo, with three frescoes on Dominican themes. These works reintroduced frescoes to Venetian art after two centuries of canvas ceiling paintings.

There is another brightly coloured Tiepolo on the first altar on the right, *The Virgin and Child with Saints Rosa, Catherine and Agnes*. Tiepolo here plays with optical effects, allowing St Rosa's habit to tumble out of the frame.

♥ Santa Maria della Salute

Dorsoduro, campo della Salute (041 274 3928, www.basilicasalute.it). Vaporetto Salute. **Open** *9.30am-noon, 3-5.30pm daily.* **Admission** *Church free. Sacristy €4. No cards.* **Map** *p136 J13.*

This magnificent Baroque church, queening it over the entrance to the Grand Canal, is almost as recognisable an image of Venice as St Mark's or the Rialto Bridge.

It was built between 1631 and 1681 in thanksgiving for the end of Venice's last bout of plague, which had wiped out at least a third of the population in 1630. The church is dedicated to the Madonna, as protector of the city. Every year on 21 November (*see p60*), a processions from San Marco makes it way across a specially erected pontoon bridge to the church.

The terms of the architectural competition won by 26-year-old Baldassare Longhena presented a serious challenge, which beat some of the best architects of the day. The church was to be colossal but inexpensive; the whole structure was to be visually clear on entrance, with an unimpeded view of the high altar, and the ambulatory and side altars coming into sight only as one approached the chancel; the light was to be evenly distributed; and the whole building should *creare una bella figura* – show itself off to good effect.

Longhena succeeded brilliantly in satisfying all of these requisites – particularly the last and most Venetian of them.

The architect said he chose the circular shape with the reverent aim of offering a crown to the Madonna as she stands on the lantern above the cupola. Beneath her, on the great scroll-brackets around the cupola, stand statues of the Apostles – the 12 stars in her crown. This Marian symbolism continues inside the church, where in the centre of the mosaic floor, amid a circle of roses, is an inscription, *Unde origo inde salus* (from the origin comes salvation) – a reference to the legendary birth of Venice under the Virgin's protection.

The three chapels on the right have paintings by Luca Giordano, a prolific Neapolitan painter. On the opposite side is a clumsily restored *Pentecost*, by

💙 Punta della Dogana

*Dorsoduro 2, campo della Salute
(041 200 1057, www.palazzograssi.
it). Vaporetto Salute.* **Open** *10am-
7pm Mon, Wed-Sun.* **Admission**
*€18; €15 reductions (Punta &
Palazzo Grassi; see p81).* **Map**
p136 K13.

Due to its strategic location
between San Marco, the Grand
Canal and the Giudecca Canal,
the Punta della Dogana served
as Venice's customs post from
the 15th century. The triangular
complex of warehouses, with the
distinctive Customs House tower
at its tip, was completed in the
late 17th century and remained in
use until the 1980s. The buildings
were left empty until 2007 when
French tycoon Francois Pinault
beat the Peggy Guggenheim
Collection (*see p143*) in a bid to

turn them into a contemporary art
gallery – much to the annoyance
of many Venetians who felt that
Pinault's outpost at Palazzo
Grassi (*see p81*) was more than
enough. Inaugurated in June 2009
after a remarkable makeover by
Japanese archistar Tadao Ando,
the Punta della Dogana gallery
masterfully mixes contemporary
architectural elements, such
as concrete floors, reinforced
steel and glass fixtures, with
the original stuccoes, exposed
brick walls and wooden beams of
the 17th-century buildings. The
gallery shows revolving themed
exhibitions based around Pinault's
own immense art collection and
has confirmed Venice's key place
on Europe's contemporary art
circuit. In 2017 it hosted a major
solo show by Damien Hirst.

DORSODURO

The Fate of a Banished Man (Damien Hirst)
at Punta della Dogana, 2017

Dome of Santa Maria della Salute

Titian, transferred here from the island monastery of Santo Spirito (demolished in 1656). The high altar has a dynamic sculptural group by Giusto Le Corte, the artist responsible (with assistants) for most of the statues inside and outside the church. In the midst of all this marble hubbub is a serene Byzantine icon of the *Madonna and Child*, brought from Crete in 1669 by Francesco Morosini, the Venetian commander later responsible for blowing up the Parthenon.

Sacristy

The best paintings are in the sacristy (open from 10am). Tintoretto's *Marriage at Cana* (1551) was described by Ruskin as 'perhaps the most perfect example which human art has produced of the utmost possible force and sharpness of shadow united with richness of local colour'. He also points out how

difficult it is to spot the bride and groom in the painting.

On the altar is a very early Titian of *Saints Mark, Sebastian, Roch, Cosmas and Damian*, saints who were all invoked for protection against the plague; the painting was done during the outbreak of 1509-14. Three later works by Titian (c1540-49) hang on the ceiling, violent Old Testament scenes also brought here from the church of Santo Spirito: *The Sacrifice of Abraham*, *David Killing Goliath* and *Cain and Abel*. These works established the conventions for all subsequent ceiling paintings in Venice: Titian chose an oblique viewpoint, as if observing the action from the bottom of a hill. More Old Testament turbulence can be seen in Salviati's *Saul Hurling a Spear at David* and Palma il Giovane's *Samson and Jonah*, in which the whale is represented mainly by a vast lolling rubbery tongue.

Cafés, bars & gelaterie

❤ Cantinone (già Schiavi)

Dorsoduro 992, fondamenta Nani (041 523 0034). Vaporetto Accademia or Zattere. **Open** *8am-8pm Mon-Sat.* **Map** *p136 F13* ⑥

Two generations of the Gastaldi family work in the Cantinone (also, confusingly, known as Il Bottegon) filling glasses, carting cases of wine, and preparing huge panini with mortadella or more delicate *crostini* with, for example, creamed pistachio or cream cheese with fish roe. Give yourself ample opportunity to select from the day's offerings by arriving before the crowds pour in at 1pm. When the bar itself is full, you'll be in good company on the bridge outside – an apt setting for the Venetian ritual of spritz and prosecco consumption.

Osteria al Squero

Dorsoduro 944, fondamenta Nani (335 600 7513 mobile). Vaporetto Zattere or Accademia. **Open** *11am-9.30pm Mon, Tue, Thur-Sun.* **No cards.** **Map** *p136 E14* ⑦

This simple, friendly *bacaro*, located opposite one of Venice's very few remaining gondola building/repairing yards (*squero, see p150* Gondolas), looks as if it has been here since time immemorial, but that's an illusion. The former teachers who run the place, however, have perfectly captured the spirit of the traditional Venetian drinking den, adding only some truly gourmet *cicheti* at very reasonable prices. There are no tables, just benches and perching places; on fine days, much of the clientele will be standing out on the *fondamenta*, gazing across at the *squero*.

Shops & services

Le Forcole di Saverio Pastor

Dorsoduro 341, fondamenta Soranzo de la Fornace (041 522 5699, www.forcole.com). Vaporetto Salute. **Open** *8am-6pm Mon-Fri.* **Map** *p136 H13* ⑥ *Oar-makers/gifts*

This is the place to come when you need a new *forcola* (walnut-wood rests) or pair of oars for your favourite gondola. Saverio Pastor is one of only three recognised *marangon* (oar-makers) in Venice; he specialises in making the elaborate *forcole* that are the symbols of the gondolier's trade. There are also bookmarks, postcards and some books (in English) on Venetian boatworks.

Marina & Susanna Sent

Dorsoduro 669 & 681, campo san Vio (041 520 8136, www. marinaesusannasent.com). Vaporetto Accademia. **Open** *10am-6pm daily.* **Map** *p136 G13* ⑦ *Accessories*

Some of Venice's finest contemporary glass jewellery is created by the Sent sisters. There's also a good selection of the work of the contemporary design house Arcade. **Other locations** San Marco 2090, ponte San Mosie (041 520 4014); Murano, fondamenta Serenella 20 (041 527 4665).

Campo Santa Margherita

💜 Gondolas

The Venetian style of rowing, in which the rower stands up, facing in the direction of travel, is known as *voga alla veneta*. Venetians find it difficult to understand why anybody would row any other way: the standing position allows one to put all one's force behind the stroke; facing forwards is also a major aid to navigation.

There are various types of *voga alla veneta*: team rowing is one (*see p59* Rowing regattas); the solo, cross-handed, two-oar method known as *voga alla valesana* is another. But the most famous type is the *voga ad un solo remo*, as practised by Venetian gondoliers. It may look effortless, but the single-oar scull is one of the most difficult rowing strokes of all.

Most other forms of rowing rely on pairs of oars, whose equal and opposite forces keep the boat travelling in a straight line. The gondolier, on the other hand, only ever puts his oar in the water on the right side of the boat – where it rests in a *forcola*, an elaborate walnut-wood rowlock. Pushing on the oar has the obvious effect of making the gondola turn to the left. The trick consists in using the downstroke (*la stalìa*), during which the oar stays in the water, to correct the direction. It has been calculated that a gondolier

uses up no more energy rowing a half-ton, 65-foot gondola with three passengers than the average person expends in walking.

Such ingenious efficiency made the gondola the most effective form of transportation in Venice for centuries, although its shape and appearance have evolved considerably over time. Originally an ornately gilded and covered craft, the classic gondola of today is painted entirely black and is exposed to the elements. A gondola comprises about 280 pieces of wood made from eight types of tree. The bottom is flat to allow it to navigate shallow waters. The Squero di San Trovaso in Dorsoduro is one of very few active gondola *squeri* or shipyards that survive in Venice today.

While gondola rides remain popular among tourists, they can be underwhelming for the price (*see p176* Getting Around). A more economical and authentic alternative exists in the form of *traghetti*, slightly larger craft manned by two gondoliers, that are used to ferry pedestrians across the Grand Canal.

If you fancy trying *voga alla veneta* for yourself, you can sign up for a lesson, combined with a tour, with www.veniceonboard.it and www.rowvenice.org.

DORSODURO

Burano

Islands of the Lagoon

The Venetian lagoon covers some 520 square kilometres (200 square miles) and has 34 islands. Of these, Giudecca and San Giorgio are considered part of the city, while Murano and Burano attract visitors in their droves. However, other islands, such as Sant'Erasmo, are always bucolically tranquil and almost entirely tourist-free. And, even at the busiest times, the views from the vaporetto of the lagoon's empty reaches are enough to soothe the most frayed of nerves. This wild, fragile environment is where Venetians take refuge from the tourist hordes, escaping by boat to picnic, fish, hunt or row.

Iconic sights

Torcello (*p161*) was the first settlement on the lagoon. The view from San Giorgio Maggiore's bell tower is unique (*p155*).

Best shopping experiences

Fortuny Tessuti Artistici (*p153*) is an Aladdin's cave of fabulous fabrics. For all your glassy needs, head to Murano (*p159*).

Best food with a view

For aperitivo head to the Skyline bar (*p153*) in Giudecca; for a meal stroll a bit eastward to Alla Palanca (*p153*).

Best entertainment

The Venice Film Festival (*p44*) is where movies meet glamour in Venice.

Best gourmet restaurants

For luxury dining in the lagoon there's Venissa (*p162*) on the island of Mazzorbo, and La Favorita (*p156*) on the Lido.

Best places to avoid the crowds

Giudecca (*p152*), San Lazzaro degli Armeni (*p157*) and Sant'Erasmo (*p162*) each offer respite from the bustle of central Venice.

La Giudecca

The Giudecca was once known as 'Spinalonga', from an imagined resemblance to a fish skeleton (*spina* means fish bone). Some claim that the present name derives from an early community of Jews; others cite the fact that the island was a place of exile for troublesome nobles, who had been *giudicati*, 'judged'. The exile was sometimes self-chosen, however, as people used the islands as a place of rural retreat: Michelangelo, when exiled from Florence in 1529, chose to mope here.

Once a place of flourishing monasteries and lush gardens, the island is less impressive today. Its nature changed in the 19th century when city authorities began converting abandoned religious houses into factories and prisons. The factories have almost all closed down, and many of the buildings have been converted into new residential complexes. The greatest transformation has been that of the **Molino Stucky**, the vast turreted and crenellated Teutonic flour mill, which closed in 1955. After decades of abandonment, it now hosts the Hilton Hotel with its rooftop Skyline Bar and swimming pool.

The *palazzi* along the northern *fondamenta* enjoy a splendid view of Venice and attract well-heeled outsiders and artists.

The main sights of the Giudecca are all on this northern *fondamenta*. **Santa Eufemia**, with its charming mix of styles ranging from the 11th to the 18th century, and the Palladian church of **Le Zitelle** ('the spinsters': the convent ran a hospice for poor girls who were trained as lace-makers) are both nearly always closed. Several fine *palazzi* are here, as well as **Il Redentore**.

Near Le Zitelle is the neo-Gothic Casa De Maria, with its three large inverted-shield windows. The Bolognese painter Mario De Maria built it for himself from 1910 to 1913, and it's the only private palazzo to have the same patterned brickwork as the Doge's Palace. It's now home to *Tre Oci* (www.treoci.org), a space hosting photography exhibitions.

Sights & museums

Il Redentore

Giudecca, campo del Redentore (041 275 0462, www.chorusvenezia. org). Vaporetto Redentore. **Open** *10.30am-4pm Mon; 10.30am-4.30pm Tue-Sat.* **Admission** *€3 (or Chorus; see p23). No cards.*

Venice's first great plague church was commissioned to celebrate deliverance from the bout of 1575-77. An especially conspicuous site was chosen, one that could be approached in ceremonial fashion. The ceremony continues today, on the third Sunday of July (*see p58*), when a bridge of boats is built across the canal. Palladio designed an eye-catching building whose prominent dome appears to rise directly behind the Greek-temple façade, giving the illusion that the church is centrally planned.

The solemn, harmonious interior, with a single nave lit by large 'thermal' windows, testifies to Palladio's study of Roman baths. But the Capuchin monks, the austere order to whom the building was entrusted, were not pleased by its grandeur; Palladio attempted to mollify them by designing their choir stalls in a plain style.

Restaurants

♥ Alla Palanca €€

Giudecca 448, fondamenta del Ponte Piccolo (041 528 7719). Vaporetto Palanca. **Meals served** *noon-2.30pm Mon-Sat.* **No cards.**
Italian

One of the cheapest meals-with-a-view in Venice is on offer at this hugely friendly bar-*trattoria* on the Giudecca quay. It's a lunch-only place: the rest of the day (7am-9pm) it operates as a bar. Sit at a quayside table and order from a good-value menu that includes some surprisingly gourmet options:

tagliatelle with prawns and *funghi porcini*, or tuna steaks in balsamic and sesame. Finish up with a delicious chocolate mousse with candied fruit.

Altanella €€

Giudecca 268, calle delle Erbe (041 522 7780). Vaporetto Palanca or Redentore. **Meals served** *noon-2.30pm, 7-10.30pm Wed-Sun.*
Venetian

The leafy canal-side terrace of this family-run *trattoria* on the Giudecca (blissfully far from the tourist trail) is one of the best places for an al fresco meal in the city. The menu is typically Venetian, including traditional dishes such as *schie* (lagoon prawns) with polenta and gnocchi with cuttlefish, and the service is friendly and professional.

Cafés, bars & gelaterie

♥ Skyline Bar

Molino Stucky Hilton Hotel, Giudecca 810, campo San Biagio (041 272 3310, www. skylinebarvenice.com). Vaporetto Palanca. **Open** *5pm-1am Tue-Sun.*

It's a hike across to the Hilton Hotel in the former Molino Stucky flour mill (*see p152*) – and the bar is an expensive extravagance – but sit out on the rooftop terrace and survey Venice beneath you, beyond the grand sweep of the Giudecca Canal, and you may well feel that it's all worth it. Meals and light snacks are served but forget the expensive food and just savour the view, with a drink in hand.

Shops & services

♥ Fortuny Tessuti Artistici

Giudecca 805, fondamenta San Biagio (393 825 7651 mobile, www. fortuny.com). Vaporetto Palanca. **Open** *Apr-Oct 10am-1pm, 2-6pm Mon-Sat. Nov-Mar 10am-1pm, 2-6pm Mon-Fri. Fabric*

This wonderful factory showroom space glows with the exquisite colours and patterns of original Fortuny prints. At €427 a metre, you may not be tempted to buy, but it's worth the trip just to see it. The marvellous garden inside the factory can be visited by appointment. Check the Fortuny blog for occasional clearance sales and cut-price discontinued lines. *See p35* Shopping.

San Giorgio Maggiore

The island of San Giorgio, facing St Mark's across the lagoon, realised its true potential under set designer extraordinaire Andrea Palladio, whose church of **San Giorgio Maggiore** (*see p155*) is one of Venice's most recognisable landmarks. Known originally as the Isola dei Cipressi (Cypress Island), it soon became an important Benedictine monastery and centre of learning – a tradition that is carried on today by the **Fondazione Giorgio Cini**, which operates a research centre and craft school on the island.

Sights & museums

Fondazione Giorgio Cini: Benedictine Monastery & Le Stanze del Vetro
041 271 0229, www.cini.it. Vaporetto San Giorgio. **Monastery** *Guided tours every hour Sat, Sun; by appt only Mon-Fri (call 338 683 4601 mobile). Apr-Sept 10am-5pm Sat, Sun. Oct-Mar 10am-4pm Sat, Sun.* **Le Stanze del Vetro** *10am-7pm Mon, Tue, Thur-Sun during exhibitions.* **Admission** *Monastery €10; €8 reductions. Le Stanze del Vetro free. No cards.*
There has been a Benedictine monastery here since 982, when Doge Tribuno Memmo donated the island to the order. After the church acquired the remains of St Stephen

(1109), it was visited yearly by the doge on 26 December, the feast day of the saint. The city authorities often used the island as a luxury hotel for particularly prestigious visitors, such as Cosimo de' Medici in 1433. Cosimo had a magnificent library built here; it was destroyed in 1614, to make way for a more elaborate affair by Longhena.

The monastery was suppressed by the French in 1806 and did ignominious service as a barracks and ammunition store. In 1951, industrialist Vittorio Cini bought the island to set up a foundation in memory of his son, Giorgio, killed in a plane crash in 1949.

The Fondazione Giorgio Cini uses the monastery buildings for artistic and musical research, and a naval college. A portion of the complex was given back to the Benedictines. The foundation is open to the public at weekends for guided tours. There are two beautiful cloisters – one by Giovanni Buora (1516-40), the other by Palladio (1579) – an elegant library and staircase by Longhena (1641-53), and a magnificent refectory by Palladio (1561). The tour also includes the splendid garden, including the **Labirinto Borges**, a maze by the late British designer Randoll Coate, behind the monastery.

Beyond the monastery complex, **Le Stanze del Vetro** (www.lestanzedelvetro.org) is an exhibition space that hosts excellent shows of Venetian glass.

The Lido

The Lido is the northernmost of the two strips of land that separate the lagoon from the open sea. It is no longer the playground for wealthy aesthetes that fans of *Death in Venice* might come in search of. These days, Venice-by-the-sea is a placidly residential suburb, full of supermarkets and

♥ San Giorgio Maggiore

*041 522 7827, www.abbazia
sangiorgio.it. Vaporetto San
Giorgio. **Open** Apr-Oct 9am-7pm
daily. Nov-Mar 8.30am-6pm
daily. **Admission** Church free.
Campanile €6; €4 reductions.
No cards.*

This unique spot cried out for a
masterpiece. Palladio provided
it. This was his first complete
solo church; it demonstrates how
confident he was in his techniques
and objectives. With no hint of
influence from the city's Byzantine
tradition, Palladio here develops
the system of superimposed
temple fronts with which he had
experimented in the façade of San
Francesco della Vigna (*see p91*).
The interior maintains the same
relations between the orders
as the outside, with composite
half-columns supporting the
gallery, and lower Corinthian
pilasters supporting the arches.
The effect is of luminosity and
harmony, decoration being
confined to the altars.

There are several good works
of art inside. Over the first altar
is an *Adoration of the Shepherds*
by Jacopo Bassano. The altar to
the right of the high altar has a
*Madonna and Child with Nine
Saints* by Sebastiano Ricci.

On the side walls of the chancel
hang two vast compositions by
Tintoretto, a *Last Supper* and
the *Gathering of Manna*, painted
in the last years of his life. The
perspective of each work makes
it clear that they were intended
to be viewed from the altar
rails. Tintoretto's last painting,
a moving *Entombment*, hangs

in the Cappella dei Morti (open
for 11am Mass on Sundays in
winter only). It's possible that
Tintoretto included himself
among the mourners; he has been
identified as the bearded man
gazing intently at Christ.

In the left transept is a
painting by Jacopo and
Domenico Tintoretto of the
Martyrdom of St Stephen, placed
above the altar containing the
saint's remains (brought from
Constantinople in 1109).

From the left transept, follow
the signs to the campanile. Just
in front of the ticket office stands
the huge statue of an angel that
crowned the bell tower until
it was struck by lightning in
1993. To the left of the statue,
a corridor gives access to the
lift that takes you up to the bell
tower. The view from the top of
the tower is extraordinary: the
best possible panorama across
Venice and the lagoon.

cars. Now, the only moment when the place stirs to anything like its former vivacity is at the beginning of September for the **Venice film festival** (*p44*).

The Lido has few tourist sights as such. Only the church of **San Nicolò** on the riviera San Nicolò – founded in 1044 – can claim any great antiquity. It was here that the doge would come on Ascension Day after marrying Venice to the sea in the ceremony known as *lo sposalizio del mare* (*see p57* Festa e Regata della Sensa).

Fans of art nouveau and deco have plenty to look at on the Lido. On the Gran Viale there are two gems: the tiled façade of the Hungaria Hotel (no.28), and Villa Monplaisir at no.14, an art deco design from 1906. For full-blown turn-of-the-century exotica, though, it's hard to beat the Hotel Excelsior on lungomare Marconi, a neo-Moorish party-piece.

In the know
Battling the sea

For Venetians, the greatest threat has always been the open sea, and efforts have been devoted over the centuries to strengthening the natural defences offered by Pellestrina and the Lido. In the 18th century, the *murazzi* were created: an impressive barrier of stone and marble blocks all the way down both islands.

Nowadays, the threat is seen as coming from the three *bocche di porto* (the lagoon's openings to the sea) between the Lido and Cavallino, between the Lido and Pellestrina and between Pellestrina and Chioggia. Works to create the highly controversial mobile dyke system known as MOSE – which when fully operational should protect the lagoon from tides of up to three metres – have experienced a series of delays.

Restaurants

♥ La Favorita €€€
Via Francesco Duodo 33 (041 526 1626). Vaporetto Lido. **Meals served** *7.30-10.30pm Tue; 12.30-2.30pm, 7.30-10.30pm Wed-Sun. Closed Jan.* Venetian

With a lovely vine-shaded pergola for summer dining, this is an old-fashioned and reassuring sort of place that does textbook Venetian seafood classics like *spaghetti ai caparossoli* or *scampi in saor* (sweet-and-sour sauce), plus a few more audacious dishes such as pumpkin gnocchi with scorpion fish and radicchio. Service is professional, and the wine list has a fine selection of bottles from the north-east.

Entertainment

Multisala Astra
Via Corfù 9, Lido (041 526 5736). Vaporetto Lido. **No cards.** Cinema
During the Film Festival (*see p44*), the Astra is home to the Venice Film Meeting, which promotes locally made films.

Southern lagoon

The southern part of the lagoon – between Venice, the Lido and the mainland – has 14 small islands, a few of which are still inhabited, though most are out of bounds to tourists. The islands of San Servolo and San Lazzaro, however, are served by Vaporetto 20, and both are well worth visiting.

From the 18th century until 1978, San Servolo was Venice's mental hospital; it is now home to Venice International University and the **Museo del Manicomio di San Servolo** (San Servolo Asylum Museum; 041 524 0119). The museum is open for guided visits only (€3; minimum five people); booking is essential. It reveals the different ways in which mental illnesses have been treated over the years. After the tour, it is possible to visit the island's extensive and charming gardens.

A further five minutes on the no.20 will take you to the island of **San Lazzaro degli Armeni**.

A black-cloaked Armenian priest meets the boat and takes visitors on a detailed tour (041 526 0104, €6) of the Monastero Mechitarista. The tiny island has been a global point of reference for Armenia's Catholic minority, visited and supported by Armenians from Italy and abroad since 1717.

The tour takes in both the cloisters and the church, rebuilt after a fire in 1883. The museum and the modern library contain 40,000 priceless books and manuscripts, and a bizarre collection of gifts donated over the years.

The island's most famous student was Lord Byron, who used to row over three times a week to learn Armenian. He helped the monks to publish an Armenian-English grammar, which you can buy in the shop just inside the monastery gate.

Towards Murano

Halfway between Venice and Murano, **San Michele** is the island where tourists begin their lagoon visit. For many Venetians, it's the last stop: San Michele is the city's **cemetery** (open Apr-Sept 7.30am-6pm daily, Oct-Mar 7.30am-4.30pm daily). Early in the morning, *vaporetti* are packed with locals coming over to lay flowers. This is not a morbid spot, though: it is an elegant city of the dead, with more than one famous resident including Igor Stravinsky, Ezra Pound and Joseph Brodsky. There's a corner dedicated to the city's gondoliers, their tombs decorated with carvings and statues of gondolas.

Before visiting the cemetery, take a look at the church of **San Michele in Isola** (open 7.30am-12.15pm, 3-4pm daily). Designed by Mauro Codussi in the 1460s, this white building of Istrian stone was Venice's first Renaissance church.

After San Michele, the vaporetto continues to **Murano**, one of the larger and more populous islands.

Murano owes its fame to the decision taken in 1291 to transfer all of Venice's glass furnaces to the island because of a fear of fire in the main city. Over the following centuries, the island refined its particular craft. Its vases, chandeliers, mirrors and drinking vessels were shipped all over the world by Venice's great merchant fleet.

Nowadays, Murano looks close to being ruined by glass tourism. Dozens of 'guides' swoop on visitors as they pile off the ferry, to whisk them off on tours of furnaces. Even if you head off on your own, you'll find yourself on fondamenta dei Vetrai, full of shops selling glass knick-knacks, most of which are made far from Murano. But behind the tack, Murano remains a special place where centuries of glass-making techniques are still jealously preserved (*see p159*).

There's more to Murano, however, than glass. At the end of fondamenta dei Vetrai is the nondescript façade of the 14th-century parish church of **San Pietro Martire**, which holds important works of art including Bellini's impressive *Virgin and Child Enthroned with St Mark, St Augustine and Doge Agostino Barbarigo*. There is also a Tintoretto Baptism, two works by Veronese and his assistants and an ornate altarpiece by Salviati. The Palazzo Giustinian holds the

Museo del Vetro, the best place to learn about the history of glass. Just beyond this is Murano's greatest architectural treasure: the 12th-century basilica of **Santi Maria e Donato** a classic of the Veneto-Byzantine style. Inside is a richly coloured mosaic floor, laid down in 1140, and a Byzantine apse mosaic of the Virgin.

Sights & museums

Museo del Vetro
Fondamenta Giustinian 8 (041 527 4718, museovetro.visitmuve. it). Vaporetto Museo. **Open** *Nov-Mar 10am-5pm, Apr-Oct 10am-6pm daily.* **Admission** *€12; €9.50 reductions (see p184 Tourist information).*
Housed in beautiful Palazzo Giustinian, built in the late 17th century for the bishop of Torcello, the museum has a huge collection of Murano glass. As well as the famed chandeliers, which were first produced in the 18th century, there are ruby-red beakers, opaque lamps and delicate Venetian *perle* – glass beads that were used in trade and commerce all over the world from the time of Marco Polo. One of the earliest pieces is the 15th-century Barovier marriage cup, decorated with portraits of the bride and groom. In one room is a collection of 17th-century oil lamps in the shapes of animals, some of which are uncannily Disney-like. On the ground floor is a good collection of Roman glassware from near Zara on the Istrian peninsula.

Restaurants

Busa alla Torre €€
Murano, campo Santo Stefano 3 (041 739 662). Vaporetto Faro. **Meals served** *noon-3.30pm daily.* *Seafood*
In summer, tables spill out into a pretty square opposite the church

of San Pietro Martire. The service is deft and professional. The cuisine is reliable, no-frills seafood cooking, with good *primi* that might include ravioli filled with *branzino* (bream) in a spider-crab sauce, or tagliatelle with *canoce* (mantis shrimps). Note the lunch-only opening.

La Perla ai Bisatei €€
Murano, campo San Bernardo 1 (041 739 528). Vaporetto Museo or Venier. **Meals served** *noon-2.30pm Mon, Tue, Thur-Sun.* **No cards.** *Traditional Venetian*
La Perla is a rare gem in Venice: spit-and-sawdust, local, family-run, unreconstructed, with great mainly fishy dishes at sub-Venetian prices and an atmosphere that makes anyone who wanders this far into the heart of Murano feel like they've stumbled across a roomful of old friends. The traditional Venetian fare – both seafood and meat – is well prepared, served in generous helpings and very fresh.

Shops & services

Davide Penso
riva Longa 48 (041 527 4634, www. davidepenso.com). Vaporetto Museo. **Open** *9.30am-6pm daily.* *Glass jewellery*
Davide Penso makes and shows exquisite glass jewellery. His own creations are all one-off or limited edition pieces with designs drawn from nature: zebra-striped, mother-of-pearl or crocodile-skinned. The shop sometimes closes from 1.30 to 2.30pm.

Marina e Susanna Sent
Fondamenta Serenella 20 (041 527 4665, www.marinaesusannasent. com). Vaporetto Colonna. **Open** *10am-5pm Mon-Fri.* *Jewellery*
In the Sent sisters' recently expanded Murano workshop, you'll find clean, modern jewellery in glass, in interesting counterpoise

💜 Murano glass

Murano glass is divided into medium to large furnace-made pieces (blown glass, sculpture and lamps) and smaller pieces (beads and animals) fashioned from sticks of coloured glass in the heat of a gas jet. Once made, these objects may be engraved or patterned with silver, and multi-piece objects need assembling – all of which keeps much of Murano's population employed.

But unless you have your wits about you, you may never get beyond shops and warehouses packed with glass shipped from the Far East. Most hotel porters and concierges in Venice have agreements of some kind with these emporia: don't expect disinterested advice on where to go. Tourist-trade Murano outlets with 'authentic' furnaces being used by 'authentic' glass-blowers rarely sell the articles you'll see produced, whatever the salesmen

tell you. Glass shops range from the excellent to the downright rip-off: labels proclaiming '*vetro di Murano*' mean very little.

So, how do you go about making sure you get the real thing? Real Murano glass is fiendishly expensive. There's no such thing as a real €30 vase, or a genuine €5 wine glass... If you want genuine without paying much for it, you'll have to resort to the odd glass bead. Moreover, the best workshops don't allow tourists in to gawp, though sometimes you can peer through an open front gate. And, occasionally, they'll invite you in if you really intend to purchase.

In the outlets listed in our Towards Murano Shops & services section (*see p158*) you'll find fine examples of the real thing. More great glass can be found at **L'Isola – Carlo Moretti** (*see p83*) and **Vittorio Costantini** (*see p116*).

Murano glass

ISLANDS OF THE LAGOON

to innovative jewellery in other materials, including wood, coral, paper and rubber.

Seguso Viro

Fondamenta Venier 29 (041 527 4255, www. segusoviro.com). Vaporetto Museo or Venier. **Open** *11am-4pm Mon-Sat. Glass*
Giampaolo Seguso comes from a long line of Venetian glass-makers. His modern blown glass pieces are enhanced by experiments working around Murano traditions.

Venini

Fondamenta Vetrai 47 (041 273 7204, www.venini.com). Vaporetto Colonna. **Open** *9.30am-5.30pm Mon-Sat. Glass*
Venini was the biggest name in Murano glass for much of the 20th century, and remains in the forefront of the industry. Classic designs are joined by more innovative pieces, including a selection designed by major international glass artists.

In the know
Building Venice

Beneath the Venetian lagoon is a layer of compacted clay called *caranto*, the remains of the ancient Venetian plain that subsided aeons ago. On top of this firm base are silt deposits that vary in depth – from very shallow by the mainland to many metres deep out by the Adriatic.

As the builders of this most unlikely of cities were soon to realise, nothing of any size would stay vertical unless it was standing firmly on the caranto. So great trunks of larch and oak trees were driven down through the mud, to bear the weight of what would then be built above. Lack of oxygen in the clay saved the wood from decomposition, turning the stakes as hard as rock. As you walk through Venice's *calli*, you are, in effect, striding over a petrified forest.

Burano & around

Mazzorbo, the long island next to Burano, is a haven of peace, rarely visited by tourists. It is worth getting off here just for the sake of the quiet walk along the canal and then across the long wooden bridge that connects Mazzorbo to Burano. The view from the bridge across the lagoon to Venice is stunning.

Burano is picturesque in the extreme, a magnet for tourists armed with cameras. The street leading from the main quay throbs with souvenir shops selling lace, lace and more lace – much of it machine-made in Asia. Lace was first produced in Burano in the 15th century, originally by nuns, and then by fishermen's wives and daughters. Today, most work is done on commission.

It was in Burano that Carnevale (*see p56*) was revived in the 1970s; the modest celebrations here are still far more authentically joyful than the antics of masked tourists cramming piazza San Marco.

The busy main square of Burano is named after the island's most famous son, Baldassare Galuppi, a 17th-century composer who collaborated with Carlo Goldoni on a number of operas. Across from the lace museum is the church of San Martino (open 8am-noon, 3-7pm daily), containing an early Tiepolo *Crucifixion*. From behind the church, there is a view across the lagoon to the idyllic monastery island of **San Franceso del Deserto**. The island, with its 4,000 cypress trees, is inhabited by a small community of Franciscan monks. Getting there can be a challenge. If you take the water taxi from Burano, expect to pay at least €60 for the return ride. Individuals or smaller groups should call the Laguna Fla boat hire service (347 992 2959, mobile), which charges €10 per person return (no credit cards).

💜 Torcello

This sprawling, marshy island is where the history of Venice began. Torcello today is a picturesquely unkempt place with a resident population of about 15 (plus infinitely more mosquitoes). It's difficult to believe that in the 14th century more than 20,000 people lived here. It was the first settlement in the lagoon, founded in the fifth century by the citizens of the Roman town of Altino on the mainland. But Torcello's dominance of the lagoon did not last: Venice itself was found to be more salubrious (malaria was rife on Torcello) and more easily defendable. But past decline is present charm, and rural Torcello is a great antidote to the pedestrian traffic jams around San Marco.

From the ferry jetty, the cathedral campanile can already be made out; to get there, simply follow the path along the main canal through the island. Halfway along the canal is the **ponte del Diavolo** (one of only two bridges in the lagoon without a parapet). For the classic Torcello restaurant, head to **Locanda Cipriani** (piazza Santa Fosca 29, 041 730 150, locandacipriani.com, Mar-Dec noon-3pm Wed-Mon, also 7-9pm Fri-Sat by appt, €€€€).

Torcello's main square has some desultory souvenir stalls, the small but interesting **Museo di Torcello** with archaeological finds from around the lagoon, a battered stone seat known arbitrarily as Attila's throne, and two extraordinary churches. The 11th-century church of **Santa Fosca** (open 10am-6pm Mon-Sat, 9am-6pm Sun, free) looks somewhat like a miniature version of Istanbul's St Sophia, more Byzantine than European with its Greek-cross plan and external colonnade; its bare interior allows the perfect geometry of the space to come to the fore. Next door is the imposing cathedral of **Santa Maria Assunta** (041 730 119, Nov-Feb 10am-5pm daily, Mar-Oct 10.30am-6pm daily, €5, €4 reductions). Dating from 639, it is the oldest building on the lagoon, with vivid mosaics on the ceiling vault and walls. Once you've explored inside, climb the campanile; the view of the lagoon from the top is memorable.

Santa Fosca

Sights & museums

Museo del Merletti

Piazza B Galuppi 187, Burano (041 730 034, museomerletto.visitmuve. it). Vaporetto 9, 12, N. **Open** *10am-6pm Tue-Sun.* **Admission** *€5; €3.50 reductions; see also p184 Tourist information. No cards.*
Following a major revamp, the Lace School's rooms with painted wooden beams are looking resplendent. In a chronological layout, the display covers elaborate examples of lace-work from the 17th century onwards. There are fans, collars and parasols, and some of the paper pattern-sheets that lace-makers use. Some of Burano's remaining lace-makers can regularly be found at work here, displaying their handicraft to visitors.

Restaurants

♥ Venissa €€€€

Mazzorbo, fondamenta Santa Caterina 3 (041 527 2281, www. venissa.it). Vaporetto Mazzorbo. **Restaurant** *(Apr-Sept) noon-2.30pm, 7-9.30pm Mon, Tue- Sun.* **Osteria** *noon-10.30pm Mon, Tue-Sun. Modern Venetian*
Inside a lovely high-walled vineyard, Venissa serves ambitious fare inspired by super-fresh produce, much of which comes from the nets of local fishermen and the on-site vegetable garden. The 2017 season saw the arrival of much-fêted young chef Francesco Brutto, who describes his creations as avant-garde. The main restaurant in the garden is a summer affair (open from April; bring mosquito repellent). Prices are high but you can avoid surprises at bill-paying time by opting for taster menus from €120 to €200. In the canalside HQ, Venissa's Osteria is open year-round. The menu here is slightly simpler and (very) slightly less demanding on the wallet.

Sant'Erasmo

The largest island in the northern lagoon, Sant'Erasmo has a tiny population that contents itself with growing most of the vegetables eaten in *La Serenissima* (on Rialto market stalls, the sign 'San Rasmo' is a mark of quality, *see p122* Mercato di Rialto).

There are also some restaurants and a fishermen's bar-*trattoria* – **Ai Tedeschi** (041 244 4139, open 9am-11pm daily in summer) – hidden away on a small sandy beach by the **Forte Massimiliano**. This latter is a moat-surrounded 19th-century Austrian fort that has been restored and is open to the public (11 am-6pm Sat, Sun).

The main attraction of the island lies in the beautiful country landscapes and lovely walks past traditional Veneto farmhouses, through vineyards and fields of artichokes and asparagus.

By the main vaporetto stop (Chiesa) is the 20th-century church, technically named Santi Erme ed Erasmo, but widely known as simply '**Chiesa**'. Over the entrance door is a gruesome painting, attributed to Domenico Tintoretto, of the *Martyrdom of St Erasmus*, who had his intestines wound out of his body on a windlass. The resemblance of a windlass to a capstan resulted in St Erasmus becoming the patron saint of sailors.

Sant'Erasmo

Venice
Essentials

Grand Canal

Accommodation

A day-trip to Venice just won't do. To appreciate the city's 24-hour magic, you have to fall asleep to the sound of gondoliers crooning and awake to the very particular bouncing echo of footsteps rushing along a narrow *calle*.

If horror tales of hair-raising prices are a deterrent, remember, this is a Jekyll and Hyde city: even the most expensive places will slash prices in the low season. Of course, peak times still pull in visitors in their thronging millions. As well as summer, Carnevale, big regattas, key Biennale events and important religious festivities including Christmas and Easter will push up prices. Outside of these times, you'll find that the Lagoon City is refreshingly quiet and relatively cheap – to sleep in, at least.

The scene

Venice's accommodation sector continues to change and expand. Some of this is retrenching: at the Gritti Palace (*see p168*) for example, a massive revamp some years ago has reduced the number of rooms, but ramped up the luxury quotient still further.

Small continues to be beautiful, and chic B&Bs proliferate: CimaRosa (*see p170*) is one of the best. But off-piste locations are also proving popular, with some of the most uncharacteristic out on the islands of the lagoon.

Where to stay

Venice is divided into six *sestieri* plus outlying islands, Giudecca being the closest of these. Though you'll be hard pushed to tell where one ends and the next begins, a closer look reveals that each has its own particular feel.

Plush hotels and tourist action centre around St Mark's square and the riva degli Schiavoni: many first-timers feel that being right in the thick of it is best, but the crowd thronging outside the front door can tarnish that pampered feel.

Remember that Venice is small and wherever you are, you'll never feel far from the sightseeing action. On the right bank of the Grand Canal, in the *sestieri* of Dorsoduro, Santa Croce and San Polo, there are chic little hideaways for those who seek style without the glam trappings. Moving away from the hub at St Mark's square, Castello and Cannaregio also harbour good options in their refreshingly residential *calli* and *campi*.

Our categories

Venice is a city of immense accommodation price swings: the same room that costs €500 in high season, or during a crowd-pulling festival or event, might plummet to €150 in the late November doldrums; and even mid-range options at around €200 will be on offer at €75 a night or less when wintry weather drives less hardy souls from the lagoon city.

For this reason, placing hotels under category headings is as difficult as it is misleading. As a general rule of thumb, however, Luxury means a double room in mid-season will start at €500 and stop at nothing; 'Expensive' means it will cost from €250 up to €500 per night; 'Moderate' means €150-€250, and 'Budget' will come in at below €150.

Whatever agency or booking site you use to find your accommodation, don't presume that it's offering the best price. Always check hotel websites carefully and look out for special deals. It's often cheaper to book directly with the selected establishment.

Getting to your hotel

Reaching your hotel in this labyrinthine city can be a challenge. Ask for very clear directions, which should include the nearest vaporetto (ferry) stop, campo (square) or church. Alternatively, ask for GPS coordinates – but bear in mind that if you plan to rely on your smartphone to get you there, you should download a map on to your device before arriving: Venice's 4G signal can disappear unexpectedly in places.

If you have mobility problems and/or don't fancy dragging your suitcase over too many bridges with steps, ask whether your hotel of choice has a *porta d'acqua* (canal-side entrance) where a water taxi can pull right up to reception.

Facilities for the disabled are scarce in Venetian hotels, partly due to the nature of the buildings. Many establishments are spread over several floors but do not have lifts; always check first. *See p178* for information on disabled travel in Venice.

What you will (and won't) get

In general, room prices include breakfast. Except in more upmarket hotels, 'breakfast included' means a continental breakfast of tea/coffee, pastries and, if you're lucky, yoghurt and/or fruit: don't expect a full cooked meal, and be aware that what's on offer varies wildly in freshness and generosity. If it's unclear whether or not you'll be given breakfast as part of your room rate, avoid surprises by asking when you book.

Most room prices also include Wi-Fi. Don't be surprised, though, if thick walls and meandering corridors make for a shaky signal.

Most hotels will charge more for rooms with canal or lagoon views. As some canals are muddy backwaters, and others are major highways with a constant procession of bellowing gondoliers (not so good for light sleepers), it pays to ask exactly what this water view consists of.

By law Italian hotels cannot provide irons in rooms, though some may have an ironing room for guests' use, or press clothes on request. The electric kettle is not a piece of equipment considered vital by Italians, so don't presume that it will feature in your hotel room.

Self-catering

If you're travelling as a family or group, or staying for an extended period, an apartment with kitchen facilities might prove a sensible option. Beside the usual plethora of AirBnB offerings, many of Venice's hotels are adding apartments to their repertoire.

Among hotels listed in this guide, La Calcina (*see p170*), the Bauer group's Villa F (*see p166*), AD Place (*see p168*) and Corte di Gabriela (*see p169*) have self-catering facilities.

The websites www.viewsonvenice.com and www.veniceapartment.com are also good resources for finding an apartment.

In the know
Price categories

Our price categories are based on hotels' standard prices (not including seasonal offers or discounts) for one night in a double room with en suite shower/bath. Breakfast is included unless otherwise stated. Given the potential for off-season discounts, it's always worth trying to negotiate a better deal.

Luxury	€500+
Expensive	€250-500
Moderate	€150-250
Budget	up to €150

The Tourist Tax

What you need to know

Like most destinations in Italy, Venice levies a tourist tax (*imposta di soggiorno*), which must be paid over and above the lodging rates when you stay in any hotel or rented accommodation. It is charged separately from your room bill and should be paid in cash, so bear that in mind when checking out. Tourist tax rates vary by type of accommodation, season and age.

In low season, the tax for those staying in a one-star hotel in island Venice is 70c per adult per day (30c ages 10-16) while a five-star hotel charges €3.50 (€1.70). In high season the rate is €1 (50c) in a one-star and €5 (€2.50) in a five-star. Under-tens are not charged. The tax is charged for a maximum five days in any given establishment.

Luxury

Aman Grand Canal Venice

San Polo 1364, calle Tiepolo Baiamonte (041 270 7333, www.aman.com). Vaporetto San Silvestro. **Rooms** *24.* **Map** *p117 F6.*

Aman's Venetian outpost is exactly what you'd expect of this Far Eastern hotel group: utter luxury, immaculate service and exceptional style. The hotel is housed in palazzo Papadopoli, the only building on the Grand Canal with two private gardens; the count-owner of the *palazzo* still lives on the top floor and often sweeps in to lend an aristocratic Venetian air – which is just as well because one complaint that could be levelled at the hotel is that it's much like any Aman hostelry anywhere in the world. The restaurant serves Italian and Asian cuisine. The bedrooms and suites are exercises in pared-back luxury: one has frescoes by GB Tiepolo; another has a magnificent fireplace designed by Sansovino.

The Bauer Venezia

San Marco 1459, campo San Moisè (041 520 7022, www.bauervenezia.com). Vaporetto San Marco Vallaresso. **Rooms** *210.* **Map** *p64 H8.*

This Venetian accommodation classic a stone's throw from St Mark's square is a hotel of different parts, spreading from a rather brutal 1930s building on campo San Moisè to a glorious antique *palazzo* with Grand Canal frontage. Appearances are deceptive, and the newer extension conceals vast halls inside, where marble, gold and black detailing give the place the air of a grand art deco ocean liner. The water-facing Il Palazzo, on the other hand, offers plusher, more traditional opulence. There are views to remember at breakfast, which is served either at canal-level, or on the Settimo Cielo (seventh heaven) terrace. The Bauer empire extends across the water to the Giudecca, where accommodation options Palladio Spa and Villa F back on to a gorgeous garden.

Belmond Hotel Cipriani

Giudecca 10, fondamenta San Giovanni (041 240 801, www.hotelcipriani.com). Hotel launch from San Marco Vallaresso vaporetto stop, or Vaporetto Zitelle. **Rooms** *95.*

Set amidst verdant gardens, the Cipriani has superb facilities as well as a private harbour for your yacht and a better-than-average chance of rubbing shoulders with an A-list film star, especially during the film festival (*see p44*) when many make this their base. Rooms are as luxurious and well appointed as you'd expect in this category. If this seems too humdrum, take an apartment in the neighbouring 15th-century Palazzo Vendramin, with butler service and private garden. Facilities include tennis courts, a pool, a sauna, a spa, a gym and a fine-dining restaurant designed by Adam Tihany.

There's a motorboat to San Marco, but many guests never even leave the premises.

Gritti Palace

San Marco 2467, campo Santa Maria del Giglio (041 794 611, www. thegrittipalace.com). Vaporetto Giglio. **Rooms** *82.* **Map** *p64 G8.*

With much fanfare, the Gritti Palace reopened in 2013 after a massive makeover that reduced the number of rooms and suites but upped the already considerable luxury quotient, while adding some handy 21st-century conveniences such as a state-of-the-art concrete lining for the ground floor, so that guests checking in during *acqua alta* (high water) will no longer have to do so with the lagoon lapping around their knees. The air of old-world charm and nobility about this 15th-century *palazzo* now feels fresher, with superb Rubelli fabrics replacing fittings that had become frayed over the decades, and every piece of antique furniture restored and polished. Refined and opulent, adorned with luscious bathroom treats and fresh flowers, each room is uniquely decorated; one is lined with antique floor-to-ceiling mirrors. If you want a canal or campo view, specify when booking: some rooms overlook a dingy courtyard. Breakfast, or just an *aperitivo* on the vast canal terrace, is an experience in itself.

Metropole

Castello 4149, riva degli Schiavoni (041 520 5044, www.hotelmetropole.com). Vaporetto San Zaccaria. **Rooms** *67.* **Map** *p88 L8.*

Of all the grand hotels that crowd this part of the riva, the Metropole is arguably the most characterful. The owners' museum-level collection of antiques and curios are dotted in the sumptuous public rooms – which have a deliciously exotic, decadent air – and through the varied bedrooms, which vary from slightly gloomy classic doubles to glorious suites shimmering with mosaics and marbles. In winter, tea and cakes are served in the velvet-draped *salone*; in summer, guests relax in the pretty garden to the sound of water trickling in the fountain. There are views over the lagoon (for a hefty supplement), the canal or on to the garden. The hotel's Met restaurant has one Michelin star and prices to match.

Palazzo Venart

Santa Croce 1961, calle Tron (041 523 3784, www.palazzovenart.com). Vaporetto San Stae. **Rooms** *18.* **Map** *p117 G6.*

New for 2016, five-star Palazzo Venart gives guests all the antiques, brocades and sparkling chandeliers of classic Venetian hotel tradition, but places them in a boutique hotel context, with very friendly service and a pretty garden leading down to the Grand Canal to boot. The 18 rooms are equally sumptuous but each has its own feel and colour scheme; the coloured marbles in the huge (for Venice) bathrooms are extraordinary. A low glassed-in structure in the palm-and-magnolia-filled courtyard is home to Glam, the latest addition to superchef Enrico Bartolini's empire and Venice's hottest new restaurant opening. Hotel guests' breakfast is served here.

Expensive
AD Place

San Marco 2557A, fondamenta della Fenice (041 241 3234, www. adplacevenice.com). Vaporetto Giglio. **Rooms** *12 + 7 apartments.* **Map** *p64 G8.*

Tucked away on a quiet canal behind the La Fenice opera house, 12-room AD Place mixes a friendly atmosphere with great service in bedrooms and public spaces, which revel in a wild combination of candy-stripe colours and baroque touches. Rooms (spread over four floors with no lift) vary in size: some of the standard rooms are fairly small but the top-floor suite, with its canopied bed in the master bedroom, is suitable for families, as is a ground-floor room that is wheelchair-adapted. The hotel's private water entrance means you can get straight here by water taxi. The glorious roof terrace is a great place to watch the sun set. AD Place has recently expanded its self-catering side, bringing to seven (three of them opening in 2017) the number of its elegant-with-a-twist apartments sleeping up to six people. In low season, the hotel slips into the moderate category.

Al Ponte Antico

Cannaregio 5768, calle dell'Aseo (041 241 1944, www.alponteantico.com). Vaporetto Rialto. **Rooms** 7. **Map** p104 H5.

With its padded reception desk, festooned curtains and lashings of brocade in public spaces and most of the bedrooms, the family-run Al Ponte Antico takes the traditional Venetian hotel decor idiom and turns it into something over-the-top, Louis Quinze-ish and faintly decadent: a pleasant change from the prudish norm. In a 16th-century palazzo on the Grand Canal, with views over the Rialto Bridge, Al Ponte Antico's exquisite little balcony overlooks the water, as do some doubles and suites. Owner-manager Matteo Peruch will make you feel totally at home from the moment you arrive, and the breakfasts here are famous and feted.

Ca' Maria Adele

Dorsoduro 111, rio terà dei Catecumeni (041 520 3078, www.camariaadele. it). Vaporetto Salute. **Rooms** 14 + mini-apartment. **Map** p136 G9.

Situated in the shadow of the basilica of Santa Maria della Salute, Ca' Maria Adele marries sumptuous 18th-century Venetian decadence with modern design, with some Moorish elements and a host of quirky tongue-in-cheek details thrown in. Brothers Alessio and Nicola Campa preside attentively over a main hotel of 12 luxurious bedrooms, five of which are themed; the red and gold Doge's Room is voluptuous, the Sala Noire ultra-sexy. There's an intimate sitting room on the ground floor with chocolate brown faux-fur on the walls and black pony-skin sofas, plus a Moroccan-style roof terrace for sultry

evenings. Breakfast can be consumed in bed or in any of the hotel's public spaces. Next door at number 113 are two more splendid rooms, which can be booked as a private suite: and 50 metres from the mother ship is the equally delightful MiniPalace where a private terrace overlooks San Giorgio Maggiore and the Salute. Service is deft but discreet.

Corte di Gabriela

San Marco 3836, calle degli Avvocati (041 523 5077, www.cortedigabriela. com). Vaporetto Sant'Angelo. **Rooms** 10, plus 2 apartments. **Map** p64 F7.

Corte di Gabriela marries classic Venetian frescoes and stucco with some molto-mod design details to produce a very stylish four-star boutique handily placed in a quiet street near campo Santo Stefano (see p81). Obliging, well-informed staff preside over a pretty courtyard and a warmly red living room complete with grand piano and a little bar. Spacious bedrooms come with iPads and kettles; the bathrooms are large and chic. The breakfast is a rich feast of home-baked goodies. Two self-catering apartments located near the hotel are perfect for groups or families. Corte di Gabriela is towards the lower end of this price range.

Palazzo Abadessa

Cannaregio 4011, calle Priuli (041 241 3784, www.abadessa.com). Vaporetto Ca' d'Oro. **Rooms** 15. **Map** p104 H4.

A beautiful, shady walled garden is laid out in front of this 16th-century palazzo, which is filled with antiques, paintings and silver, and where the prevailing atmosphere is that of an aristocratic private home (which it is), restored and opened to guests. Service is charming but discreet. A magnificent double stone staircase leads to the impressive bedrooms, all of which are beautifully appointed with richly coloured brocade-covered walls, and some of which are truly vast. Beware, however: the three low-ceilinged doubles on the mezzanine floor are rather cramped. Bathrooms tend to be on the small side. In low season, prices at this lovely place fall into the affordable end of the 'moderate' category, especially if you book ahead.

Palazzo Stern

Dorsoduro 2792A, calle del Traghetto (041 277 0869, www.palazzostern.com). Vaporetto Ca' Rezzonico. **Rooms** *24.* **Map** *p136 D8.*
Built in the early 20th century in eclectic pastiche style, Palazzo Stern is now home to this elegant hotel. A magnificent wooden staircase leads up to rooms done out in classic Venetian style in pale shades. Pricier rooms have views over the Grand Canal but the standard doubles at the back face towards a lovely garden. There's a view that stretches across the city to the Dolomites from the rooftop terrace, where there's a jacuzzi for guests' use. A wonderful breakfast terrace overlooks the canal.

Moderate
Al Ponte Mocenigo

Santa Croce 2063, fondamenta Rimpetto Mocenigo (041 524 4797, www. alpontemocenigo.com). Vaporetto San Stae. **Rooms** *15 + 8 + 6.* **Map** *p117 F4.*
This delightful hotel, which has its own little bridge over a quiet canal near campo San Stae, has expanded recently into two nearby structures, taking the number of rooms and suites to 29. It remains, however, one of Venice's best-value accommodation options. It has tastefully decorated mod-Venetian rooms – some in a luscious shade of deep red, others in rich gold – and well-appointed bathrooms, not to mention Wi-Fi access throughout, a bar, a Turkish bath, a pretty courtyard garden and genuinely charming owners – Walter and Sandro – who manage to be warm and laid-back in just the right ratio. This hotel is at the less expensive end of the moderate price range, becoming remarkably budget in low season.

La Calcina

Dorsoduro 780, fondamenta delle Zattere (041 520 6466, www.lacalcina. com). Vaporetto Accademia or Zattere. **Rooms** *29.* **Map** *p136 E9.*
La Calcina is a perennial favourite – Victorian critic John Ruskin opted to stay here – but remains great value at quieter moments. The open vistas of the Giudecca canal provide the backdrop for meals taken on the terrace of this hotel, a view shared by the bedrooms at the front of the building. With an air of civilised calm, La Calcina is one of the best-value hotels in its category. Rooms have parquet floors, 19th-century furniture and a refreshingly uncluttered feel; one single is without private bath. There is an *altana* (suspended roof terrace), and a number of suites and self-catering apartments are available in adjacent buildings.

CimaRosa Boutique B&B

Santa Croce 1958, calle Tron (www. cimarosavenezia.com). Vaporetto San Stae. **Rooms** *5.* **Map** *p117 G6.*
The supremely stylish B&B in the quiet northern Santa Croce district has just five beautiful rooms, their colours picking up the hues of the city. On the ground floor, the water of the Grand Canal laps outside the windows of a chic but comfortable living room where breakfast is served. Upstairs, a kitchenette has tea- and coffee-making equipment plus a fridge to keep your wine cool. Three of the bedrooms overlook the canal. Owner-manager Brittany and her architect husband created this Venetian home-from-home; her all-female team cossett guests through their stay. Book early because returnee guests fill the place up quickly.

Locanda Novecento

San Marco 2683-4, calle del Dose (041 241 3765, www.novecento.biz). Vaporetto Giglio. **Rooms** *9.* **Map** *p64 F8.*
This home-from-home with a gently exotic edge is a real pleasure to come back to after a hard day's sightseeing, especially when it's warm enough to

relax in the delightful little garden. With its friendly, helpful staff, and reading and sitting rooms, Novecento is a very special place to stay. Wooden floors, ethnic textiles, oriental rugs, Indonesian furniture and individually decorated rooms make a refreshing change from the ubiquitous pan-Venetian style. Art shows are regularly mounted in the public rooms.

Locanda Orseolo

San Marco 1083, corte Zorzi (041 520 4827, www.locandaorseolo. com). Vaporetto Rialto or San Marco Vallaresso. **Rooms** *15.* **Map** *p64 H7.*
This wonderfully welcoming *locanda* has beamed ceilings, painted wood panelling, leaded windows and rich colours; there's even a tiny water entrance. The immaculate bedrooms are ranged over three floors (there's no lift) and are furnished in a fairly restrained Venetian style. Choose between a canal view (which can be noisy) or quieter rooms overlooking the square. Breakfast is exceptionally generous. The team that runs the place bend over backwards to ensure their guests are happy. This delightful hotel is fiendishly difficult to find: go through the iron gate almost opposite the church in campo San Gallo, bear left into a smaller campo and you'll see the sign.

Oltre il Giardino

San Polo 2542, fondamenta Contarini (041 275 0015, www.oltreilgiardino-venezia.com). Vaporetto San Tomà. **Rooms** *6.* **Map** *p117 E6.*
Tucked away at the end of a *fondamenta* and accessed through a *giardino* (garden), this attractive villa was once owned by Alma Mahler, widow of the composer Gustav. Today, host Lorenzo Muner welcomes guests to this stylish yet homely hotel. Going against the deep-hued, brocaded Venetian grain, Oltre il Giardino's neutral/pastel shades and wood floors provide the backdrop for a mix of antique furniture, contemporary objets and unexpected splashes. Subtly colour-themed bedrooms vary considerably in size;

the large suites and junior suites can be equipped with beds in their living room, and are perfect for groups or families. All are equipped with LCD TVs, robes, slippers and luxurious bath goodies.

Budget

B&B San Marco

Castello 3385L, fondamenta San Giorgio degli Schiavoni (041 522 7589, 335 756 6555, http://www.realvenice.it/smarco_index.htm). Vaporetto San Zaccaria. Closed Jan; 2wks Aug. **Rooms** *3.* **Map** *p88 L7.*
One of the few Venetian B&Bs that come close to the British concept of the genre, Marco Scurati's homely apartment lies just behind San Giorgio degli Schiavoni. Two of the three cosy, antique-filled bedrooms share a bathroom and so work particularly well as a suite for a family or group; the other is en-suite. Marco and his wife Alice serve breakfast in their own kitchen and guests are treated very much as part of the family.

Generator

Giudecca 86, fondamenta delle Zitelle (041 877 8288, http://generatorhostels. com). Vaporetto Zitelle. **Beds** *240.*
Venice's once-dowdy youth hostel has undergone the Generator treatment, emerging with some hip decor, infinitely more inviting public spaces, a lively nightlife scene and a restaurant. There are double, triple and quad rooms suitable for families, and dorms sleeping up to 16 people, some of which are women-only. Though prices are low when the city's quiet, they do follow the trend elsewhere and rise sharply at busy times; breakfast and other meals are extra. People travelling on a tight budget should factor in the cost of a *vaporetto* pass, because most of what you'll be wanting to visit is over the water.

Hotel Rio

Castello 4358, campiello Santi Filippo e Giacomo (041 520 8222, www. hotelriovenezia.com). Vaporetto San Zaccaria. **Rooms** *18.* **Map** *p88 M10.*
Spread over four adjoining buildings and dotted around narrow corridors, the 18

rooms of the Rio are surprisingly chic and comfortable after a recent makeover. Friendly young staff and services such as beverage-making equipment in a small common room compensate for downsides such as tiny bathrooms. Some rooms sleep up to four people. The hotel's position is perfect for intense sightseeing, just minutes away from St Mark's square and very handy for a busy *vaporetto* stop.

San Samuele

San Marco 3358, salizada San Samuele (041 520 5165, www.hotelsansamuele. com). Vaporetto San Samuele or Sant'Angelo. **Rooms** *10.* **Map** *p64 E7.*
Flowers cascade from the window boxes of this delightful, friendly little hotel in an excellent location. The spotlessly clean rooms have a simple, sunny aspect and the welcome is always warm. The San Samuele is several notches above most of its fellow one-star establishments, although both the single rooms and one of the doubles have bathrooms in the corridor, and walls are rather thin. There's free Wi-Fi throughout and staff are always ready with well-informed advice and recommendations. Plans are afoot to add further 'superior' rooms upstairs, all with air-con. San Samuele is very popular, so book well in advance. Breakfast is not included, though there's a coffee machine in reception for guests, and a fridge to keep your supplies in.

Silk Road

Dorsoduro 1420E, calle Cortelogo (388 119 6816, www.silkroadhostel.com). Vaporetto San Basilio. **Rooms** *5.* **Map** *p136 C9.*
Sparse, basic but well placed and extremely clean, Silk Road offers four-bed women's, men's and mixed dorms, plus one double room. There are good-sized lockers for all in the dorms, and the kitchen – where Alex will spontaneously cook up meals for guests from time to time – is equipped with a big fridge and other facilities. The vibe is convivial, and lone women travellers will feel totally safe.

Venice Certosa Hotel

Isola della Certosa (041 277 8632, hotel. ventodivenezia.it). Vaporetto Certosa. **Rooms** *18.*
Facing across the lagoon towards the eastern end of Castello and a short hop from Venice proper on the 4.1/4.2 *vaporetto*, this bright, modern hostel/hotel on the quiet island of Certosa has a pine forest on one side and a forest of masts on the other – and a large percentage of yachties from the neighbouring marina occupying its clean, simple rooms. There's a night shuttle service from the city centre, and a restaurant for those times when you can't face another lagoon crossing. The hotel lies somewhere between the budget and moderate range.

Generator *p171*

Getting Around

ARRIVING & LEAVING

By air

Low-cost carriers fly visitors to Venice through Venice, Treviso and Verona airports. National carriers fly principally to Venice, although some have services to Verona.

Venice Marco Polo Airport

Switchboard 041 260 6111, flight & airport information 041 260 9260, www.veniceairport.it.

You can get a bus or taxi (*see below*) to piazzale Roma, but you may find that the **Alilaguna boat service** (041 240 1701, www.alilaguna.it) drops you nearer your hotel. The dock is seven minutes' walk from arrivals; porter service costs €5 per bag. Various Alilaguna services call at San Marco, Rialto, Fondamenta Nove, Guglie, Zattere, Ca' Rezzonico, Sant'Angelo, San Stae, Zitelle, San Zaccaria, Arsenale, Lido, Bacini, Ospedale, Murano Colonna and Madonna dell'Orto vaporetto stops, as well as the Mulino Stucky Hilton on the Giudecca island, and at the Stazione Marittima cruise ship terminal: check which is handiest for your final destination. Main services are hourly, others less frequent. Tickets (€15 to Venice, the Lido or the Stazione Marittima) can be purchased at Alilaguna's counter in the arrivals hall or on board. Allow 70 mins to San Marco.

Two **bus** companies operate services from the airport. The slower bus 5, run by **ACTV** (041 272 2111, timetable information 041 24 24, www.actv.it), travels between the airport and piazzale Roma, leaving every 15 mins; journey time 25-30 mins. Tickets (€8; €15 return) can be purchased at the machine next to the bus stop at the airport, or at any ACTV/ Hellovenezia ticket office; discounted fares are available when purchased together with tourist transport passes; see p174.

The quicker, non-stop bus service (20 mins) between the airport and piazzale Roma is run by **ATVO** (0421 594 671/672, www.atvo.it). Buy tickets (€8; €15 return) from the ATVO counter at the airport, or at their piazzale Roma office. You may also be able to just pay the driver directly if you have exact change.

A regular **taxi** from the airport to piazzale Roma costs €40 and takes about 20 mins. You can pay in advance by credit card in the arrivals hall at the **Cooperativa Artigiana Radio Taxi** desk (041 59 64).

The most luxurious way to reach the centre is by **water taxi**. **Consorzio Motoscafi Venezia** (041 522 2303) charges from €100 for the half-hour crossing. *See p175* Water taxis.

Sant'Angelo Airport (Treviso) *0422 315 111, www.trevisoairport.it.*

ATVO (0422 315 381, www.atvo.it) bus services run between the airport and Venice's piazzale Roma to coincide with flights – if the flight arrives late, the bus will wait. The journey takes about 70 mins, and costs €12 one way, €22 return (valid for ten days). Buses from piazzale Roma to Treviso airport leave ridiculously early, so ensure your timely arrival.

Alternatively, there are **trains** between Treviso and Venice (35 mins), with connections between the airport and station by bus or taxi (**Taxi Padova**, 049 651 333); **ACTT** (0422 32 71) bus 6 does the 20-minute trip at frequent intervals throughout the day and costs €1.30.

Major airlines
Alitalia *89 20 10, www.alitalia.com.*
British Airways *199 712 266, www.britishairways.com.*
Easyjet *848 887766, www.easyjet.com.*
Ryanair *(Treviso Airport) 895 895 8989, www.ryanair.com.*

By train

The **Trenitalia** website (www.trenitalia.com) gives exhaustive information on rail timetables, in English as well as Italian. Tickets can be booked through the website with a credit card; you'll receive an email with a barcode and a booking code, either of which should be presented (on your smartphone, tablet, computer and so on, or in a print-out) to inspectors on board the train. Trenitalia's national rail information and booking number is 892 021 (24hrs daily). Press 1 after the recorded message, then say 'altro' to speak to an operator (who may not speak English). Tickets can also be purchased at the station (*see below*) or at travel agents around the city bearing the Trenitalia logo.

The slowest trains are prefixed **R** (Regionale) or **RV** (Regionale Veloce) and are remarkably cheap; **IC** (Intercity) trains are slightly faster and cost a little more. **Frecce** high-speed trains are more expensive still, though there are large discounts to be had if you book online and well in advance: you will be given a reserved seat number when you book on Frecciarossa and Frecciargento trains.

If you have a regular railways-issued ticket, you must **validate** it in the machines on the platform before boarding or face a fine; if you forget, locate the inspector as soon as possible to waive the fine.

The private train operator **Italo** (www.italotreno.it) also runs high-speed services from Venice's Santa Lucia to Rome, Florence, Bologna, Naples, Padua and Salerno. It's worth checking the website, as prices can be competitive.

Stazione di Venezia Santa Lucia

Vaporetto Ferrovia. **Open** *Information 7am-9pm daily. Tickets 6am-9pm daily.* **Map** *p117.*
This is Venice's main station. Most trains arrive here, though a few will only take you as far as Mestre on the mainland; if so, change to a local train (every ten minutes or less during the day) for the short hop across the lagoon. Tickets can be bought from the counters in the main hall (all major credit cards accepted) or from vending machines throughout the station. (For other options, *see left.*)

By bus

Long-distance buses to Venice all arrive at piazzale Roma.

By car

Prohibitive parking fees make cars one of the least practical modes of arrival, and you won't want your car in the city (*see p176* Driving). Many Venetian hotels offer their guests discounts at car parks, and VeneziaUnica (*see p184*) has special offers too.

PUBLIC TRANSPORT

Public transport – including vaporetti (water buses) and local buses – in Venice itself and in some mainland areas is run by **ACTV** (www.actv.it). **ATVO** (0421 594 671, www.atvo.it) runs more extensive bus services to numerous destinations on the mainland.

Information

Venezia Unica's extremely helpful call centre (041 2424) provides information on vaporetto and bus schedules. Its outlets at many vaporetto stops sell tickets and Venezia Unica passes (*see p184*) which allow users to buy multiple services and access them all through one ticket. Timetables are posted at all vaporetto stops.

The free VeneziaUnica app has real-time transport information and can be downloaded from Google Play or the iTunes store.

Vaporetti

Venice's vaporetti (water buses) run to a very tight schedule, with sailing times for each line marked clearly at stops. Strikes sometimes occur, but are always announced in advance; look out for notices posted inside vaporetto stops bearing the title *sciopero* (strike). Services are also curtailed and rerouted for Venice's many rowing regattas; these disruptions are also announced with posters in vaporetto stops.

Regular services run from about 5am to around midnight, after which a frequent night service (N) operates.

Taking a boat in the wrong direction is all too easy. Remember: if you're standing with your back to the station and want to head down the Grand Canal, take Line 1 (slow) or Line 2 (faster) heading left.

Not all passenger ferries are, strictly speaking, vaporetti. A **vaporetto** has room for 230 passsengers and follow routes along the Grand Canal.

The **motoscafo** carries 160 passengers, has outside seats only at the back and runs on routes encircling the island. **Motonave** take 600-1,200 passengers, and cross the lagoon to the Lido.

A **single trip** by vaporetto costs €7.50 (valid for 75 mins on multiple boats); a **shuttle journey** (ie one stop across the Grand Canal, the hop across to the Giudecca, or from Sant'Elena to the Lido) is €5. Passes for **24hrs** (€20), **36hrs** (€25), **48hrs** (€30), **72hrs** (€40) or **1 week** (€60) are also available and can be purchased as part of a Venezia Unica package (*see p184*). Tickets and passes can be bought from *tabacchi* (*see p183*) and at Venezia Unica counters at many vaporetto stops; stops without ticket counters have automatic ticket-dispensing machines. Once you're on board, you can only buy single tickets.

Tickets must be validated prior to boarding the vaporetto, by swiping them in front of the machines at the jetty entrance. For multiple-journey tickets you need only stamp your ticket once, at the start of the first journey.

Traghetti

The best way to cross the Grand Canal when you're far from a bridge is to hop on a *traghetto*. These unadorned *gondole* are rowed back and forth at fixed points along the canal. At €2 (70c for resident travel card holders), this is the cheapest gondola ride in the city – Venetians make the short hop standing up.

Traghetti ply between the following points:

Santa Sofia–Pescheria *7.30am-8pm Mon-Sat; 8.45am-7pm Sun.* **Map** *p117 J7.*

Riva del Carbon–Riva del Vin *8am-12.30pm Mon-Sat.* **Map** *p64 J9.*

Ca' Garzoni–San Tomà *7.30am-8pm Mon-Sat; 8.30am-7.30pm Sun.* **Map** *p64.*

San Samuele–Ca' Rezzonico *7.45am-12.30pm Mon-Sat.* **Map** *p136 F10.*

Santa Maria del Giglio–Santa Maria della Salute *9am-6pm daily.* **Map** *p136 H13.*

Punta della Dogana–Vallaresso *9am-2pm daily.* **Map** *p64 K12.*

Buses

ACTV buses operate to both Mestre and Marghera on the mainland, as well as serving the Lido, Pellestrina and Chioggia. Services for the mainland depart from piazzale Roma (*see map p118*). From midnight until 5am, buses N1 (leaving every 30 mins) and N2 (leaving every hour) depart from Mestre for piazzale Roma, and vice versa. There are also regular night buses from the Lido (departing at least hourly) to Malamocco, Alberoni and Pellestrina.

Bus tickets, costing €1.50 (also available in blocks of ten tickets for €14), are valid for 75 mins, during which you may use several buses, though you can't make a return journey on the same ticket. They can be purchased from ACTV/ Venezia Unica ticket booths (*see p184*) or from *tabacchi* (*see p183*) anywhere in the city. They should be bought before boarding the bus and then stamped on board.

WATER TAXIS

Water taxis are hugely expensive: expect to pay €100 from the airport (*see p173*) directly to any single destination in Venice, and more for multiple stops. The minimum possible cost for a 15-minute trip from hotel to restaurant is €60, with most journeys averaging

€110 once numbers of passengers and baggage have been taken into account. In all cases, tariffs are for five people or less, with each extra passenger charged €10 up to a maximum of ten people. Between the hours of 10pm and 7am, there is a surcharge of €10.

Taxi pick-up points can be found at piazzale Roma, outside the train station, next to the Rialto vaporetto stop, and next to San Marco-Vallaresso vaporetto stop, but it's more reliable to call and order yourself. Pre-booking through the **Motoscafi Venezia** website can give discounts on some routes. Avoid asking your hotel to book a taxi for you, as they frequently add a 10% mark-up. Beware of unlicensed taxis, which charge even more than authorised ones. The latter have a black number on a yellow background.
Consorzio Motoscafi Venezia 041 240 6711, 522 2303, www.motoscafivenezia. it. **Open** 24hrs daily.

GONDOLAS

For an overview of gondola trips in Venice, see p150 Gondolas. Official gondola stops can be found at (or near) the following locations:

Fondamenta Bacino Orseolo **Map** p64 K11.
Riva degli Schiavoni in front of the Hotel Danieli. **Map** p64 M11.
San Marco Vallaresso vaporetto stop. **Map** p64 K12.
Santa Lucia railway station. **Map** p117 D6.
Piazzale Roma bus terminus. **Map** p118 B7.
Santa Maria del Giglio vaporetto stop. **Map** p64 H13.
Piazzetta San Marco jetty. **Map** p64 M11.
Campo Santa Sofia near Ca' d'Oro vaporetto stop. **Map** p117 J6.
San Tomà vaporetto stop. **Map** p118 F10.
Campo San Moisè by the Hotel Bauer. **Map** p64 K12.
Riva del Carbon at the southern end of the Rialto Bridge, near the vaporetto stop. **Map** p64 J9.

Fares
These are set by the **Istituzione per la Conservazione della Gondola e Tutela del Gondoliere** (Gondola Board; 041 528 5075, www.gondolavenezia.it). Prices are €80 for 30 mins and €40 for each additional 20 mins during the day (8am-7pm), and €100 for 40 mins, €50 for each additional 20 mins, at night (7pm-8am). Prices are for six passengers or fewer; having your own personal crooner will push the fare up. In the event that a gondolier tries to overcharge you – and it does happen: be prepared to stick to your guns – complain to the Gondola Board.

DRIVING

Driving is an impossibility in Venice: you'll need to park on the outskirts and walk or use alternative means of transport.

You can drive on the Lido, but there aren't many places to go. A car ferry (route 17) leaves from the Tronchetto ferry stop for Lido San Niccolò every 50 mins and the cost is determined by the size of your car, starting at €26 per car, plus a regular vaporetto ticket per person.

CYCLING

Bicycles are banned – and otiose – in Venice itself, but are a great way of exploring the Lido (see p154) or Sant'Erasmo (see p162).

Cycle hire
Lido on Bike Gran Viale 21B, Lido (041 526 8019, www.lidoonbike.it). **Open** Mar-Sept 9am-7pm daily. **Rates** €5/1.5hr; €9/day.
Venice Bike Rental Gran viale Santa Maria Elisabetta 79A, Lido (041 526 1490, www. venicebikerental.com). **Open** Mar-Oct 8.30am-8pm daily. **Rates** €4/hr; €9/day. No cards.

WALKING

Most sightseeing is done on foot. Be aware that there are over 400 bridges, all with steps. For tour guides, see p185.

Resources A-Z

ACCIDENT & EMERGENCY

For ambulance, police or fire services, call the **Numero Unico Emergenze** 112.

Medical emergencies

For urgent medical advice from local health authority doctors during the night, call 041 238 5600 (8pm-8am Mon-Fri; 10pm Sat-8am Mon). **Ospedale Civile** *Castello 6777, campo Santi Giovanni e Paolo (041 529 4111, casualty 041 529 4516). Vaporetto Ospedale.* **Map** *p88 N6.* Housed in the 15th-century Scuola di San Marco (*see p94*), Venice's main civic hospital has helpful staff and doctors who are quite likely to speak English.

Other emergencies

Thefts or losses should be reported immediately at the nearest police station (either the Polizia di Stato or Carabinieri; *see p182*). Report the loss of your passport to the nearest consulate or embassy (*see p179*). Report the loss of credit cards or travellers' cheques to your credit card company (*see p181*).

ADDRESSES

Postal addresses in Venice consist of the name of the *sestiere* (district) plus the house number. With only this information, you will probably never reach your destination. For convenience, we have also given the name of the *calle* (street) or *campo* (square) etc, where each place is located. But finding your way around remains a challenge, especially as matters are sometimes complicated by there being an official Italian and several unofficial Venetian dialect names in use for the same location. When asking for directions, make sure you ascertain the nearest vaporetto stop, church, large square or other easily identifiable local landmark.

AGE RESTRICTIONS

Buying/drinking alcohol 18.
Driving 18.
Sex (hetero- & homosexual) 14.
Smoking 16.

Travel Advice

For up-to-date information on travel to a specific country – including the latest on safety and security, health issues, local laws and customs – contact your government's department of foreign affairs. Most have websites with useful advice for would-be travellers.

Australia
www.smartraveller.gov.au

Canada
www.voyage.gc.ca

New Zealand
www.safetravel.govt.nz

Republic of Ireland
www.dfa.ie

UK
www.fco.gov.uk/travel

USA
www.state.gov/travel

CUSTOMS

If you arrive from an EU country you are not required to declare goods imported into or exported from Italy as long as they are for personal use.

For people arriving from non-EU countries the following limits apply:

• 200 cigarettes or 100 cigarillos or 50 cigars or 250g of tobacco.
• 1l of spirits or 2l of wine.
• one bottle of perfume (50ml), 250ml of eau de toilette.
• gift items not exceeding €430 (€150 for children under 15).

Anything above these limits will be subject to taxation at the port of entry. For more information, call customs (*dogana*) at Marco Polo Airport on 041 269 9311 or consult www. agenziadoganemonopoli.gov.it.

If you are not an EU citizen, remember to keep your official receipt (*scontrino*) as you are entitled to a rebate on IVA (sales tax) paid on purchases of personal goods costing more than €155, as long as they leave the country unused and are bought from a shop that provides this service. Make sure there's a sign displayed in the window, and also ask for the form that you'll need to show at customs on departure. For more information about customs, see the Italian government website, **www. agenziadoganemonopoli.gov.it**, which has a section in English.

DISABLED

With its narrow streets, 400-plus stepped bridges and lack of barriers between canals and pavements, this city is no easy task for anyone with impaired mobility or vision to negotiate. But with determination and forward planning, Venice is far from impossible, and recent efforts to make the city more negotiable for disabled travellers have helped.

Start your research on the city council website, **www.comune.venezia.com**. Type '*Venezia accessibile*' into the search box; once you reach the page,

Climate

Average temperatures and monthly rainfall in Venice

	High (°C/°F)	Low (°C/°F)	Rainfall (mm/in)
January	6/42	-1/30	58/2.3
February	8/47	1/33	54/2.1
March	12/54	4/39	57/2.2
April	16/61	8/46	64/2.5
May	21/70	12/54	69/2.7
June	25/77	16/61	76/3.0
July	28/82	18/64	63/2.5
August	27/81	17/63	83/3.3
September	24/75	14/58	66/2.6
October	18/65	9/49	69/2.7
November	12/53	4/40	87/3.4
December	7/44	0/32	54/2.1

you'll find the English option button. Here you'll find itineraries and a useful map of barrier-free zones; at the time of writing, the map still showed long-removed stairlifts previously installed on some bridges.

VeneziaUnica (041 2424, www. veneziaunica.it) also provides information and shows itineraries without barriers, as well as hosting a helpful FAQ section on its 'Accessible Venice' pages.

Alilaguna (www.alilaguna.it) services between the airport and Venice proper can carry wheelchairs, as can most vaporetti: these will move you between bridge-free areas of the city in an enjoyable fashion. Staff will help you on and off the boats, and ensure that assigned areas are available; if they're short-tempered at peak times, don't take offence – they're like that with everyone. Tickets for wheelchair users cost €1.50 for 75 mins; if you have an *accompagnatore*, s/he travels free.

Transport
Public transport is one area where Venice scores higher than many other destinations, as standard vaporetti and *motonavi* have a reasonably large, flat deck area and there are no steps or steep inclines on the route between quayside and boat, enabling easy travel along the Grand Canal, on lines 1 and 2. Lines that circle the city use *motoscafi*; some of their older models have not yet been adapted to accommodate wheelchairs, although the onboard ACTV personnel are unerringly helpful. The vaporetto lines that currently guarantee disabled access (though peak times should be avoided if possible) are 1, 2, LN and N. Some of the buses that run between Mestre and Venice also have wheelchair access. For further details, consult the Accessible Venice site; for train- or plane-related information, phone **Trenitalia** (199 303 060) or **Marco Polo Airport** (041 260 9260).

DRUGS

Anyone caught in possession of any quantity of drugs of any kind will be taken before a magistrate. There is no distinction between possession for personal use and intent to supply. All offenders are therefore subject to stiff penalties, including lengthy prison sentences. Foreigners can expect to be swiftly deported. Couriering or dealing can land you in prison for up to 20 years.

ELECTRICITY

Italy's electricity system runs on 220/230V. To use British or US appliances, you will need two-pin adaptor plugs: these are best bought before leaving home, as they tend to be expensive in Italy and are not always easy to find. If you do need to buy one here, try any electrical retailer (look for *Casalinghi*, *Elettrodomestici* or *Ferramenta* in the yellow pages).

EMBASSIES & CONSULATES

There are a handful of diplomatic missions in Venice. But for most information, and in emergencies, you will probably have to contact offices in Rome or Milan. There is no longer a British Consulate in Venice; for assistance, refer to the duty officer at the Milan consulate. There is a US Consular Agency in Venice, open by appt only (041 541 5944). Citizens of other countries should refer to http://embassy.goabroad.com/.

Consulates in Milan
Australia 02 7767 4200.
Ireland 02 5518 7569.
New Zealand 02 7217 0001.
South Africa 02 885 8581.
United Kingdom 06 4220 2431.
United States 02 290 351.

Embassies in Rome
Australia 06 852 721.
Canada 06 85444 2911.

Ireland 06 585 2381.
New Zealand 06 853 7501.
South Africa 06 8525 4262.
United Kingdom 06 4220 0001.
United States 06 46741.

HEALTH

The *pronto soccorso* (casualty department) of public hospitals provides free emergency treatment for travellers of any nationality. The public relations department of Venice's **Ospedale Civile** (041 529 4588) can provide general information on being hospitalised in Venice. EU citizens are entitled to reciprocal medical care if they have an EHIC (European Health Insurance Card) card, which, in the UK, can be applied for online (www.dh.gov.uk) or by post using forms that you can pick up at any post office. For minor treatments, take your EHIC card with you to any doctor for a free consultation. Drugs they prescribe can be bought at pharmacies (*see below*) at prices set by the health ministry. Tests or appointments with specialists in the public system (*servizio sanitario nazionale*, SSN) are charged at fixed rates (*il ticket*) and a receipt issued.

Non-EU citizens should review their private health insurance plans to see if expenses incurred while travelling are covered. If not, some form of travel health insurance is strongly advised (*see p180 Insurance*).

Pharmacies

Pharmacies (*farmacie*), identified by a green or red cross above the door, are run by qualified chemists who will dispense informal advice on, and assistance for, minor ailments, as well as filling prescriptions. Over-the-counter drugs are much more expensive in Italy than in the UK or US. They can be purchased in some larger supermarkets.

Most chemists are open 9am-12.30pm, 3.45-7.30pm Mon-Fri and 9am-12.45pm Sat. A small number remain open on Sat afternoon, Sun and at night on a duty rota system, details of which are posted outside every pharmacy.

Most pharmacies carry homeopathic medicines, and will check your blood pressure. If you require regular medication, bring adequate supplies with you. Ask your GP for the generic rather than the brand name of your medicine: it may be available in Italy under a different name.

ID

You are legally obliged to carry photo-ID with you at all times. Hotels will ask for an identification document when you check in, but they should take the details and return the ID to you immediately.

INSURANCE

EU nationals are entitled to reciprocal medical care in Italy, provided they are in possession of a European Health Insurance Card (EHIC; *see left*). Despite this provision, short-term visitors from all countries are advised to get private travel insurance to cover a broad number of eventualities (from injury to theft). Non-EU citizens should always ensure that they take out comprehensive medical insurance with a reputable company before leaving home. Visitors should also take out adequate property insurance before setting off for Italy. If you rent a car, motorcycle or moped, make sure that you pay the extra for full insurance and sign the collision damage waiver before taking off in the vehicle. It's also worth checking your home insurance first, as it may already cover you.

INTERNET & WI-FI

Most hotels, of all standards, offer Wi-Fi. Very few now charge for it, but to avoid surprises, it's best to enquire before you use. A city-wide Wi-Fi service is accessible for a fee through VeneziaUnica (*see p184*). However, you will find no shortage of cafés and bars offering free Wi-Fi. If you opt to use an internet café, you will be asked to present ID to conform with anti-terrorism laws.

LANGUAGE

Although Italian is the official language, some locals speak the Venetian dialect, too; this is also used interchangeably with Italian for local place names, which can be confusing. English is spoken by staff in hotels, at major sights and in all but the most spit-and-sawdust restaurants, but a smattering of Italian will help you get the most from your trip. *See also p186* Vocabulary.

LEFT LUGGAGE

Marco Polo Airport *Arrivals hall, ground floor, behind the bar (041 260 5043). **Open** 5am-9pm daily. **Rates** €6 per item per day. No cards.*
Piazzale Roma bus terminus *041 523 1107. **Open** 6am-9pm daily. **Rates** €7 per item per day. No cards. **Map** p118 B9.*
Santa Lucia railway station *041 785 670. **Open** 6am-11pm daily. **Rates** €6 per item per 5hrs; 90¢ every additional hour from 6am to midnight, 40¢ every additional hour after midnight. No cards. **Map** p104 C6.*

LGBT

The national gay rights group **ArciGay** (www.arcigay.it) sponsors activities, festivals, counselling and AIDS awareness. In Venice, the city council's **Osservatorio LGBT** keeps a weather eye out for acts of discrimination or intolerance around the lagoon and posts news of any LGBT-related events and initiatives on its blog queervenice. blogspot.it (Italian only). **Anddos** (www.anddos.org) membership (€10-17) is often needed to enter gay venues in Italy; it can be purchased at the door, though many venues will waive the requirement for tourists. In a city so used to, and tolerant of, an immense diversity of travellers, you'll be hard pressed to find a hotel that *isn't* gay-friendly. That said, there are some clear favourites, including **Al Ponte Mocenigo** (*see p170*) and **San Samuele** (*see p172*). Others include

B&B Fujiyama (Dorsoduro 2727A, calle lunga San Barnaba, 041 724 1042, www.fujiyama.life), **Alle Guglie B&B** (Cannaregio 1308, calle del Magazen, 320 360 7829, www.alleguglie.com) and the **Molino Stucky Hilton** (Giudecca 810, fondamenta San Giacomo, 041 272 3311, www.molinostuckyhilton.com).

LOST PROPERTY

Your mislaid belongings may end up at one of the *uffici oggetti smarriti* listed below. You could also try the police (*see p182*), or get in touch with **Veritas**, the city's rubbish collection department (041 729 1111).

ACTV *Santa Croce, piazzale Roma c/o Garage comunale AVM (041 272 2179). Vaporetto Piazzale Roma. **Open** 7am-7.30pm daily. **Map** p118 B9.* Items found on vaporetti or buses.
Comune (City Council) *San Marco 4136, riva del Carbon (041 274 8225). Vaporetto Rialto. **Open** 9am-1pm Mon-Fri. **Map** p64 J9.*
FS/Stazione Santa Lucia *(041 78 55 31).* Staff hand over all lost and found items to the Comune of Venice (*see above*).
Marco Polo Airport *Arrivals Hall (WFS and GH Venezia 041 260 9228; AVIA Partner 041 260 9226/7, lost objects 041 260 9260). Bus 5 to Aeroporto. **Open** WFS and GH Venezia 10am-12.30pm; 2-6pm. AVIA Partner 10am-1pm; 3-6pm.*

MONEY

Italy's currency is the euro (€). There are euro banknotes of €5, €10, €20, €50, €100, €200 and €500, and coins worth €1 and €2 as well as 1¢ (*centesimo*), 2¢, 5¢, 10¢, 20¢ and 50¢. Notes and coins from any euro-zone country are valid.

Banks & ATMs

Most banks (*banche*) have cash dispensers accepting cards with the Maestro, Cirrus or Visa Electron symbols; the daily withdrawal limit is usually €250.

Most banks are open 8.20am-1.20pm and 2.45-3.45pm Mon-Fri. All banks are closed on public holidays and work reduced hours the day before a holiday, usually closing at 11am.

Changing money

The best exchange rates are to be had by withdrawing cash from ATMs. The exchange rates and commissions for currency transactions at banks vary greatly, but most offer more generous rates than bureaux de change (*cambio*). Travellers' cheques are almost a thing of the past: many banks no longer accept them and those that do charge large commissions.

Note that anywhere with a 'no commission' sign will probably offer dire exchange rates. There is no longer an American Express office in Venice.

Travelex *San Marco 5126, riva del Ferro (041 528 7358, www.travelex.it). Vaporetto Rialto.* **Open** *9.30am-6.45pm Mon-Sat; 9am-5pm Sun.* **Map** *p64 J9.* Cash and travellers' cheques exchanged. MasterCard and Visa cardholders can also withdraw cash – but note that you will need your passport or other valid photo ID. **Other locations** San Marco 142, piazza San Marco (041 277 5057); Marco Polo Airport arrivals (041 269 8271).

Lost or stolen cards

Report lost credit or debit cards to your issuing bank.

OPENING HOURS

Food shops traditionally close on Wed afternoon; non-food shops on Mon morning. In practice, larger shops are open six or even seven days a week, as are smaller ones at busier times of the year. Note that ticket offices often shut an hour (or even more) before final closing time. *See also right p181* Banks & ATMs, *p180* Pharmacies, *right* Postal services, and *right* Public holidays.

POLICE

For emergencies, *see p177.*

Both the (nominally military) **Carabinieri** and the **Polizia di Stato** deal with crimes and emergencies of any kind. If you have your bag or wallet stolen, or are otherwise made a victim of crime, go as soon as possible to either force to report a *scippo* ('bagsnatching'). A *denuncia* (written statement) of the incident will be made for you. Give police as much information as possible, including your passport number, holiday address and flight numbers. The *denuncia* will be signed, dated and stamped with an official police seal. It is unlikely that your things will be found, but you will need the *denuncia* for making an insurance claim.

Carabinieri *Castello 4693A, campo San Zaccaria (041 27411). Vaporetto San Zaccaria.* **Map** *p88 N10.*
Polizia di Stato *Questura Santa Croce 500, piazzale Roma (041 271 5511, http://questure.poliziadistato.it/ Venezia). Vaporetto Piazzale Roma.* **Map** *p118 B7.*

POSTAL SERVICES

Italy's postal service (www.poste.it) is generally reliable. Postage supplies – such as large mailing boxes and packing tape – are available at most post offices; stamps can be bought at post offices and *tabacchi* (*see p183*). Each district has its own sub-post office, open 8.20am-1.45pm Mon-Fri, 8.20am-12.45pm Sat.

Italy's standard postal service, *posta prioritaria*, gets letters to their destination within 48hrs in Italy, three days for EU countries and four or five for the rest of the world. A letter of 20g or less in Italy costs 85¢, within the EU €1, and to the rest of the world €2.20 or €2.90 (Oceania. Express and parcel post services are also available).

Postboxes are red and have two slots: *Per la città* (for Venezia, Mestre and Marghera), and *Tutte le altre destinazioni* (all other destinations).

Posta Piazzale Roma *Santa Croce
511, fondamenta Santa Chiara (041
244 6811). Vaporetto Piazzale Roma.
Open 8.20am-7.05pm Mon-Fri;
8.20am-12.35pm Sat.* **Map** *p118 B8.*

PUBLIC HOLIDAYS

On official public holidays (*giorni
festivi*), public offices, banks and post
offices are closed. So, in theory, are
shops – but in tourism-oriented Venice,
this rule is often waived. Some bars
and restaurants may observe holidays:
if in doubt, call ahead. You won't find
much open on Christmas Day and New
Year's Day.

Public transport is reduced to a
skeleton service on 1 May, Christmas
Day and New Year's Day, and may be
rerouted or curtailed for local festivities,
especially those including regattas (*see
p59*); details are posted at vaporetto
stops and at the bus terminus in
piazzale Roma.

Holidays falling on a Sat or Sun are
not celebrated on the following Mon.
By popular tradition, if a public holiday
falls on a Tue or Thur, many people will
also take the Mon or Fri off as well, a
practice known as *fare il ponte* ('doing
a bridge').

New Year's Day *(Capodanno)* 1 Jan
Epiphany *(Befana)* 6 Jan
Easter Monday *(Pasquetta)*
Liberation Day *(Festa della Liberazione)*
and patron saint's day *(San Marco)* 25
Apr
Labour Day *(Festa del Lavoro)* 1 May
Assumption *(Ferragosto)* 15 Aug
All Saints' Day *(Ognissanti)* 1 Nov
Festa della Salute *(Venice only)* 21 Nov
Immaculate Conception
(L'Immacolata) 8 Dec
Christmas Day *(Natale)* 25 Dec
Boxing Day *(Santo Stefano)* 26 Dec

SAFETY & SECURITY

Venice is, on the whole, an
exceptionally safe place at any time
of day or night, and violent crime is
almost unknown. Lone women should
steer clear of dark alleyways (as far as is

possible in labyrinthine Ven,
night, though they are more l
harassed than physically attack

Bag-snatchers are a rarity, mos
because of the logistical difficultie
of making a quick getaway. However,
pickpockets operate in crowded
thoroughfares, especially around San
Marco and the Rialto, and on public
transport, so make sure you leave
passports, plane/train tickets and at
least one means of getting hold of
money in your hotel room safe.

If you are the victim of theft or other
serious crime, contact the police (*see
p182*).

SMOKING

Smoking is banned anywhere with
public access – including bars,
restaurants, stations, offices and on
all public transport – except in clearly
designated smoking rooms.

Tabacchi

Tabacchi or *tabaccherie* (identified by a
white T on a black or blue background)
are the only places in Italy where you
can legally buy tobacco products.
They also sell stamps, telephone cards,
individual or season tickets for public
transport, lottery tickets and the
stationery required when dealing with
bureaucracy.

TELEPHONES

Dialling & codes

Italian landline numbers must be
dialled with their prefixes, even if you're
phoning within the local area. Numbers
in Venice and its province begin **041**.

Numbers generally have seven or
eight digits after the prefix; some older
ones have six, and some switchboards
five. If you try a number and can't get
through, it may have been changed
to an eight-digit number. Check the
directory (*elenco telefonico*) or with
directory enquiries (see below).

Numeri verdi ('green numbers') are
free and start 800 or 147. Numbers

...inning 840 and 848 are charged at a nominal rate. These numbers can be called from within Italy only, and some are available only within certain regions. Mobile phone numbers always begin with a 3.

When calling an Italian landline from abroad, the whole prefix, including the 0, must be dialled; so, to call a number in Venice from the UK, dial 00 39 041.... . To make an **international call** from Venice dial 00, then the country code (+44 for the UK; +1 for the USA), then the area code (usually without the initial 0) and the number.

Mobile phones

Standard European handsets will work in Italy, but your service provider may need to activate international roaming before you leave. There are no longer roaming charges within the EU, but you should always check exactly what your contract allows (in terms of calls, texts, minutes and data usage) to avoid unexpected charges. Tri-band US handsets should also work; check with the manufacturer.

If your phone is not locked to your home SIM card/service provider, you can buy an Italian pay-as-you-go SIM card available from mobile phone shops for around €10, allowing you to make cheaper calls within Italy. In theory you have to provide an Italian tax code to purchase one of these; in practice, many vendors will waive this requirement.

Operator services

You can call 1254 for **directory enquiries** but charges for information are steep. Instead, get the information for free at www.1254.it or www.paginebianche.it.

TIME

Italy is one hour ahead of London, six ahead of New York, eight behind Sydney and 12 hours behind Wellington.

TIPPING

There are no hard and fast rules on tipping in Italy, though Venetians know that foreigners tip generously back home, and expect them to be liberal. Some upmarket restaurants (and a growing number of cheaper ones) will add a service charge to your bill: ask *il servizio è incluso*? If not, leave whatever you think the service merited (Italians leave 5-10%). Bear in mind that all restaurants include a cover charge (*coperto*) – a quasi-tip in itself.

TOILETS

Public toilets (*servizi igienici pubblici*) are numerous and relatively clean in Venice, but you have to pay (€1.50) to use them, unless you have invested in the appropriate Venezia Unica package (*see below*). Follow blue and green signs marked WC. By law, all cafés and bars should allow anyone to use their facilities; however, many Venetian bar owners don't. The website https://wctoilettevenezia.com/ has a map of public toilets in the city and an associated app: Bagni a Venezia.

TOURIST INFORMATION

Information

Both the official tourist board's website, www.veneziaunica.it, and the extremely helpful call centre (041 2424) have useful information for visitors, including transport timetables, events listings and a host of other information, in English and Italian. There's also a free VeneziaUnica app in English. Several free publications – available at tourist offices and in some bars –provide supplementary information. There's also *Un'ospite di Venezia* (*A Guest in Venice*), a bi-weekly bilingual booklet compiled by hoteliers. For details of upcoming events, consult the local press and look out for posters plastered on walls across the city.

Venezia Unica *San Marco 71F, piazza San Marco (041 2424, www.veneziaunica. it). Vaporetto San Marco-Vallaresso.* ***Open*** *9am-7pm daily.* ***Map*** *p64 K11.*

The official City of Venice tourist service provides information on sights and events, a list of hotels and walking itineraries with maps for sale. It also issues and adds services to the Venezia Unica City Pass (see below). Staff will put you in touch with registered guides and give details of guided tours (see p185). Tickets for special events are sold at some offices. In addition to the branches listed here, there are outlets (generally open 8am-8pm daily) at the following vaporetto stops: Tronchetto, Piazzale Roma, Ferrovia, Rialto, San Marco-Vallaresso, San Marco-San Zaccaria, Fondamenta Nove, Lido. **Other locations** Santa Lucia railway station (7am-9pm daily); Marco Polo Airport Arrivals Hall (8.30am-7pm daily).

Venezia Unica City Pass

This all-in-one pass is available from Venezia Unica outlets in the city (see above) or online at www.veneziaunica. it (not easy to navigate but worth the effort). It combines access to public transport with admission to tourist attractions, tickets for cultural events and many other useful services, including the two museum passes and Chorus church pass (see p23), city-wide Wi-Fi, use of public toilets, transport to and from the airport, car parks, guided tours and audio-guides. The Pass allows you to select and pay for only the services you require, and the total price is slightly less than if you'd bought everything separately. If you buy online, you will be sent a code which you will need in order to collect your City Pass from a Venezia Unica outlet in the city. Additional services can be added online or in person at any time.

Other passes

For the museum and Chorus passes, see p65. Travellers aged between 6 and 29 should consider buying the **Rolling Venice** card (€6), which allows you to purchase a three-day travel pass for €22 instead of the usual €40, and gives discounts at many sights, shops and restaurants.

Guided tours

Venezia Unica provides information on guides by language and area, or try the following:

Context *www.contexttravel.com/cities/ venice. Rates vary.* The university professors and experts at Context take groups of visitors (maximum six) on customised and/or themed tours.
Cooperativa Guide Turistiche *041 520 9038, www.guidevenezia.it. Rates €140 for half-day tour, for up to 30 people; €4 for every extra person. No cards.* This cooperative offers made-to-measure tours in English and other languages. In high season, book at least a week in advance.
Guide to Venice *328 948* 5671 mobile, www.guidetovenice.it. Rates €50-€70/ person.
Historian Martino Rizzo specialises in tours of the islands, including cruises on traditional boats such as the Nuovo Trionfo. He also runs tours of Venice itself.
See Venice *349 084 8303, www. seevenice.it. Rates from €70-80/hr.* Luisella Romeo organises tours of sights, a range of interesting themed visits and shopping tours.
Venice with a Guide *www. venicewithaguide.com. Rates €150 for 2hrs or €30/person.*
Ten qualified multilingual guides.

VISAS

For EU citizens, a passport or a national identity card valid for travel abroad is sufficient. Non-EU citizens must have full passports. Citizens of the US, Canada, Australia and New Zealand do not need visas for stays of up to 90 days. In theory, visitors are required to declare their presence to the local police within a few days of arrival, unless they are staying in a hotel, where this will be done for them. In practice, you will not need to report to the police station unless you decide to extend your stay and you apply for a *permesso di soggiorno* (permit to stay).

Vocabulary

Italian is pronounced as spelled. Stresses usually fall on the second-last syllable; a stress on the final syllable is indicated by an accent.

There are three 'you' forms: the formal singular *lei*, the informal singular *tu*, and the plural *voi*. Masculine nouns and accompanying adjectives generally end in 'o' (plural 'i'), female nouns and their adjectives end in 'a' (plural 'e').

VENETIAN

The distinctive nasal Venetian drawl is more than just an accent: locals have their own vocabulary too. Venetians tend to ignore consonants, running vowels together in long diphthongs (explaining how *vostro schiavo* – 'your servant' – became *ciao*.) *Xè* is pronounced 'zay'; *gò* sounds like 'go' in 'got.' For more, visit www.veneto.org/language.

PRONUNCIATION

Vowels

a *as in* a**s**k
e *like* a *in* a**g**e *(closed e) or* e *in* s**e**ll *(open e)*
i *like* ea *in* e**a**st
o *as in* h**o**tel *(closed o) or in* h**o**t *(open o)*
u *as in* b**oo**t

Consonants

c *before a, o or u – like* c *in* **c**at
c *before an e or an i – like the* ch *in* **ch**eck *(sh as in* **sh**ip *in Venetian)*
ch *like* c *in* **c**at
g *before a, o or ui – like* g *in* **g**et
g *before an e or an ii – like the* j *in* **j**ig
gh *like the* g *in* **g**et
gl *followed by an ii – like* **ll**i *in* mi**lli**on
gn *like* **ny** *in* ca**ny**on
qu *as in* **qu**ick

r *always rolled*
s *two sounds, as in* **s**oap *or* ro**s**e
sc *before an e or an ii – like the* **sh** *in* **sh**ame
sch *like the* **sc** *in* **sc**out
z *two different sounds, like* **ts** *or* **dz**

USEFUL PHRASES

hello and goodbye *ciao (used informally in other parts of Italy; in all social situations in Venice)*
good morning, hello *buongiorno*
good afternoon, good evening *buonasera*
please *per favore, per piacere*
thank you *grazie*
you're welcome *prego*
excuse me *mi scusi (polite), scusami (informal) scusime/me scusa*
I'm sorry *mi dispiace/me dispiaxe*
I don't understand *non capisco, non ho capito/no gò capìo*
do you speak English? *parla inglese?*
open *aperto/verto*
closed *chiuso*
when does it open? *quando apre?*
it's closed *è chiuso/xè serà*
what's the time? *che ore sono?*
do you have a light? *hai d'accendere?/ti gà da accender, ti gà fógo?*

Transport

car *macchina*
bus *autobus*
taxi *tassì, taxi*
train *treno*
plane *aereo*
stop (bus/vaporetto) *fermata*
station *stazione*
platform *binario*
tickets biglietto, biglietti
one way *solo andata*
return *andata e ritorno*
I'd like a ticket to... *Vorrei un biglietto per...*

Communications

phone *telefono*
mobile phone *cellulare*
postcard *cartolina*
stamp *francobollo*
email *(messaggio di) posta elettronica*

Directions

entrance *entrata*
exit *uscita*
where is...? *dov'è...?/dove xè?*
(turn) left *(giri a) sinistra*
(it's on the) right *(è sulla/a) destra*
straight on *sempre dritto*
could you tell me the way to...? *mi può indicare la strada per...?*
is it near/far? *è vicino/lontano?*

Eating & drinking

▶ *For other words and phrases associated with Venetian food and drink, see p43* The Venetian Menu.

I'd like to book a table for four at eight *vorrei prenotare una tavola per quattro alle otto*
that was poor/good/delicious *era mediocre/buono/ottimo*
the bill *il conto*
I think there's a mistake in this bill *credo che il conto sia sbagliato*
is service included? *è incluso il servizio?*

Accommodation

I'd like to book a single/ twin/double bedroom *vorrei prenotare una camera singola/doppia/matrimoniale*
I'd prefer a room with a bath/shower/ window over the courtyard/canal *preferirei una camera con vasca da bagno/doccia/finestra sul cortile/canale*

Shopping

shop *negozio/botega*
how much does it cost/is it? *quanto costa?, quant'è?/quanto xè?*

do you accept credit cards? *si accettano le carte di credito?*
do you have small change? *ha delle monete?*
I'd like to try on the blue sandals/ black shoes/brown boots *vorrei provare i sandali blu/le scarpe nere/gli stivali marroni*
I take (shoe) size *porto il numero...*
I take (dress) size *porto la taglia...*
it's too loose/too tight/just right *mi sta largo/stretto/bene*

a litre *un litro*
100 grams of *un etto di*
200 grams of *due etti di*
one kilo of *un kilo di*

Days & times

Monday *lunedì*
Tuesday *martedì*
Wednesday *mercoledì*
Thursday *giovedì*
Friday *venerdì*
Saturday *sabat*
Sunday *domenica*

yesterday *ieri*
today *oggi/ancùo*
tomorrow *domani*
morning *mattina*
afternoon *pomeriggio*
evening *sera*
this evening *stasera*
night *notte*
tonight *stanotte*

Numbers

0 *zero;* **1** *uno;* **2** *due;* **3** *tre;* **4** *quattro;*
5 *cinque;* **6** *sei;* **7** *sette;* **8** *otto;* **9** *nove;*
10 *dieci;* **11** *undici;* **12** *dodici;* **13** *tredici;*
14 *quattordici;* **15** *quindici;* **16** *sedici;*
17 *diciassette;* **18** *diciotto;* **19** *diciannove;*
20 *venti;* **21** *ventuno;* **22** *ventidue;*
30 *trenta;* **40** *quaranta;* **50** *cinquanta;*
60 *sessanta;* **70** *settanta;* **80** *ottanta;*
90 *novanta;* **100** *cento;* **1,000** *mille;*
2,000 *duemila*

Index

Photo credits

Inside front cover: Viacheslav Lopatin/Shutterstock.com Pages 2 (top) Frederico Nero; 2 (bottom) MR_ross/Shutterstock.com; 3 Funkystock/age fotostock/SuperStock.com; 4 Catarina Belova/Shutterstock.com; 7 InnaVar Shutterstock.com; 11 (bottom) ju.grozyan/Shutterstock.com; 11 (top) Ioan Florin Cnejevici/Shutterstock.com; 12 (bottom) Christian Mueller/Shutterstock.com; 13 (bottom) Smith Mark Edward/AGF/SuperStock.com; 13 (top) pisaphotography/Shutterstock.com; 14(middle) Tina Bour/Shutterstock.com; 14 (top) Andrew Angelov/Shutterstock.com; 14 (bottom), 101 bepsy/Shutterstock.com; 15 (top) Melodia plus photos/Shutterstock.com; 15 (middle) Yulia Grigoryeva/Shutterstock.com; 16 (top) Anibal Trejo/Shutterstock.com; 16 (bottom), 53, 93, 129, 131 Renata Sedmakova/Shutterstock.com; 17 (bottom) S.Borisov/Shutterstock.com; 17 (top) HUANG Zheng/Shutterstock.com; 18 (top) Peter Barritt/SuperStock.com; 18 (bottom) taniavolobueva/Shutterstock.com; 19 Buffy1982/Shutterstock.com; 21, 62 Viacheslav Lopatin/Shutterstock.com; 23 artjazz/Shutterstock.com; 25 (bottom), 66 s74/Shutterstock.com; 25 (top) Pfeiffer/Shutterstock.com; 26 (top) kyrien/Shutterstock.com; 26 (middle) LALS STOCK/Shutterstock.com; 26 (bottom) Happy Moments/Shutterstock.com; 27 Stanislav Samoylik/Shutterstock.com; 29 S-F/Shutterstock.com; 32 canyalcin/Shutterstock.com; 33 Cristiano Bendinelli; 34 Yulia Grigoryeva/Shutterstock.com; 35 AgathaK/Shutterstock.com; 37 Signor Blum Snc; 39 Bevilacqua; 40 Asim Verma/Shutterstock.com; 41, 44 La Biennale de Venezia/Andrea Avezzù ; 43 Michele Crosera/Teatro Malibran; 45 ©Marie-Anne Bacquet; 47 ChiccoDodiFC/Shutterstock.com; 48 Helena G.H/Shutterstock.com; 50 vvoe/Shutterstock.com; 51 BasPhoto/Shutterstock.com; 52 Vela Spa; 54 Vladimir Korostyshevskiy/Shutterstock.com; 55 Alexxxey/Shutterstock.com; 56 Pecold/Shutterstock.com; 59, 114 Simone Padovani/Shutterstock.com; 61, 111, 117 Dreamer Company/Shutterstock.com; 67 Mark Edward Smith/Museo Correr; 68 Ideo/Shutterstock.com; 69 cge2010/Shutterstock.com; 70 ansharphoto/Shutterstock.com; 72 PlusONE/Shutterstock.com; 73 Bob Noto; 75 JopsStock/Shutterstock.com; 76 Verkhovynets Taras/Shutterstock.com; 76 Henryk Sadura/Shutterstock.com; 77 Reeed/Shutterstock.com; 79 4kclips/Shutterstock.com; 82 Heracles Kritokos/Shutterstock.com; 85 Michele Crosera/La Fenice; 87 Aleksandr Vrublevskiy/Shutterstock.com; 91 canadastock/Shutterstock.com; 94, 108 anyaivanova/Shutterstock.com; 96 VizioVirtù; 98 Phant/Shutterstock.com; 102 Nicolas Ruel; 103 trabantos/Shutterstock.com; 107 Ivan Marc/Shutterstock.com; 112, 132 Oleg Znamenskiy/Shutterstock.com; 116 Vittoria Costantini; 122 EQRoy/Shutterstock.com; 133 sbellott/Shutterstock.com; 140 Estro Vino e Cucina. Ph. Matteo de Fina; 143 © Peggy Guggenheim Collection. Ph. Matteo de Fina; 145 José Luiz Bernardes Ribeiro, via Wikimedia Commons; 147 simona flamigni/Shutterstock.com; 148 Ioan Panaite/Shutterstock.com; 149 Javen/Shutterstock.com; 150 Taweep Tang/Shutterstock.com; 151 Mirelle/Shutterstock.com; 155 Elzloy/Shutterstock.com; 159 underworld/Shutterstock.com; 161 keko64/Shutterstock.com; 162 Rita1/Shutterstock.com; 163 Csehak Szabolcs/Shutterstock.com; 172 Nikolas Koenig.

Credits

Crimson credits
Editor Luisa Grigoletto
Contributors Chiara Barbieri, Luisa Grigoletto, Anne Hanley, Clara Marshall
Proofreader Liz Hammond
Layouts Emilie Crabb, Patrick Dawson
Cartography Gail Armstrong, Simonetta Giori

Series Editor Sophie Blacksell Jones
Production Manager Kate Michell
Design Mytton Williams

Chairman David Lester
Managing Director Andy Riddle

Advertising Media Sales House
Marketing Lyndsey Mayhew
Sales Joel James

Photography credits
Front cover zoran1/iStockphoto.com
Back cover Slavko Sereda/Shutterstock.com
Interior Photography credits, see p191.

Publishing information
Time Out Venice Shortlist 3rd edition
© TIME OUT ENGLAND LIMITED 2018
February 2018

ISBN 978 1 78059 261 9
CIP DATA: A catalogue record for this book is available from the British Library

Published by Crimson Publishing 21d Charles Street, Bath, BA1 1HX (01225 584 950, www.crimson publishing.co.uk) on behalf of Time Out England.

Distributed by Grantham Book Services
Distributed in the US and Canada by Publishers Group West (1-510-809-3700)

Printed by Replika Press, India.